The Light of the Living

The Light of the Living

Studies in the Interpretation of Scripture

D. E. R. ISITT

EPWORTH PRESS

7162 0456 8

First published 1989
by Epworth Press
Room 195, 1 Central Buildings
Westminster, London SW1H 9NR

Typeset at The Spartan Press Ltd,
Lymington, Hants.
and printed in Great Britain by
Richard Clay Ltd,
Bungay, Suffolk

Contents

Preface

I believe there are a good many people who try to read the Bible seriously but are put off, either by the technicalities of biblical scholarship, or by the suggestion that Bible Reading requires a particular devotional attitude and will Do You Good. This book is meant for such general readers rather than for students or group leaders or others with ulterior motives. But its origins need to be explained.

In the early 1980s I worked with the late Donald Walters in preparing men and women for ministry in the Church of England and the United Reformed Church. Our students, mostly between 30 and 60 years of age, came from Gloucester and Hereford and Swindon and Bristol and thereabouts. Virtually all were in full-time secular employment, and would continue to be so after ordination as non-stipendiary ministers. Many were highly trained in their own fields, but most of them started with virtually no knowledge of theology. They took their studies very seriously (which is not always the case with candidates for ordination), and found themselves involved in a process of shared learning to which they could all contribute, and from which they could all benefit.

A special part of this process was what came to be known as the CAT Session. CAT stands for Close Attention to the Text, and the students were required to look hard at a selected passage from the Bible and learn to read the scriptures closely, with a view to expounding them responsibly and intelligently.

Over the years, CAT Sessions began to circulate beyond the circle of those for whom they were first devised, and some of them are now offered to a wider audience still.

This book therefore has a limited range and a rather odd shape. There is very little here about St Paul or St John, who need a separate volume. The chapters vary a good deal in length. Some points of interpretation have been laboured by repetition, as the

experience of working with adult students has proved necessary. Passages were chosen for comment, not for their intrinsic
importance, and not with a view to completeness, but in the
hope of demonstrating the variety of the scriptural witness. The
result is bound to be fragmentary, as Close Attention to the Text
has remained the principal concern, and CAT Sessions were
always concerned with representative samples of scripture
rather than with systematic study of particular books. However,
at the end of either part of this selection there's a brief exposition
of an entire book, Malachi and Ephesians respectively, to show
how the principles of CAT can be applied over a wider range,
albeit inevitably in less detail.

This is obviously not a work of technical scholarship, but I
have drawn heavily on the published work of many people.
Acknowledgments are not made in the text itself, as I have tried
to clear it of notes and to print almost all biblical references in
full, since I believe people don't usually look them up otherwise. You will find at the end of the volume a list of books
consulted, and suggestions for further reading. Most of the
quotations from the Bible are from the Authorized Version,
except in chapter 17 where the Revised Standard Version is
used, and in certain places where there are special problems of
translation.

I want to express my gratitude to a number of scholars and
friends who have helped and taught me: Jeanne Forster, Ken-
neth Grayston, C. F. D. Moule, D. E. Nineham, Lars Oesterlin,
H. P. Steer, A. R. Vidler, and to some who died before this
book was finished – Mark Gibbs, C. P. M. Jones and G. W. H.
Lampe. They are, of course, in no way responsible for the
shortcomings of what follows.

I am specially indebted to Bishop John Tinsley, under whose
leadership the Bristol School of Ministry was encouraged towards theological exploration and new forms of training. My
other colleagues in that venture will know of my gratitude to
them: Sue Walrond-Skinner, Mary Wyman, Betty Millard, John
Furst, Evelyn Saward (who most kindly read the manuscript),
Noel and Adele Bailey, and many others who supported and
taught the students.

Above all, my wife Verity has been an unfailing support
during the writing of the book and the work out of which it
grew.

But the dedication must be

TO THE STUDENTS
and in memory of
DONALD

Introduction

The Light of the Living

When it's announced that the next hymn will be number 444 omitting verse 2, it's to verse 2 that you immediately turn, to see why you're not supposed to sing it. When the Lectionary directs you to read some parts of the Bible and not others, you speculate at once about what's being left out. (A Lectionary, by the way, is a table of readings for private or public use: valuable, because in private it discourages you from reading only those parts that you enjoy, and because in public worship it gives you some protection from the individual tastes of the clergy.) Quite a lot gets left out, for shortage of time, or because a good deal of Holy Scripture really isn't very appropriate for use in an act of public worship. So if you are perverse or inquisitive enough to explore the obscurer corners of the Bible, you find yourself reading about strange happenings and queer people. It will be a recurrent theme of this book to show how often the Bible, and not only the obscure parts of it, offers an intriguing mixture of the strange and the familiar.

Take the story of Doeg the Edomite and the priests of Nob. You'll find it in chapters 21 and 22 of the First Book of Samuel. Part of it is familiar, because there's a reference to it in the Gospel according to St Matthew: the rest of it is both strange and rather repulsive. David, son of Jesse, is on the run from King Saul who suspects him of treason. He and his companions are unarmed and hungry. They go for help to Ahimelech and the priests of the Lord at Nob, saying that they are on a secret mission for the King. Ahimelech says they have nothing to eat except the Shewbread which is reserved for the priests, and no weapon except the sword of Goliath which is wrapped up and treasured as a votive offering. These suit David admirably: he takes the food and the weapon, and he and his men go their way to find refuge with

Achish, the Philistine king of Gath. So far, so good. But lurking in the priests' house is one of Saul's men. He's an Edomite, which means he's a hereditary enemy of Israel. He is also the king's chief herdsman, and if we're to grasp the significance of that, we have to make a short digression.

Cattlemen, in the ancient Near East, were often no more than inferior servants. To the Egyptians, you may remember, they seem to have been an abomination, at certain times: this may be why Jacob and his family, when they settled in Egypt, were relegated to the land of Goshen so as not to contaminate the neighbours; though the rather mysterious business of the 'Hyksos Invasion' may have something to do with this. At a much later date, at Bethlehem on Christmas night, the shepherds apparently represent the poor. On the other hand David himself looked after his father's livestock, as did Joseph and Moses before him. There was no disgrace in that. Indeed, there are ancient texts from Assyria and Egypt in which the King himself is pictured as Shepherd of his people. The Hebrew psalmists and prophets, especially Isaiah and Ezekiel, took up this theme, so that it became something of a cliché in Jewish religious writing. 'The Lord is my Shepherd . . .' In the Greek world too the shepherd sometimes serves as a model for the good ruler: he can represent the *philanthropos*, the figure of the benefactor. So, by the time you come to the earliest Christian art, in the catacombs and on the mosaics of fourth-century Rome, you find Christ represented as both Shepherd and Lamb. If that's confusing, so much the better. You need to keep such confusions in view, my point being that very often the picture-language of the Bible (as of any other literature) is not as simple as it looks, and you have to realize that its imagery can bear different meanings in different contexts, and can even carry contradictory overtones at the same time.

Back to Doeg. There he is in the house of the priests, 'detained before the Lord' – what had he been up to? – and in due course he reports to Saul what has been going on. The king sends for the priests and accuses them of conspiring with David against him. Ahimelech, having been hoodwinked by David, makes an innocent answer:

> And who is so faithful among thy servants as David, which is the king's son in law, and goeth at thy bidding, and is honourable in thine house? Is this the first time that I have enquired of the Lord

for him? God forbid. Let not the king impute anything to his servant.

But the king is beyond reason. He tells his guards to kill the priests. Nobody moves.

> And the king said to Doeg, Turn thou, and fall upon the priests. And Doeg the Edomite turned, and he fell upon the priests, and slew on that day fourscore and five persons that did wear the linen ephod. And Nob, the city of the priests, smote he with the edge of the sword, both men and women, children and sucklings, and oxen, and asses, and sheep, with the edge of the sword.

A grim little story of bloodshed and revenge. History is full of such deeds, and you read them and pass on. Except that in this case, if you have one of those old-fashioned Bibles with a column of cross-references down the middle, your eye may be caught by the words 'Psalm 56, title'. And if you turn to the book of Psalms you'll find that in your Bible, though not in your Prayer Book, almost all the psalms do indeed have titles attached to them. And very intriguing they are:

> Psalm 52. David, condemning Doeg, prophesieth his destruction. To the chief Musician, Maschil, a Psalm of David, when Doeg the Edomite came and told Saul, and said unto him, David is come to the house of Ahimelech.

> Psalm 56. David complaineth of his enemies. To the chief Musician upon Jonath-elem-rechokim, Michtam of David, when the Philistines took him in Gath.

Goodness knows what all that means, except that there are clearly instructions about the music, and Jonath-elem-rechokim apparently means 'The Dove in the Far-off Terebinths', and wouldn't you love to know how that tune went? There's also the suggestion that these poems were written by David. It's pretty certain they weren't, and that calls for another digression.

Anyone who handles the material of the Bible very soon discovers that when it is suggested that David didn't write the Psalms and Moses didn't write Genesis and St Paul didn't write Ephesians, nobody wants to listen. People feel threatened, as the jargon goes; principally because, according to the custom of the twentieth century, it is plain dishonest to put out a document under the name of somebody who didn't write it, and nobody

wants to hear the Bible accused of dishonesty. It's only slightly
reassuring to learn from the scholars that in the ancient world it
didn't look like that at all, and that it was quite acceptable to write
'pseudepigraphically', attributing your work to some venerated
figure of the past. People did it all the time. All right; so perhaps it
doesn't matter much, not on the fringes of the scriptures, so to
speak. But then comes the suggestion that many of the words
attributed in the gospels to our Lord himself turn out to date from
a rather later period; and that is profoundly shocking. It seems to
cast doubts on the reliability of the good news itself, and those
who say such things are seen as undermining the simple faith of
ordinary folk. It's a minefield, and we shall have to look at it in
more detail in later chapters, especially when we come to texts
from the New Testament. For the moment, let's leave open the
question of who wrote these psalms (for my part, I'm happy to
think that there were a good many fine psalmists in Israel) and
whether they did in fact originally relate to the particular historic
context which the titles have attributed to them. They are in any
case fine poems. This is how Psalm 56 begins:

> Be merciful unto me, O God, for man goeth about to devour me: he
> is daily fighting and troubling me.
>   Mine enemies are daily in hand to swallow me up: for they be
> many that fight against me, O thou most Highest.
>   They daily mistake my words: all that they imagine is to do me
> evil.
>   They hold all together and keep themselves close: and mark my
> steps, when they lay wait for my soul.

It could certainly be a lament for the priests of the Lord, or the
appeal of a young man in fear of his life. But equally it could
belong to almost any moment in the history of the Jewish people –
a voice from Treblinka? – because nowhere in the Old Testament
is the voice of lamentation far away. Sometimes the voice is
dignified in acceptance of the will of God, sometimes strident in
protest against it, and often turning remarkably into praise at the
conclusion. This is how Psalm 56 ends:

> In God's word will I rejoice: in the Lord's word will I comfort me.
>   Yea, in God have I put my trust: I will not fear what man can do
> unto me.

Unto thee, O God, will I pay my vows: unto thee will I give thanks.

For thou hast delivered my soul from death, and my feet from falling: that I may walk before God in the light of the living.

I have taken the title of my book from that last line, because there are two things about the Bible which strike me as more important than anything else.

First, it was the supreme privilege of the servants of the Lord to 'walk before God'. It's true of the people of the Old Testament. It's just as true of the people of the New Testament, who described themselves as 'followers of The Way' long before their opponents saddled them with the offensive nickname of 'Christians'. It's also true of many people who do not call themselves Christians at all, because to do so would imply subscription to beliefs and practices which it would be wrong for them to subscribe to, but who nonetheless walk before God in the light of the living. I hope it's not patronizing to say that the Bible is their book, if only they can prise it away from the grip of those who think they own it.

The second thing needs more unwrapping. Speaking on television in the 1970s about the persecution of the Jews, the composer Michael Tippett said:

I knew that they stood for every kind of scapegoat, every outcast, whether it was in Russia, or America, or in England, and that for these people (and for myself) I had to sing songs. And suddenly, in fact the day after war broke out, the whole thing welled up in me in a way which I can exactly remember. I simply had to go and take the pencil and begin to write 'A Child of Our Time' as it stood.

The Bible has grown out of a compulsion to sing songs, songs in prose and verse, in Hebrew and in Greek. Some of them are fragments from primitive antiquity, like the triumph song of the Red Sea:

I will sing unto the Lord, for he hath triumphed gloriously: the horse and his rider hath he cast into the sea.

The Lord is my strength and my song: and he is become my salvation.

Others are formal masterpieces, like the heart-rending acrostics of the book of Lamentations:

> From the daughter of Zion all her beauty is departed: her princes are become like harts that find no pasture, and they are gone without strength before the pursuer.
>
> All they that pass by clap their hands at her: they hiss and wag their head at the daughter of Jerusalem.
>
> Is this the city that they call the Perfection of Beauty: the Joy of the Whole Earth?

The compulsion to sing songs isn't just an urge to compose, a kind of literary itch. In Tippett's case it was a response to the events of 1939, of which he remained an appalled spectator until the moment when he took up his pencil. At that point he became part of the story he was telling. The same thing can happen to any of us, at all sorts of different levels. For instance, in 1936 we used to sing in the school playground a song about the abdication of the King:

> Who's this coming down the street?
> Mrs Simpson's fairy feet . . .

I have no notion who wrote it, and we didn't have much idea what it was all about. But by singing it, by giving it currency, we became part of the story. We took part in the history of our time. Singing songs, telling stories, spraying the walls with graffiti, writing oratorios, are different ways of stepping in to the history which is being created around you, at whatever level you do it.

Tippett says he had to sing songs for a persecuted people and for himself. When the Old Testament writers speak of Doeg, they aren't simply telling yarns: they are taking part in their own history by giving currency to a point of view about Edomites and priests and herdsmen and paranoid autocrats. When the New Testament writers speak of Jesus they are doing the same thing: they don't just tell the stories, they give them currency as good news, gospel, *kerygma*, and take their place within their own history. So does anyone who takes pencil in hand as preacher, scholar, commentator, gospel singer; in the pulpit, in the playground, in the study. You give currency to the Lord's song, and take part in the history. What's important is not to misrepresent the history or debase the currency.

1

The Tower of Babel

Genesis 11. 1–9

And the whole earth was of one language, and of one speech. And it came to pass, as they journeyed from the east, that they found a plain in the land of Shinar; and they dwelt there. And they said one to another, Go to, let us make brick, and burn them throughly. And they had brick for stone, and slime had they for mortar. And they said, Go to, let us build us a city and a tower, whose top may reach unto heaven; and let us make us a name, lest we be scattered abroad upon the face of the whole earth. And the Lord came down to see the city and the tower, which the children of men builded. And the Lord said, Behold, the people is one and they have all one language, and this they begin to do; and now nothing will be restrained from them, which they have imagined to do. Go to, let us go down, and there confound their language, that they may not understand one another's speech. So the Lord scattered them abroad from thence upon the face of all the earth: and they left off to build the city. Therefore is the name of it called Babel; because the Lord did there confound the language of all the earth: and from thence did the Lord scatter them abroad upon the face of all the earth.

Everybody knows that story. So you'd have said, not so long ago. I don't suppose that's the case any longer. We can't assume any common knowledge of Bible stories. Take a census in a London street and how many people will you find who know about the Garden of Eden, Cain and Abel, Noah's Ark? Those stories which seemed to belong to all of us, which were experienced as the bedrock of a universal culture, have very largely gone out of circulation, and it's hard to see what, if anything, has taken their place.

The Tower of Babel is quite well-known, all the same, and it's a particular favourite in the textbooks because you can illustrate it with photographs. Look at any handbook of biblical studies, and you'll find somewhere in chapter 1 a picture of one of those great stepped mounds called *ziggurats* whose remains are still to be seen here and there in the Middle East, monuments of 2000 BC, and earlier. Many of them are just mounds of earth now, the brick having slurped into shapelessness over the centuries. But there they still are, evidence of one of those reassuring correspondences between literature and archaeology, like Mycenae or Knossos or Glastonbury Tor.

The temptation as you consider this evidence is to go overboard and say, 'There you are, the archaeologists have proved what the Bible (or Homer) has been saying all along. It's all true, so now let's have a serious look at Mount Ararat: surely Noah's Ark must be up there somewhere . . .'

But that, of course, is not what the archaeologist is about. His concern is to discover what's there, not to dig around for support for this theory or that legend, as Schliemann did at Troy with results which have confused us all ever since. The serious reader of the Bible, similarly, has to concentrate attention on discovering what's there, in the text and on the ground, not beaver around in search of biblical support for the favoured belief or point of view. The different sciences do indeed enlighten one another, but there needs to be mutual respect for the autonomy of the different scientific disciplines. Practitioners need to take one another seriously, not like one clergyman I used to know, who would telephone an expert in (say) economics and ask, 'Would it be true to say that . . . ?' The expert would cautiously say, 'Well ye-es, I suppose so, but . . .' and be astonished to find himself later quoted in support of some half-baked opinion he didn't hold at all. Theologians are rather given to that sort of simplification, so don't be deceived into thinking that ziggurat pictures actually prove anything except the existence of ziggurats. You may want to make the connection, but you must first look hard at the text.

It's surprising to discover how little serious theological comment there has been about the Babel story. There are, as we shall see, very few echoes of Genesis 11 elsewhere in either the Old or the New Testament. The commentators don't have much to say about it, nor do the textbooks of Old Testament theology. It seems that the Fathers make little of it: I can't claim to be sure of that, but certainly St Augustine, in devoting forty-three chapters of *The City of God* to an elaborate exposition of the book Genesis, passes by the Tower of Babel with scarcely a mention. You're left with the impression that this may be an engaging story, but it's marginal, not important like the Flood or the Fall of Man. And this is the more surprising when you consider how, recently, in the study of linguistics writers like George Steiner have claimed Babel as a formative myth for literature.

What exactly is it, then, this account that we're looking at? One answer might be that, like everything else in the Bible, it's a direct historical account of something that happened at a particular place and a specific time: and that if that strikes you as unlikely, it's because your vision has become blurred so that you're no longer able to receive the word of God straight, in the clear and literal way you're meant to take it. That's one view, and it's widely and passionately held. Literal fundamentalism is stronger than it has ever been; unfortunately it's a closed system which cannot be argued with.

So is the Babel story a folk-tale? If so, what sort of folk-tale? Oddly enough, it doesn't figure (as the Creation narratives and the Great Flood do) in other ancient Near Eastern literature. We're told that it's unique to the Hebrew scriptures. And that's surprising, because you would expect to find something like it cropping up here and there in other contexts. In folk tales you often come across the figure of the innovator, the semi-divine or heroic person like Prometheus or Herakles who brings heavenly gifts to earth and is made to suffer for it. At first sight you don't find that in the Genesis texts, but a closer look reveals some strange hints:

> And Cain knew his wife; and she conceived and bare Enoch: and he builded a city, and called the city after the name of his son.

There's a revolutionary act for you. If the city-dweller is always an object of suspicion and contempt to the nomadic community, how much more the man who actually builds cities! As we've seen, the children of Israel had no doubt that God favoured the herdsman and the hunter rather than the cultivator, Abel rather than Cain, Jacob rather than Esau. They were particularly uneasy with those who settled down to the cultivation of the vine:

And Noah began to be an husbandman, and he planted a vineyard: and he drank of the wine, and was drunken; and he was uncovered within his tent . . .

with deplorable results. Even though the protagonists in the Babel story are unspecified 'children of men' (who are they, exactly?) rather than characters in the Hebrew tradition, you can spot traces of this same conflict between tent-dweller and townee: 'There you are, you see: that's what comes of your new-fangled notions.'

It's fairly obvious that the story doesn't come to us direct from the lips of the storyteller. They hardly ever do. This one has been worked over, probably at a variety of levels. A pun has been introduced: the tower is called Babel because the Hebrew word for confusion is *balal*. That's a trivial enough point, but before we go any further we need to consider what other editorial activities there may have been, and this means considering how these early chapters of Genesis came to assume the form in which they have come down to us.

It has become a bit of a joke, really. People deride the pomposities of biblical scholarship and research (quite right, too) and make particular sport with J, E, D and P, mysterious symbols which have to be mastered before you can take your first steps in theology. In fact these four characters are quite amiable, once you understand them: they are shorthand terms for a long process by which the first six books of the Old Testament, the Hexateuch, came into being. Let me try and explain.

It can be demonstrated that these early accounts of the origins of the Jewish people have been quite heavily 'edited' at various stages. The editing was probably done under the influence of schools of thought rather than by individual scribes; and these schools of thought, or traditions, have been identified as the Jahwist, the Elohist (because of two different Hebrew words for God – Jahweh and Elohim – which are used in two different traditions), the Deuteronomic and the Priestly revisers. We can't concern ourselves too much with the technicalities of this, but it should be obvious what happened. It's the work of many centuries to bring together collections of ancient material (songs, tales, genealogies) and weave them into something coherent.

Now, the result of that weaving will depend on the point of view from which you start, as you realize when you look at accounts of Richard III or Oliver Cromwell in our own history books. So you're not surprised to find in the Old Testament narratives strong evidence of what the scholars call 'editorial activity'. This activity accounts for the fact that there we find not one but two creation stories in Genesis 1 and 2, and not one but two accounts of the enslavement of Joseph intertwined in Genesis 37, and goodness knows how many intermingled stories in I Samuel dealing with the emergence from obscurity of David, son of Jesse. It makes an engrossing study, the history of the way different traditions come together in the making of this history, and it's a pity that scholarship has given it the disconcerting name of 'source criticism'. This frightens people a good deal, and it's necessary to insist that the word 'criticism', as the scholars use it, doesn't in the least imply censure or disparagement; it means, simply, using the analytical tools of literary study in order to sharpen our understanding of how the writings of scripture have come to be as they are.

What concerns us here is the overall purpose of the Hexateuch as it now stands, the compilers having finished with it, and how the Tower of Babel came to be part of the weaving of it.

A key passage in this enquiry is to be found in the twenty-sixth chapter of Deuteronomy. There Moses is depicted giving instructions for the proper observance of the festival of Firstfruits:

> Thou shalt speak and say before the Lord thy God, A Syrian ready to perish was my father, and he went down into Egypt, and sojourned there with a few, and became there a nation, great, mighty and populous: and the Egyptians evil intreated us, and afflicted us, and laid upon us hard bondage: and when we cried unto the Lord God of our fathers, the Lord heard our voice, and looked on our affliction, and our labour, and our oppression: and the Lord brought us forth out of Egypt with a mighty hand, and with an outstretched arm, and with great terribleness, and with signs, and with wonders; and he hath brought us into this place, and hath given us this land, even a land flowing with milk and honey.

That in a nutshell is what the Hexateuch is all about. Or, more precisely, it's what the final editors of the Hexateuch thought it was all about. It's a kind of conspectus of how traditional Judaism has come to understand the relation between God and his people, in the context of the land in which they lived and which they believed God had given to them. It's how later generations of Jews have seen and interpreted God's action in their earliest history. That's the story they wanted to tell; that's how they underlined, so to say, the parts they wanted to underline.

This has brought us a long way from the Tower of Babel. But the point is that, before they could tell the story proper, the compilers of these opening books of the Old Testament had other things to say. And that's why the first eleven chapters of Genesis are different from the rest – rather like the Prologue in 'I Pagliacci' or 'Ariadne auf Naxos'. In the Jewish traditions there were, as well as history-proper, a good many primaeval stories, a sort of pre-history made up of legends and folk-tales and bits and pieces borrowed from the neighbours. And this farrago is in no way to be despised, because it has something to say about the way things are. The technical term is 'aetiological narrative'. Kipling's *Just So Stories* are of the same kind, even though he tells them more in terms of 'how' (the elephant got his trunk) than why. The ancient pre-history of Israel is concerned less with how, more with why. Why do we feel as we do about sex, nakedness, menstruation? Why do weeds grow faster and stronger than crops? Why are snakes sinister, and work difficult, and childbearing painful, and incest unthinkable? And why do foreigners have strange habits and talk gibberish? These are questions worth asking, worth telling tales about. These are some of the themes of Genesis 1–11.

It looks, then, as though we have here, in the Tower of Babel, an ancient story, origin unknown, of a just-so type, attached to similar stories as a prologue to the main narrative of the first six books of the Old Testament, and making its own contribution to that narrative. It addresses itself to questions about foreigners. It is followed at once, or almost at once, by the great drama of the Patriarchs and God's covenants with them; then by the formative experience of captivity in Egypt, deliverance at the Red Sea, settlement in Canaan, and the fulfilment of the promises made to Abraham.

If that's the shape of it, how does Babel contribute to that shape, and does it help me to understand foreigners and their funny ways? To this question there may be a clue in the preceding chapter. Chapter 10 at first sight is as unpromising as it could be – a rigmarole in which, for instance, we're told that Shem begat Aram, and the sons of Aram were Uz, Hul, Gether and Mash. (Yes, really.) Emphatically, it's one of the bits that don't get read in church or chosen for private devotional reading. But as we look more closely we'll see that it's quite a significant list for the historian. And this means that we have to digress again.

It appears that some time after 1200 BC a series of catastrophes shook the lands of the eastern Mediterranean basin, bringing to an end a number of early civilizations, such as those of Minoan Crete and Mycenean Greece, and making an impact on the mainland of Asia Minor and Egypt and North Africa. It's not clear exactly what happened. There seems to have been earthquake, tidal wave, perhaps linked with the eruption of Thera/Santorini; and on top of all, marauding invasions by a mysterious group of outsiders widely known as The People from the Sea. Traces of them turn up in the records of the Hittites and on an Egyptian inscription called the Stele of Merneptah. Just who these invaders were, nobody is quite sure: but it seems likely that they included people who came later to be known as Ionians, Tyrrhenians (Etruscans?), Aeolians, Danaans. And is it possible that here they are, in chapter 10 of Genesis of all places, disguised as Javan, Tiras, Elishah, Dodanim, the descendants of Japheth, the son of Noah? It's a fascinating possibility, if nothing else.

It's never easy to interpret very ancient evidence, or to be sure of making the right connections, but there is one conclusion which appears fairly convincing. It seems that those who compiled the Jewish sacred writings decided to include in them a number of rather incongruous elements. And they did so, not for antiquarian but for theological reasons. They wanted to insist that all humanity comes ultimately under the hand of a God who was not just one tribal deity among others, but who had come to be seen (by the time the editors have done their work) as Lord of *all* peoples,

. . . after their tongues, in their lands, after their nations . . .

which is why the story of Babel had to be told.

But that's not quite all. The compiler who found room for Babel in his history found in it a very individual idea of God. Supranational he may be, but he's not a God to stand by and let history take its course. The story is told in very personal terms. ('Anthropomorphism' is the technical term for speaking of God as though he were a man.) The Lord comes down to see what's going on. What's all this, then? this urban development, these settlements on the plains, this building with brick and slime? This isn't going to find much favour with the mountain God of Sinai, of Horeb, whose word is engraved on *stone*, and who summons his people to go up the mountain when he wants to meet them. Who are these people who are so far from any real hills that they have to try and build their own? 'Go to!' says God; *'yahab!'* and inevitably, in Jewish story-telling it is by the initiative of God that these outlandish folk get their come-uppance and are scattered across the face of the earth, their speech turned to barbarism.

Put it another way: in the view of those who compiled this history, there's not a chance that the rapidly expanding nations of the Middle East are going to fulfil the purposes of God through the random process of history, by the survival of the fittest, through self-generating migrations or the dictates of Malthusian economics. God has *something else* in mind. In a moment we'll see what that is, but first we need to attend to two loose ends in the story.

The first is this: I suggested earlier that it's surprising how little attention is paid to the Tower of Babel by commentators, whether ancient or modern; and even more surprising that other biblical documents refer to it hardly at all. But there is an oblique reference in chapter 51 of Jeremiah, where the writer seems to identify Babel with Babylon, as a model of arrogance; and in chapter 10 of the book of Wisdom, where we read of 'the nations in their wicked conspiracy being confounded'. The suggestion, in both cases, is that the Tower of Babel is a parable about human sin. But Genesis 11 doesn't actually make that point. It doesn't talk about sin at all. And here archaeology may really help us get our theology right, because the evidence from other ancient civilizations is that the ziggurats aren't after all monuments to human arrogance. They weren't built in order that evil men might climb up to heaven and challenge God, like Greek giants piling Pelion on Ossa. The great ziggurat structures of ancient Mesopotamia seem to have been built as 'the place of the terrace between heaven and earth' – a meeting-point, in other words, as the name Babel (? = Gate of God) may very well imply. And that would mean that what we're looking at is not a story about wickedness at all. About futility, more like, as man vainly tries to make a name for himself, and sets out to meet God on some sort of intermediate ground of his own devising. To attach a note of moral condemnation to the story is surely to misunderstand it. Moralistic interpretations, as we shall see when we look at the

Psalms and the Prophets, can be very misleading; even when –
especially when – such interpretations have centuries of weight
behind them.

The second loose end is this: the Babel narrative, the last of the
primaeval stories in Israel's pre-history, appears to be the only
one which is, in Gerhard von Rad's phrase, 'without grace'.
You'll see what that means if you compare it with the other
narratives in these chapters. In the story of the Garden of Eden,
for instance, despite their disobedience, man and woman apparently find some degree of rehabilitation through hard work and
childbearing. In the sequel, Cain is condemned as a murderer,
but God carefully protects him from the full implication of
outlawry. The Flood has some survivors. Noah's drunkenness is
not terminal in its effects. But for the men of Babel there seems to
be no hope. Unless God really does have *something else* in mind.

And indeed he has. The opening of the next chapter tells us
what it is:

> Now the Lord had said unto Abram, Get thee out of thy country,
> and from thy kindred, and from thy father's house, unto a land
> that I will shew thee: and I will make of thee a great nation, and I
> will bless thee, and make thy name great; and thou shalt be a
> blessing: and I will bless them that bless thee, and curse him that
> curseth thee: and in thee shall all the nations of the earth be
> blessed. So Abram departed, as the Lord had spoken unto him.

In other words, the people of God are to fulfil their purpose not
by making a name for themselves, not by having the highest
ziggurats or the most beautiful temples or the strongest armies;
they are not to depend upon their kinship alliances, or the
protection of their father's house. The chosen of God are not
necessarily the firstborn or the highly born. The choice lies solely
and unpredictably in the hand of God. That's what is meant by
the biblical doctrine of election: and if the story of Babel affirms
this, then it is not 'without grace'.

If God can scatter, he can also gather. In the New Testament
there may be no direct reference to Babel. But if there are still
loose ends, then they are tied up for sure in chapter 2 of the Acts
of the Apostles when, on the Day of Pentecost, the Holy Spirit is
given to the disciples of Jesus, and the confusion of tongues is put
into reverse:

There were dwelling at Jerusalem Jews, devout men, out of every nation under heaven . . . And they were all amazed and marvelled, saying one to another, Behold, are not these which speak Galileans? And how hear we every man in his own tongue, wherein we were born? Parthians and Medes and Elamites, and the dwellers in Mesopotamia, and in Judaea, and Cappadocia, in Pontus, and Asia, Phrygia and Pamphylia, in Egypt, and in the parts of Libya about Cyrene, and strangers of Rome, Jews and proselytes, Cretes and Arabians, we do hear them speak in our tongues the wonderful works of God.

2

The Burning Bush

Exodus 3. 1–12

Now Moses kept the flock of Jethro his father in law, the priest of Midian: and he led the flock to the backside of the desert, and came to the mountain of God, even to Horeb. And the angel of the Lord appeared unto him in a flame of fire out of the midst of a bush: and he looked, and, behold, the bush burned with fire, and the bush was not consumed. And Moses said, I will now turn aside, and see this great sight, why the bush is not burnt. And when the Lord saw that he turned aside, God called unto him out of the midst of the bush, and said, Moses, Moses. And he said, Here am I. And he said, Draw not nigh hither: put off thy shoes from off thy feet, for the place whereon thou standest is holy ground. Moreover he said, I am the God of thy father, the God of Abraham, the God of Isaac, and the God of Jacob. And Moses hid his face; for he was afraid to look upon God. And the Lord said . . . Come now, and I will send thee unto Pharaoh, that thou mayest bring forth my people the children of Israel out of Egypt. And Moses said unto God, Who am I, that I should go unto Pharaoh, and that I should bring forth the children of Israel out of Egypt? And he said, Certainly I will be with thee; and this shall be a token unto thee that I have sent thee: When thou hast brought forth the people out of Egypt, ye shall serve God upon this mountain.

What do you suppose he *really* saw?
In the old days (have they quite gone?) when schoolchildren were taught scripture in school, we were asked that sort of question. As though underneath the extravagances of biblical language there was always some *real* event waiting to be

unearthed. Miracles, visions – the miraculous, were an embarrassment, something for which one had to apologize or at least make
allowances. They were the sort of thing that deterred intelligent
people from taking seriously what was otherwise an impeccable
moral and spiritual system. So you had to demythologize,
though that word wasn't yet in common use, and a good deal of
ingenuity was deployed in trying to explain away any supernatural ingredients in the scriptural text. The results could be
hilarious. For instance: in the first chapter of Zechariah the
prophet records a vision of four horns and four carpenters. It is
explained to him by God's angel that the horns represent the
gentile nations who have scattered Judah and Israel, and the
carpenters are there to eject them. Now, that is entirely typical of
Jewish prophetic utterance. But the author of one standard
commentary, constrained to find some rational explanation of the
vision of four horns, solemnly tells us that what the prophet very
probably saw was – two oxen, in very long grass.

It's all too easy to make a fool of yourself, when you're
applying the criteria of your own time to the mysteries of an
ancient text. We've all heard the Feeding of the Five Thousand
'explained' by the theory that all those present actually had
brought their sandwiches with them, but weren't going to
share them round until they were put to shame by the little
boy with his scraps of bread and fish. And at once, what the
evangelist saw as an act of divine power is reduced to a piece
of trivial moralizing.

So here is Moses at the Burning Bush, which is afire but is not
consumed. Ah yes, we are told, the Middle East is rich in mineral
oils of a most combustible kind . . . and in parts of the desert
volatile vegetable substances like $C_{10}H_{15}O$ can be distilled from
shrubs such as *dryobalanops camphora* . . . could it be that what
Moses *really* saw was a turpentine tree?

I've laboured this point because although one would like to
think that such interpretation was a thing of the past, clearly it
isn't. And perhaps it never will be, because after all people do
want to know what actually happened.

Q. Did Jesus in fact walk on the water?
A. Well, it's hard to say, but the real point of the story is. . . .
Q. Did Jesus really rise from the dead?
A. Well of course nobody wants to cast doubts on the historical

truth of the resurrection, but is that really the question we should be asking. . . . ?

We all know how agitated people become when that kind of discussion is allowed to develop and when theologians, especially bishop-theologians, try to engage in them. The result is inevitably that people feel outraged, left with the suspicion that they've been fobbed-off with evasion and double-think.

It's not only a problem for bishops and theologians. A few days before writing this I was asked to visit someone in hospital who had become very disturbed by the death of the patient in the next bed. She felt that she should have been able to prevent it. She talked about it for a while in perfectly straightforward terms. Then I asked her if she had been anxious or frightened. She replied, without any change of gear, that it had all been perfectly all right, because she had seen the woman taken, 'and the lights, and the hands taking her up'. Later on, I thought a good deal about this. I could have pointed out that, of course, what she *really* saw was the nurses coming and going, and the doctor shining his ophthalmoscope, and the bedsheets swiftly changed. My rationalization would probably have been near the truth. From my angle. But wasn't it necessary to try and see it from hers? Her 'vision', triggered off no doubt by physical stimuli, had a meaning for her which needed to be taken seriously on her own terms. Equally, I have a perfect right to hold, if not to express, my interpretation of what she 'saw'. There's a contradiction involved, of course, which has to be expressed gently or endured silently. I can see no way of avoiding prevarication and double-think – not simply because pastoral considerations demand it, but, more simply, because it's part of the process by which people have to try and make sense of one another's experiences.

And so, to the Burning Bush. There is no way of rediscovering Moses' Own View of this experience. That's lost in the very distant past. There are doubts, even, as to whether Moses was a 'real person' or a mythical representative figure, as his name 'Drawer-Out' might suggest. What's certain is that we have before us the account of that event, as it was understood by the compiler of the book Exodus. So we can look hard at that account, helped by the scholars, and consider it from three particular angles: the sources of the story, the shape of it, and its significance in terms of Jewish tradition and expectation. When we've done that, we can look at some of the details, see how they've been interpreted in later traditions, and how they may still resonate within ours. Then it may be possible to draw our own conclusions about the religious value of the text (and, by implication, of other ancient texts), taking one stage further what we attempted when we looked at the Tower of Babel.

The Sources of the Story

As we've already seen, the ancient stories of the Old and New Testaments come to us in a final 'edited' form. The Burning Bush is no exception. If you peer over the editor's shoulder, you can see evidence of various strands being woven together. For instance, you find that rather mysterious figure, Moses' father-in-law, confronting you in various different forms. He is called sometimes Jether or Jethro, sometimes Raguel or Reuel. (Names, in both Old and New Testament, are frequently subject to change: elsewhere Moses' wife is named as Asenath, daughter of Potipherah, priest of On; but that may be another story about another wife, polygamy being acceptable in those days.) In the same way, we find the holy mountain where God appears to his people sometimes called Horeb, sometimes Sinai. This variation in nomenclature is one reason among others which lead to the conclusion that here we have two or more versions of the same story, originating perhaps as far back as the fourteenth century BC, but combined into their present form as much as a thousand years later. And that's pretty much what you'd expect, when you consider that this early material comes from a pre-literate society where everything was handed down by word of mouth and well and truly embroidered in the process.

The details of this process needn't concern us, but it's important for people reading the Bible to remember that although we may indeed be handling an inspired text, the Revealed Word of God, we are not dealing with something which has come direct from a single source, as though dictated to an ammanuensis in a once-for-all form. It has gone through a great many hands on the way. And I would want to argue that the stages through which this material has passed are in themselves part of the revelation, and an essential part of it: so that to try and peel away (as used to be done) the later additions and embroideries, in an attempt to get back to some sort of 'original', is as misguided as the passion for stripped-pine furniture. Much more helpful, surely, is the image which C. F. D. Moule uses, of the Bible being like a great flow of water, which may have originated in a stream of primal purity, but which in its journey to the sea is fed by all kinds of tributaries, and gathers to itself detritus of all sorts, making up a very rich silt indeed. It would follow from this that you don't get any nearer the fundamental truths of scripture by attempting to filter out the contribution of the countless minds through which they have passed on their way to us. This process of handing-down is surely a vitally important and valuable stage through which men and women learn about God. The Latin word for it is *traditio*, and it's one of the tragedies of religious history that we've allowed 'tradition' to be contrasted with 'revelation' as though it were something which obscures the word of God, when in fact it can so much enrich our understanding and experience of it.

In short, then, it seems that we have in these verses a fragment of ancient narrative, originally current probably in more than one oral form, which was seen to be of formative importance for the religion of the Hebrews, and therefore handled in various ways by different editors as that religion developed.

The Shape of the Story

Story-tellers in pre-literate societies had very special techniques, and needed to have their landmarks carefully worked out, to ensure that they didn't forget their lines. We know a good deal about this because Greek and Latin textbooks of rhetoric give a detailed picture of how lawyers and other public speakers, who never allowed themselves to use notes, could contrive to remember, word-for-word, long and detailed arguments They associated (for instance) different parts of their speeches with different parts of the building they were speaking in. Such-and-such a pillar or arch would locate for the speaker a particular point in his argument, and act as a spur for his memory. Dame Frances Yates in her book *The Art of Memory* made a special study of this. And Milman Parry discovered that as late as 1928 there were folk-singers in southern Yugoslavia who could memorize poems of enormous length by the use of repetitive and 'formular' structures. All this scholarly research has been very important in bringing home to us how much ancient literature circulated originally in oral form. That this isn't simply a literary puzzle becomes clear when you begin to think seriously about the sayings of Jesus. The heart of Christianity, after all, consists in the verbal utterances of someone who never, as far as we know, wrote anything down.

That's really very important, and we'll come back to it.

Unfortunately there's not much evidence in the Old Testament to show just how this verbal material was passed down from generation to generation. Poetry, of course, is easier to memorize than prose, and a lot of early stories were poetic in structure. Puns and other verbal tricks played their part. Religious teachers are apt to express themselves in oracular, gnomic utterances, and these stick easily in the mind. 'Render unto Caesar the things that are Caesar's . . .' And there were certainly lots of formulas used in the telling of Jewish history. Like this:

> In the two and twentieth year of Azariah king of Judah Pekah the son of Remaliah began to reign over Israel in Samaria, and reigned twenty years. And he did that which was evil in the sight of the Lord: he departed not from the sins of Jeroboam the son of Nebat, who made Israel to sin . . . And the rest of the acts of Pekah, and all that he did, behold, they are written in the chronicles of the kings of Israel.

If that formula comes once in the books of Kings, it must come fifty times. It suggests that one way of telling stories was by means of theological-historical set-pieces (blocks, my word processor calls them) which recur time and again. Whole passages of the book of Judges are, in the same sort of way, designed according to a set programme:

> And the children of Israel did evil in the sight of the Lord, and forgot the Lord their God, and served Baalim and the groves. Therefore the anger of the Lord was hot against Israel, and he sold them into the hand of Chushan-Rishathaim king of Mesopotamia, and the children of Israel served Chushan-Rishathaim eight years. And when the children of Israel cried unto the Lord, the Lord raised up a deliverer to the children of Israel, who delivered them, even Othniel the son of Kenaz, Caleb's brother. And the spirit of the Lord came upon him, and he judged Israel, and went out to war: and the Lord delivered Chushan-Rithanaim king of Mesopotamia into his hand . . . and the land had rest forty years. And

Othniel the son of Kenaz died. And the children of Israel did evil again in the sight of the Lord . . . and the Lord strengthened Eglon the king of Moab against Israel . . . and the children of Israel served Eglon eighteen years. But when the children of Israel cried unto the Lord, the Lord raised them up a deliverer, Ehud the son of Gera, a Benjamite, a man left-handed, and Moab was subdued under the hand of Israel. And the land had rest forty years . . . And the children of Israel again did evil in the sight of the Lord . . .

The Lord gives them rest. They do evil. The Lord sends an oppressor. They cry to the Lord. He sends a deliverer. The oppressor is destroyed. The land has rest. They do evil again. The pattern is established, and a great part of Israelite history is written according to this pattern, more or less precisely.

The same is true not only of the early narratives, and not only of the 'history books'. If you look at the first chapter of a fairly sophisticated writing, the seventh-century book of Jeremiah, you find God's dealings with the prophet set out according to a quite clear pattern:

The words of Jeremiah the son of Hilkiah, of the priests that were in Anathoth in the land of Benjamin: (a) to whom the Lord came in the days of Josiah the son of Amon, in the thirteenth year of his reign . . . (b) The word of the Lord came unto me saying, Before I formed thee in the belly I knew thee; and before thou camest out of the womb I sanctified thee, and I ordained thee a prophet unto the nations. (d) Then said I, Ah, Lord God: behold, I cannot speak; for I am a child. (c) But the Lord said unto me, Say not, I am a child; for thou shalt go to all that I shall send thee, and whatsoever I command thee thou shalt speak. (e) Be not afraid of their faces, for I am with thee to deliver thee, saith the Lord. (f) Then the Lord put forth his hand and touched my mouth. And the Lord said unto me, Behold, I have put my words into thy mouth.

What some scholars have identified, here and elsewhere, is a six-part scheme:
  (a) a divine confrontation
  (b) an introductory word
  (c) a commission
  (d) an objection

    (e) reassurance
    (f) a sign in confirmation
In the call of Jeremiah (d) comes before (c) – the pattern, after all isn't obligatory – but it's surprising how often this kind of scheme underlies accounts of God's dealings with his people.

What does all this have to do with Moses, whom we left standing in the wilderness? Well, the Burning Bush, to be sure, isn't a piece of historiography like the book of Judges. But the way the story is told, the form of the narrative, is surprisingly close to what we've just been looking at. The call of Moses, like that of Jeremiah, follows the expected course. There is a clear commission. Moses demurs exactly as might be expected. He is reassured. Signs are given, both verbal and visual. All is as it should be. But before getting back to the text we need to think a bit more about the whole matter of expectation – and these may prove to be the most difficult paragraphs in this whole book if we're to understand the full implication of this event.

The Significance of the Story

We've been looking at some formal patterns used by story-tellers and editors in the Old Testament. This patterning seems to imply (don't you think?) that people expected and wanted God to act reliably, predictably, in role. Read Psalm 37 and see for yourself. So we shouldn't be surprised, when we move forward into the New Testament, to find this same outlook. There are some particular words which express it. *Prosdokao* is a verb used in Luke/Acts for those who 'look for' the kingdom. St Paul uses an even more vigorous word for 'eager expectation' – *apokaradokia*, which means a thrusting forward of one's head, sticking the neck out. And what was it that they were looking forward to? Many different things, no doubt: the Day of the Lord, the end of time, the inauguration of the Lord's rule and judgment, and 'the manifestation of the sons of God'. All of them things worth sticking your neck out for. And, surprisingly perhaps, we find that what New Testament people were looking forward to wasn't so very different from the expectations of Old Testament people. So, when Jesus of Nazareth appears out of the wilderness, walks on water, cures lepers, feeds a multitude, brings back a widow's son from the dead, ascends into heaven, leaves a portion of his spirit with his disciples, he is doing precisely what it is expected that a man of God will do. Elijah and Elisha between them did all these things. They are part of the pattern, of what is to be expected when God and man act in role.

So what's the problem? Well, the problem lies in another and contrary expectation, which comes mainly from St John, that Jesus should emphatically not be seen as acting in role, or according to expectations, should not be seen standing alongside Moses and Elijah, because he is unique. Now, this notion of uniqueness, which is really only hinted at in the New Testament, has taken such a grip on later Christian theology and piety that now, particularly in the evangelical tradition, virtually everything seems to depend upon it. As a result, people of our time look into the scriptures expecting to find a Christ who is essentially different from everybody else; while the New Testament writers themselves seem for the most part to have been concerned to show how closely he conformed to what was expected of him.

If that's a surprising and upsetting notion, perhaps the Burning Bush may help. As a manifestation of God it is central to the Jewish experience of God – central to it, but not without parallels. Put it like this: instead of proclaiming one unrepeatable epiphany of the Divine Will, the Old Testament offers a number of epicentres. There's the whole business of the covenants with the Patriarchs ('I am the God of thy father, the God of Abraham, of Isaac and of Jacob'). There's the promise to Abraham on Mount Moriah, after he has shown himself willing to sacrifice his only son. There's Jacob's dream. There's the pivotal experience of the Passover, the deliverance at the Red Sea, the appearance of God as pillar of fire and smoke. There's the Law given on Sinai. There's the settlement of Canaan, the promises made to David, the building of the Temple, the exile and the return from Babylon. All of these events, each of which is unrepeatable and immensely significant, are yet seen as part of a pattern, the fulfilment of expectation and promise. That's how God is. He acts in character. He is dependable, or, to use a favourite Hebrew turn of phrase, 'his tender mercies endure for ever'. It was always vital to the Jews that they should be assured that God behaves like God.

The Details of the Story

The Rabbis who comment on Jewish scriptures maintain that no detail is without significance. I don't know about that. There's

that good old cliché about the wood and the trees. However, all
the details of this story are worth pondering, even if some of them
turn out to be merely trivial.

1. 'He led the flock to the backside of the desert.' Years ago
RAF personnel, faced with a posting to some remote station in
the Middle East, used to make jokes about the Persian Gulf being
the backside of the world and that particular airfield being right
up it. Nowadays, on the other hand, you'll find devotional
writers romanticizing the desert for its purity as a place for
meeting God. Much is written about the Desert Fathers, those
Egyptian ascetics of the early church, who moved out of the
corrupt urban world of Alexandria and lived, first as hermits and
then in groups, in the isolation of the wilderness. We are told that
we all need to find our own desert place, so that God may find us
there. Well, possibly. It may be true that the Jews, from a later
standpoint, came to look back at the desert as the place where
their experience of God was pristine and uncorrupt. It is certainly
true that Christians have been inclined to imitate Christ in
withdrawing to remote places for prayer and reflection. But it's
also true that the Jews were quite unidealistic about their desert
places. You only have to stand on the Mount of Olives and look
east into the Wilderness of Judaea to know what a 'howling
waste' is. The desert, in Jewish imagery, is a place of danger
where evil spirits and obscene creatures abound. It's not a lovely,
unpolluted place you can escape to, but a place where you
confront evil out of a need to be delivered from it. The saints of
the Egyptian desert certainly knew that. Anyone who thinks of
the wilderness as a bolt-hole needs to think again. But even the
remotest places, *āchārim*, the uttermost parts of the earth, have
their place in the atlas of human experience:

> Whither shall I go then from thy spirit? or whither shall I flee from
> thy presence? If I ascend into heaven thou art there; if I make my
> bed in hell, behold thou art there. If I take the wings of the
> morning and dwell in the uttermost parts of the sea, even there
> shall thy hand lead me. (Psalm 139)

As Jonah discovered, you can't escape God even in the backside
of the world, the place beyond which you can't go. Desert and
ocean are as bad as one another, chaotic and godforsaken, and
that's where Moses was, on the run from the Egyptians and from
his own people. It's an odd setting for such a turning-point: it's

perhaps even odder that we've almost come to expect that God will find us in unlikely places.

2. 'The flock of Jethro the priest of Midian.' Strange, too, what company Moses kept. This father-in-law Jethro/Reuel is a Midianite. They were mysterious people about whom we know nothing much because they were nomads who came out of nowhere on very fast camels and raided you and disappeared as suddenly as they had come. And yet these are the people with whom Moses, brought up in court circles in Egypt, has allied himself by marriage. When you consider how important marriage ties were in the ancient world, and the taboos which existed between tribes of differing habits, this becomes even stranger as a context for God's self-revelation to his chosen people. Yet it was from this Jethro, according to the eighteenth chapter of Exodus, that Moses was to learn the arts of government.

3. 'And the angel of the Lord appeared unto him.' Is it after all a self-revelation of God, or merely of some supernatural created being appearing like Wagner's Loge in a flame of magic fire? The Jews weren't and aren't much given to speaking directly about God. They talk more easily about the word of God, the finger of God, the power of the most high, the hosts of heaven, the kingdom – they speak of him by periphrasis (as the technical word goes) and this angel at the Bush surely stands for God, and isn't to be seen apart from him. This encounter is with the Most High. Moses is in the Presence, though he doesn't yet know it, because he hasn't understood what he has seen. In the Jewish religion faith is much less a matter of seeing than of hearing. You can't always believe your eyes, but when God speaks, then you know. In the meantime there is this strange sight, fire holding its fascination and representing the power of God. Samson's parents, Elijah on Carmel, Malachi the prophet, the disciples of Jesus at Pentecost – there's strong testimony in the Bible to the spiritual truth that our God is a refining fire.

4. 'And Moses said, I will now turn aside and see this great sight.' There's no knowing whether Luke had these words in mind when he tells of the shepherds in the fields saying one to another, 'Let us now go even unto Bethlehem and see this thing which is come to pass, which the Lord has made known unto us.' Certainly no direct link can be made. But the response is the same there as here. Whether from reverence or from curiosity, the people who learn most are those who turn aside to see.

5. 'And when the Lord saw that he turned aside to see, God called unto him out of the midst of the bush and said, Moses, Moses. And he said, Here am I.' The vision could have been anything. The voice was unmistakable. As with the child Samuel, and Simon Peter, and Saul of Tarsus, the intimate and personal word of God leaves no room for doubt. It speaks of a relationship which may be unsought, but is certainly inescapable. And what you can't miss in God's address, incontrovertible for those who experience it, is that it has nothing to do with your worth or suitability or your moral qualities. St Paul insisted that it's not the wise or powerful who come within range of that voice, but the weak and foolish. It comes as a shock, after all those Hollywood epics, to find that Moses is no nationalist super-hero but a man of diffidence, remembered even within Judaism as a model of meekness (of all things), who had no powers of persuasion, who needed Aaron at his side as spokesman, Jethro to teach him the arts of leadership, and Joshua as captain; who himself wasn't allowed into the land of promise. Moses was in many ways a failure, and the commissioning and the task given him in no way relate to his gifts or the excellence of his character. To realize that is to glimpse something of the ways of God which the Jews knew about and the Christian churches, in their selection procedures, have largely forgotten.

6. 'And he said, Draw not nigh hither: put off thy shoes from off thy feet, for the place whereon thou standest is holy ground.' The voice from the bush speaks out for the holiness of God. Moses must keep his distance and humble himself. That this can cause problems for the contemporary mind came home to me as I saw the outrage on the face of an English gentleman on being told he couldn't go into the Blue Mosque at Istanbul unless he first took off his good brown Oxfords and left them on the rack outside. The same sense of outrage affects many people when they find the service of God conducted behind a screen, or in a monastery, in an unfamiliar language, with strange music. It was sad to read of the church leader from the West Indies who felt obliged to walk out of the Christian Millennium celebrations in Moscow, because (he said) there was no opportunity for congregational participation; sad how we isolate ourselves through feeling that we have a right of access, that we are entitled to draw near and keep shod. And so the fear of God degenerates into alienation, or anxiety in the face of the unfamiliar. There is not much holy ground left.

7. 'Moreover he said, I am the God of thy father . . .' Even in this backside of the wilderness the people of Israel were to find, not a stranger deity, but the God of their fathers. Whether Moses himself was in the direct line of the Patriarchs is not at all clear. He doesn't figure in the genealogies and there's mystery attaching to his birth and upbringing. But the editors, at least, are determined to show that this theophany, this appearance of the divine power in the desert place, is the act of that same God who brought Abram from Ur of the Chaldees and was now about to bring his descendants out of slavery. He claims no territorial rights. God is sovereign, not in a particular place, but over a particular people.

8. 'Come now therefore, and I will send thee unto Pharaoh.' As we shall see when we come to read about Isaiah, the role of the prophet in Israel, almost without exception, was to stand in the places of power, before kings, and proclaim the word of God. Samuel and Nathan have this task, so do Elijah, Amos, Jeremiah, John the Baptist. When Paul the Apostle appeals to Caesar he is insisting on the prophet's privilege to stand at the heart of things and make the Lord's name known. Those who in our day want the churches to avoid political involvement are surely blind to one of the great claims of the Bible.

A Conclusion

This third chapter of Exodus takes us very deep into the mysteries of Jewish and Christian faith. If we went further, we should be confronted with the Name of the Lord. What does it mean? 'Tell the children of Israel that I AM hath sent thee unto them.' You need to know Hebrew before you can begin to unravel that mystery. But what seems to have mattered to the ancient Jews was not what titles you used for God (they preferred not to name him at all) but the knowledge that he was and is the God of their fathers – invisible, dwelling apart, infinite in holiness, yet bound to them by ties of intimacy which meant he could call them by name. When you read accounts of the Holocaust you come up against this, time after time; this mixture of awe and familiarity which the people of God take with them even into those places where you might expect to find only an appalling absence – *āchārim*, the uttermost parts. It's something they learnt when they were slaves, from the burning bush, in the backside of the desert.

3

The God of our Fathers

I remember being badly caught out by the owner of a stately home who was taking us round his house. He showed us some magnificent tapestries: 'Here,' he said, 'we have Jacob at the well. And that's his wife, whatever her name was. The vicar will be able to tell us.' But the vicar couldn't, dammit, his mind having gone blank. Rebekah? Leah? Rachel? It didn't take very long to work it out, but by then it was too late: we had moved to the next room, and my reputation was in ruins.

There's no excuse, of course, for the clergyman who doesn't know his Bible, but we can always blame somebody else. You see, most of us who learnt to read the Bible as children learnt to do it in a very selective way, through lectionaries, which is very useful, but it can leave you knowing the Bible as a collection of incidents, largely unrelated and out of context. It's the same with secular history: you may know something about the Greeks, something about the Romans, then you take a great leap to the England of 1066, and remember snippets thereafter; but most of us are shamefully ignorant of the bits in between, and have little idea of how different ages and civilizations relate to each other. So what do you do about these gaps in your knowledge of the scriptures? You don't want to get caught out, so perhaps you decide to read your Bible from beginning to end – it's surprising how many people do this – beginning with Genesis 1, which is presumably Year 1, and going through to Revelation, which has to be The End: and that surely must give you a comprehensive overview of this most perplexing book. Wouldn't you think?

It's not fair, but it doesn't work out like that, and it's sad to think how many people have set out on that journey only to find it doesn't lead anywhere. The Old Testament is emphatically not a chronological account of the history of Israel from beginning to end. Parts of it certainly set out to tell the story from scratch – Psalm 78 for instance, or the closing chapters of Ecclesiasticus – but when you look closely even at the 'historical' books you find, as we saw in chapter 2, that they are compilations of material from all kinds of different sources and periods, often arranged so as to lend support to a particular theological or political point of view. Perfectly reasonable, that. But it does mean that you need some sort of guideline if you are to grasp the overall shape of Jewish history, and the place of individual people or groups of people – the Patriarchs for example – within it.

This chapter is an attempt at such a guideline.

Taken at face value the 'historical' books of the Old Testament tell us how a group of nomads, after various adventures, settles in Palestine and becomes a political unit, and what happens to it then. Broadly speaking, very broadly speaking, the story goes like this:

Abram/Abraham, elderly and childless, is required by God to leave his ancestral home in Mesopotamia, near the Persian Gulf, so that God may make of him a great nation. In obedience he goes first north-west to Haran, close to the Syrian border, then south-west into Palestine, 'the land of Canaan'. Famine drives him briefly into Egypt, but he returns to stake out a claim to territory around Hebron in the southern part of Palestine. There's continual warfare with neighbouring groups, and evidently some dissension within Abraham's own clan: his nephew Lot figures as the ancestor of Moab and Ammon, Transjordanian tribes who later become bitter enemies of Israel. Intermarriage is out of the question, so wives are fetched from Mesopotamia for Abraham's son Isaac and his grandson Jacob/Israel. The bond between Abraham and God is close and personal. It is described as an intimate and exclusive covenant relationship, sealed by rites of blood, of circumcision and sacrifice. Human sacrifice of the only son is narrowly averted.

Two or three generations later it's once again famine which drives the twelve sons of Israel into Egypt: at first they prosper there, but later decline into servitude from which they are rescued by a deliverer, Moses, who leads them north again across the desert into Palestine. There they settle by right of conquest into the inland parts of the country and around the Jordan valley, but don't succeed in dislodging the Philistines of the coastal area, who seem to have been a 'people from the sea' with a more advanced culture than that of the pastoral and nomadic Hebrews. The Children of Israel are understood to be composed of twelve tribes descended from the Patriarchs, the twelve sons of Jacob/ Israel. They are subject to constant attack from north and east, but settlement takes place according to a tribal arrangement, and the map at the end of your Bible will almost certainly show you The Promised Land neatly parcelled out between The Twelve Tribes.

There the tale of the Hexateuch, the first six books of the Old Testament, comes to its end. We shall return to it in a moment, but it's as well to take the story further, through the remainder of the Old Testament and beyond:

The Old Testament writers take up the narrative as follows. The tribes of Israel lived for some time under local leaders or Judges, charismatic figures who come forward to deal with particular emergencies as they arose. But in the time of the prophet Samuel, around 1020–1000 BC (we're now moving into datable history), they were moulded into a single unit under king Saul. Saul is killed in battle against the Philistines. His successor David captures the Jebusite stronghold of Jerusalem. He and his son Solomon are determined to establish it as a national shrine and capital city for a united Jewish nation. But on Solomon's death there is a secession of the northern tribes under 'Jeroboam the son of Nebat who made Israel to sin'. Jeroboam and his successors take the title of King of Israel and establish a northern kingdom with its capital first at Shechem and later at the new city of Samaria. The much smaller southern group, now called the Kingdom of Judah, remains loyal to the descendants of David and Solomon. Israel survives until 722 BC, Judah until 597, before being overrun and taken into captivity by Assyria and Babylon respectively. A few impoverished Jews are left behind to till the fields, both in Judaea and Samaria; but when in 539 Babylon falls to the Persians, more influential groups are allowed to return from exile. Jerusalem is rebuilt, and the nation (now without a king) achieves a degree of prosperity, semi-independent at first, but subject after 332 to Hellenistic-Greek domination under Alexander the Great and his successors.

The Hebrew books of the Old Testament don't take us beyond this point, but there are Greek writings in the Apocrypha which describe how the Jews, led by the family of the Maccabees, resist their Hellenistic overlords who are by this time based on Antioch in Syria. In the last two centuries BC Greek dominance gives way to Roman, Palestine being sometimes under puppet kings of the Herodian or Hasmonaean dynasty, sometimes directly under Rome. This period is in part chronicled in the New Testament, supplemented by the Jewish historian Josephus who describes the appalling consequences of the Jewish revolt of AD 66 and the destruction of Jerusalem in 70. Further revolts lead to further destruction in the next century, and in due course Palestine comes successively under Byzantine, Arab, Turkish and European domination until the present century.

That, or something like it, is what comes down to us in the books of the Bible and of later historians. Much of this story is supported by archaeological findings: other parts are open to question. Especially, for our present purposes, we need to look again at the way they depict those early migrations of the Jewish people and their settlement in Palestine.

It's doubtful whether those early journeyings of the people of God, and their entry into their promised land, can really be understood as the activity of a single group of people, moving as a unit from Mesopotamia, into Palestine, in and out of Egypt, and finally back to Palestine to claim their particular allotment of land according to their twelve tribes. Not that there's anything necessarily impossible about all that. But there are broad hints which suggest other possible scenarios. Arguments go on among the scholars, which you'll find in the Old Testament Handbooks, but which are outside the range of this study. The early history of the Semitic peoples is certainly complex and probably indecipherable. One attractive theory, however, is that there were two and possibly more than two main migrations of Hebrew peoples into Palestine, some coming from the north and some from the south. At times these disparate groups seem to have formed a loose federation or 'amphictyony'. At other times they evidently found themselves quite seriously at odds with one another, as closely related clans easily do: the book of Joshua provides an instance in chapter 22, where a breakaway group tries to set up its own cult centre, and civil war is only narrowly averted. Certainly there seems to have been a very considerable number of cult centres, holy places – Mamre, Bethel, Gilgal, Shechem, Shiloh – some of which survived well beyond the time when, according to the official Deuteronomic account, Jerusalem had

become the national place of worship because God had chosen 'to
set his name there'. So it's tempting to see, in the later rivalries
between north and south, something more ancient and deep-
seated than a simple act of rebellion by Jeroboam in the year 922.
If the original Hebrew settlement took place piecemeal, in
successive waves of immigration rather than in One Big Happy
Family under Moses, then even the later fierce hatred between
Judaean and Samaritan is more easily understood. Especially
when you consider that the surviving records come almost
without exception from the southern kingdom, and claim as their
spiritual centre Jerusalem, the city of the living God. Northerners
get a bad press throughout the Old Testament, though it's clear
from other sources that among their kings were several powerful,
capable and farsighted men.

If this or something like it is accepted as a reinterpretation of
early Israelite history, where does that leave the Patriarchs? At
one level, I suppose, it calls into question their very existence as
individual persons, and presents them in a new light as representative figures, standing for particular groups of wanderers. This
doesn't necessarily mean that there was 'no such person' as
Abraham, Isaac, or Jacob with his twelve sons. But you only have
to reflect on characters in our own folklore like King Arthur or
Twm Shôn Catti to realize how easily the individual can come to
stand for the community, and how smudgy is the boundary
between history and legend.

More importantly, it has to be remembered (and I'll keep
harping on this) that later editors have vigorously reworked the
material which came down to them, and no doubt brought the
stories of the Patriarchs into line with much later notions of the
nature and character of the God of Israel. For instance, it's highly
unlikely that at the time of the settlement (the middle of the
second millennium BC?) the Hebrew peoples were anywhere
near to an understanding of the One True God who had, by the
time of our written records, come to be worshipped at Jerusalem.
Monotheism, like monogamy, is a fairly late development in
most cultures. Jahweh was their God, certainly, and for the most
part they felt a fierce loyalty to him, a loyalty born perhaps and
fostered in the desert: but there were other gods around, and it
didn't do to antagonize them. It was the general practice, even
among the Kings of Judah, even at a quite late date (see
II Kings 23) to pay respect to neighbouring heathen deities. In

II Kings 23 you can read how, only a few years before the Kingdom of Judah came to an end, King Josiah had to reckon with firmly-established heathen practices within Jerusalem itself. It seems that through much of their history conflicting religious observances co-existed within the various Hebrew communities. We've seen how this may well be reflected in the stories of Cain and Abel, of Jacob and Esau, where there seems to be a reflection of that tension between the worship of Jahweh and the fertility cults of the Baals. All in all, one of the fascinating things about reading the early books of the Old Testament is to find that they preserve vestiges of something much more ancient than what is being presented on the surface. You find indications of a religion more primitive, more sinister even, than the editors of a later age would like us to suppose.

It's time, then, to think about the religious significance of the patriarchs. What happens when they are regarded, as they generally have been, as Real Live Men? Whether that's what they were or not, has to remain (I believe) an open question. What matters is that the stories about them are presented as stories about real people. They are stories of God's dealings with real people. Indeed, what strikes you and surprises you about these patriarchal characters is their very humanity. They are not supermen, like Herakles or Prometheus. And this brings with it another problem: if these stories about God and man are set before us as Holy Scripture, and if religious instruction is based on such stories, as most of it is, then the characters in the narrative clearly acquire great spiritual and moral importance. Which means that teachers of religion have usually felt themselves obliged to treat the stories as moral stories. And in that case you may have to show that Abraham and Sarah weren't murderously inclined and Jacob wasn't really a cheat and a liar. Couldn't have been, dash it. These are the Fathers. God's people *par excellence*. The Bible is for guidance, so surely we should look to these heroes of religion as models to be followed? Shouldn't we?

This is a real problem. A matter of different levels. At one level you could read Genesis from scratch as a secular literary text and not concern yourself much with the morality of the participants. (Though, my goodness, when you think how lovely people like Bernard Levin go on about Wagner's *Ring* you begin to wonder whether anything's secular any more.) You can't insist on history, even religious history, being read on this uncommitted level. You may not be disposed to think of Genesis as Holy Writ, to treat it as the Word of God or find inspiration in it. But you have to acknowledge that for the most part people have indeed treated it just like that. Let me give you an example. In the sixteenth-century glass of King's College Chapel in Cambridge you'll find a great series of New Testament scenes paralleled by Old Testament 'types', in a characteristic mediaeval scheme. For instance, Joseph is cast into a pit by his brothers, and this is offered as a type of the entombment of Christ. The reunion of Joseph and Jacob in Egypt becomes a type of the appearance of the risen Christ to his disciples. The burial of the Virgin is typified in the burial of Jacob. Now, you may think this typology a rather perverse way of treating the Old Testament, but for centuries it was by far the commonest way, sometimes the only way of treating it, and therefore (this is my point) the stories came to be invested with an immense spiritual significance, by the very fact that they were set alongside the saving events of the gospel. And so they still are. When a church lectionary prescribes that a reading about the sufferings of Christ in the ninth chapter of St Luke is to be preceded by the story of the sacrifice of Isaac from the twenty-second chapter of Genesis, some kind of equation is implied: a very high religious value is being claimed for the figures of Abraham and Isaac, higher than is proper to the story itself.

That's the way it is and always has been for most Bible-reading people. In the religion of Israel, and equally strongly in the religion of the New Testament as it developed, the Patriarchs served as models: not because they were paragons of virtue, but because of the place they occupy in the scheme of salvation. Abraham, by this token, is to be seen not only as an object-lesson for faith, going out into the unknown, but more importantly as the actual physical source from which comes our inheritance as the people of God. 'To Abraham and his seed were the promises made', says St Paul. And in the speeches of Peter and Stephen in the book of Acts (which preserve, so we're told, elements of Christian teaching even earlier than St Paul) the Jews are repeatedly assured that the God who raised Jesus from the dead is none other than the God of their fathers, of Abraham and of Isaac and of Jacob. It was important to harp on this, not only for the sake of the story-line, but in order to root the new revelation immovably in the same soil as the old.

'As in Adam all die, even so in Christ shall all be made alive.'
It's hard to imagine how that point could be made more concisely
or more concretely. Adam may not strictly be counted as one of
the patriarchs, and we may find St Paul's conception of the First
Man as strange to us as Milton's is: none the less, isn't it
astonishing to find such swiftness of communication across the
centuries? But if such language is to retain its usefulness we need,
of course, to know who Adam was. Or who St Paul thought he
was. Somehow we need to keep the channels clear, back into that
pre-history, back to the fathers, since that's where Jews and
Christians alike have presumed to find their spiritual origins, and
still do.

I once asked a friend who was alienated from her parents what
she thought she could learn from them. She looked surprised by
the question, but answered without hesitation. 'Nothing at all',
she said. That's sad. I'm more impressed by the witness of, say,
Psalm 77:

> I will remember the works of the Lord: and call to mind thy
> wonders of old time. I will think also of all thy works: and my
> talking shall be of thy doings. Thy way, O God, is holy: who is so
> great a God as our God? Thou art the God that doeth wonders: and
> hast declared thy power among the people. Thou hast mightily
> delivered thy people: even the sons of Jacob and Joseph.

4

The Witness of Isaiah of Jerusalem

Isaiah 6. 1–9. 7

At first sight The Book of the Prophet Isaiah is unreadable. Sixty-six chapters of obscurity, relieved occasionally by a text from Handel's 'Messiah'. It doesn't help much when you're told that there wasn't one Isaiah but three, and that the book is made up of prophecies from various times, the first part dating from the eighth century BC, when the kingdom of Judah was still prosperous, the second and third parts assembled after the destruction of Jerusalem by the King of Babylon in 597.

Why should you be bothered with all this? There doesn't seem to be much here for today's readership. And there are other factors which make the prophetic books of the Old Testament hard going.

First, you're likely to have at the back of your mind the idea that the prophet's main function is to foretell the future, and that of course makes you ask, Did he get it right? In fact, as we'll see, forecasting in this sense is not the most important part of what Old Testament prophecy was about; but success or failure in this department did, and still does, affect the way the prophet's message was received.

Secondly, and connected with my first point, you'll sometimes find as you read the prophets that your Bible has printed headings saying things like 'Christ's Birth Foretold'; and when you attend public worship and hear the prophets read, the reader may introduce the reading by announcing 'Christ's Kingdom is Foreshown' or some such formula. So you can easily get the idea that Old Testament prophets are chiefly significant as witnesses to the coming of Christ. And that view does them less than justice.

Thirdly, there's the fact that as they stand these books are extremely bitty. You can't read them straight through and make sense of them. This is because in their original oral form prophetic utterances were usually brief, obscure and oracular in style, and often ambiguous in content. Even when these pronouncements were collected and written up, with connecting narratives and comments, the resulting book may be higgledy-piggledy indeed.

The word 'prophet' can be used to describe a wide variety of people. On the one hand there were those bands of ecstatics at large in ancient Palestine, whose activities you can read about as they encounter Saul in the tenth chapter of the First Book of Samuel, and Elisha in the second chapter of the Second Book of Kings. Very odd they seem, as we read how they went into transports and cut themselves with stones. The prophet or prophetess might continue to wander from village to village, or might settle and be venerated as a seer or wise woman in some holy place. On the other hand there were prophets who were much more firmly established either at court or in the temple. They could be figures of great social and political significance like Elijah or Jeremiah, influential in high circles. But all those within the prophetic tradition whose words have come down to us have one thing in common. The prophet is someone who, as E. M. Forster said of the poet Cavafy, 'stands at a slight angle to the universe', who gives testimony first and foremost as the critic of those who are powerful in politics and in religion. It's this element in Hebrew society which still attracts attention today. People still expect the religious leader to exercise a prophetic role in the world, not by claiming to see any further into the future than anyone else, not by holding the crystal ball, but standing as one who is ready to question authority and influence, to speak in the hearing of nations or of individuals, 'telling it slant' but insisting that what is being said is indeed the word of the Lord. That's the legacy of the Hebrew prophets.

If you think this legacy is important, it's worth reading this prophetic literature with a good deal of care. You have to put yourself to the trouble of discovering what the prophet had to say in its own context. You're not searching, necessarily, for a message for your own time, or using the prophetic book (or any other scripture) as a quarry for uplifting or reassuring texts. The Bible needs to be taken more seriously than that. Taken and read on its own terms it will bring you face to face with much that is strange, and much again which is strangely familiar.

Isaiah of Jerusalem, the 'First Isaiah' of chapters 1–39, seems to have belonged to a well-connected family of priests, and to have had access both to the temple community and to the royal household. He lived in the public eye, and you can get a glimpse of his career through the nineteenth and twentieth chapters of the Second Book of Kings. The chapters we're studying in the book of Isaiah itself, from the beginning of the sixth to half-way through the ninth, can be read as a self-contained unit within the larger collection. They shed a great deal of light on how the prophets experienced their own calling and understood the task they had to fulfil. In Isaiah's case we shall see that there are six stages in this process:

> The prophet's vision
> The prophet's response
> The prophet meets the king
> The prophet in action
> The prophet and his problems
> The prophet's end in view

The Prophet's Vision

In the year that King Uzziah died I saw also the Lord sitting upon a throne, high and lifted up, and his train filled the temple. Above it stood the seraphims: each one had six wings; with twain he covered his face, and with twain he covered his feet, and with twain he did fly. And one cried unto another, and said, Holy, holy, holy, is the Lord of hosts: the whole earth is full of his glory. And the posts of the door moved at the voice of him that cried, and the house was filled with smoke.

There was nothing very special about the year 742 BC when King Uzziah (Azariah) died. Just as there was nothing special about the fifteenth year of the reign of Tiberius Caesar, when Pontius Pilate was procurator of Judaea, and Herod tetrarch of Galilee, and his brother Philip tetrarch of Ituraea . . . None of this is of any great matter; except that in both cases there were pennies dropping, 'disclosure situations' as Ian Ramsey used to say, whether for

Isaiah the prophet in the temple or for John the son of Zacharias in the wilderness. And in both cases there was a need to fix the experience in terms of where and when. Roughly, at any rate. The precise dating of biblical events is a frustrating business, if you want a tidy chronological scheme, or if you're trying to decide for instance why St Paul's dates are so different from St Luke's, or whether Jesus died on a Thursday or a Friday. Exact dates don't always matter tremendously, and in some respects the ancient world sat more lightly to its calendars than we do to ours. What did matter to them, and it matters to us, is that when the moment of disclosure occurs, when the word comes from God, it doesn't drop into a vacancy in some imaginary world; it relates to the actual events surrounding people as they live and die. The search for 'historicity' can of course be a red herring, but it's a true instinct which leads us to look for connections between religious truth and the material world in which and through which it is communicated. It's these connections which inevitably bring together the strange and the familiar.

What is at issue here in the sixth chapter of Isaiah is the human capacity for seeing and hearing. It's surely pointless to enquire whether Isaiah's vision was, so to say, externalized; or whether it was a matter of the inward eye. We've nothing to go on, other than what the prophet says: 'I saw the Lord.' What does concern us is the language, the form in which the vision came. Why did God look like that to him? In other words, what is the background, the mental and spiritual equipment, which creates this particular imagery and imprints it on the retina?

To begin with, the vision is set unmistakably in the Temple. To appreciate the vision you have to understand the Temple, a very particular building with its own history and its specific shape. From its foundation by King Solomon in about 950 BC until its destruction by Nebuchadnezzar of Babylon in 587 it remained virtually unchanged, except that idolatrous kings like Manasseh might interfere with it and reforming kings like Josiah might restore it. It was built to reflect and represent the dwelling-place of God. The earthly Temple is a microcosm of the heavenly, as is a Byzantine church or a Gothic cathedral. But the Temple is also a place of assembly adapted to the requirements of those who worship there, and it seems that the shape of the Temple of Jerusalem had to recognize not one but two viewpoints which belonged to the people of God. We've already seen that some

centuries earlier the people of Israel had come into their promised
land, probably in more than one migration, in a series of separate
waves. It may well be that one group centred its worship on a
Tabernacle, a Tent of Meeting, whereas another venerated the
Ark of the Covenant, a wooden box which they could carry with
them on their travels and into battle. Solomon's planning may
have had to take account of both these traditions, which would
account for the shape which the Temple assumed. First, a great
open courtyard where the people could assemble and hold their
sacrifices and their feasts; secondly, a holy place indoors, where
the priests went to burn incense and display the shewbread;
thirdly, the Holy of Holies, a perfect cube of thirty feet square,
perfectly dark, where once a year the high priest went and where
the Ark was installed as the throne of God and guarded by carved
seraphim fifteen feet high.

All of this could be of merely antiquarian interest. Guesswork
too, some of it. But it's precisely these details, these exterior
representations of the presence of God, which give shape to the
vision of the prophet Isaiah. The externals of religion profoundly
affect the way people worship and the way they experience God.
So we need to look at this a bit more closely, and consider what
happened in Solomon's Temple. Once a year, for instance, what
happened was a re-enactment of the arrival of God when he first
came to take up his residence there. It took the form of an annual
Covenant festival. And the remarkable thing about it is that we
still sing, both in Christian and in Jewish worship, the songs
written for that festival. Look at Psalms 80, 99 and 132:

> Hear, O thou Shepherd of Israel, thou that leadest Joseph like a
> sheep: shew thyself also, thou that sittest upon the cherubims.
> The Lord is King, be the people never so unpatient: he sitteth
> between the cherubims, be the earth never so unquiet.
> The Lord is great in Sion: and high above all people . . .
> O magnify the Lord our God, and worship him upon his holy
> hill: for the Lord our God is holy.
> We will go into his tabernacle: and fall low on our knees before
> his footstool.
> Arise, O Lord, into thy resting-place: thou and the ark of thy
> strength.

The Temple of Yahweh Sebaoth, the Lord of Hosts, the Ark of
the Covenant with its attendant angels, it's all there in the

worship of Israel, and it's still there in the worship of the
Christian church. You're using the same furniture, so to say,
when you sing a hymn like

> Bright the vision that delighted
>   once the sight of Judah's seer;
> sweet the countless tongues united
>   to entrance the prophet's ear.
>
> Round the Lord in glory seated
>   cherubim and seraphim
> filled his temple, and repeated
>   each to each the alternate hymn:
>
> 'Lord, thy glory fills the heaven;
>   earth is with its fulness stored;
> unto thee be glory given,
>   holy, holy, holy, Lord.'

It's part of our mental furniture, ingrained into our religious
imagery as surely as it was for Isaiah in 742 BC. It's always
important to acknowledge our religious ancestry, and to recognize that the impulse for it comes from a level which is both
primitive and deep. The young couple who want to get married
in church find that the place of worship on their housing-estate is
a dual-purpose building erected in 1976, and it simply won't do;
what they need is a proper church, and that means stained glass
and pews and an organ. Crematorium chapels must have them
too. Now, it's all too easy to mock, but this goes deep. It's not just
a matter of ancient and modern: I have stood more than once in
the sixth-century church of Sancta Sophia in Istanbul, even in its
present state one of the great religious buildings of the world, and
heard dismayed visitors from the west saying that it doesn't feel
like a church at all. The furniture and the imagery are all wrong,
and for most of us, if we are to express our religious aspirations,
the surroundings need to be right.

It's at this level, then, that the testimony of Isaiah begins. It's in
this conventional, ecclesiastical, cultic context that his meeting
with God takes place. Once again, it's a meeting-point of the
strange and the familiar: familiar, because the enthronement of
God in his Temple was the background of his daily life and
priestly work; strange, because the Holy of Holies was impenetrable and shrouded in utter darkness. Isaiah never saw inside it.

The seraphim, too, were strangers from another world: yet it's by familiar gestures that they cover their faces and their genitals ('feet' is a euphemism), for these are created beings like ourselves, in awe at the presence of God. The song that they sing is a mixture, too. Like Jacob's Ladder it has its feet on the earth and its top in heaven. Holy, holy, holy – it's the familiar Jewish New Year song, as hackneyed as Good King Wenceslas; strange words, all the same, so that even in our own culture musicians of however agnostic a persuasion respond to them with peculiar reverence. Listen to the Sanctus in Vaughan Williams' Mass in G, or in Britten's War Requiem.

Not only heaven but the whole earth is full of this glory. Irenaeus, who wrote at the end of the first century AD, has a famous remark to this effect: *Visio Dei gloria hominis: gloria Dei vivens homo*. The vision of God is man's glory: God's glory is a living man – man and woman, both. That quotation has become fashionable because, I suspect, people aren't any longer at ease with the concept of glory. It has uncomfortable overtones of flag-waving, Pomp and Circumstance, *La Gloire*, until you make it manageable by associating the divine with the human. Maybe Irenaeus did so because he too was uncomfortable with the 'glory' ideology which pervaded the Roman Empire. Glory makes us fidget, even the glory of God. It needs to be hidden behind the veil, the iconostasis, shadowed by seraphim. But the vision comes through just the same. V. Herntrich goes further than Irenaeus when he says of Isaiah's vision, 'God's holiness is his hidden glory: but his glory is his hiddenness revealed.' In the New Testament context the concept of glory largely gives way to a theology of mystery; and Geoffrey Lampe used to insist that Christian mystery, especially as St Paul expounds it, is not something clandestine, to be safeguarded or shrouded in secrecy, but is to be proclaimed, made known, shared.

The strange and the familiar complement one another. There's a powerful paradox at work here, as you'd expect when the hidden God is revealed. It's from this point that all religious vision starts, and all prayer. So how is the visionary to respond?

The Prophet's Response

Then said I, Woe is me! for I am undone; because I am a man of unclean lips, and I dwell in the midst of a people of unclean lips: for mine eyes have seen the King, the Lord of hosts.

It's not quite what you might expect, and it's not what preachers often want you to think it is. Here's a young man hesitating, admittedly. 'Woe is me.' He has seen the Lord, and that's supposed to be lethal. Moreover, he has unclean lips. Pause for a moment on that; it's not easy to interpret, because the ancient Jewish concept of uncleanness is rather different from ours. Uncleanness, as they saw it, was incurred chiefly by contact; contact with certain kinds of animal, with almost any kind of sickness of mind or body, with any kind of discharge from the human body, and most especially with death. You didn't have to be the victim: any contact with these things, even with the shadow of them, could make you unclean. It had nothing to do with morality. To get rid of uncleanness you didn't have to be sorry or repent, but you did have to take the proper steps for ritual purification before you could do anything else at all. So when Isaiah said of himself and his associates that they were men of unclean lips, he didn't mean that they talked dirty, or were conscious of sin or unworthiness in the interiorized way we use those words; he meant that he was in some way disqualified, inhibited from speaking in the name of God, even though he had not yet been required to do so. That was to be the next stage, the removal of inhibition:

Then flew one of the seraphims unto me, having a live coal in his hand, which he had taken with the tongs from off the altar: and he laid it upon my mouth, and said, Lo, this hath touched thy lips; and thine iniquity is taken away and thy sin purged. Also I heard the voice of the Lord, saying, Whom shall I send, and who will go for us? Then said I, Here am I; send me.

It seems a strange way of proceeding. First the vision, then the response, and only then the commission. Even stranger is the charge which the prophet receives:

And he said, Go, and tell this people, Hear ye indeed, but understand not; and see ye indeed, but perceive not. Make the heart of this people fat, and make their ears heavy, and shut their eyes; lest they see with their eyes, and hear with their ears, and understand with their heart, and convert, and be healed.

What do you make of that? The words probably ring a bell, because you'll remember them from the fourth chapter of St Mark, where Our Lord is justifying his method of teaching. Why parables? they asked. Because, says Jesus, although you can know the mystery of the kingdom, they have to be taught obliquely, so that they may see without perceiving and hear without understanding, and *not* be converted and forgiven. It's a very perplexing passage which we'll consider at length in a later chapter. St Mark quotes from Isaiah, but he uses the Greek version, called the Septuagint, which is a bit different from the Hebrew. The Hebrew, however, is no less puzzling. The prophet is sent out specifically to fatten the hearts of the people, to obscure their vision and occlude their hearing. And that really is very difficult to understand. So the prophet lodges the age-old protest that everybody makes when the will of God becomes more impenetrable than usual:

> Then said I, Lord, how long?

As a protest, that doesn't usually expect or get an answer. But in this case it does:

> Until the cities be wasted without inhabitant, and the houses without man, and the land be utterly desolate, and the Lord have removed men far away, and there be a great forsaking in the midst of the land. But yet in it there shall be a tenth, and it shall return (to be destroyed again) as a terebinth or an oak, whose stock remains even when the tree is felled. The holy seed is its stump.

That's hard going, too, even with some help from modern translators, and with an editor's comment at the end. The message, at all events, is a grim one. But is it possible, the world being what it is, to conceive of a prophetic message being anything but grim? On the morning I write this, there's an item in my newspaper about a two-year-old child in Leeds infected with venereal disease after sexual abuse from her father. The heart waxes fat, the cities are desolate indeed. What are we to expect? What message can there be? except to claim, as prophets always have and as Isaiah shortly will, that the future like the past lies under the judgment of God, whether it's a judgment of condemnation, as it must be, or one of faint hope for a remnant to survive even the cutting down and burning of the tree. That's the message which somehow has to be delivered.

The Prophet's Meeting with the King

And it came to pass in the days of Ahaz the son of Jotham the son
of Uzziah king of Judah, that Rezin the king of Syria and Pekah the
son of Remaliah king of Israel, went up toward Jerusalem to war
against it, but could not prevail against it. And it was told the
house of David, saying, Syria is confederate with Ephraim. And
his heart was moved, and the heart of his people, as the trees of the
wood are moved with the wind. Then said the Lord unto Isaiah,
Go forth now to meet Ahaz, thou and Shear-Jashub thy son, at the
end of the conduit of the upper pool in the highway of the fuller's
field; and say unto him, Take heed and be quiet; fear not, neither
be fainthearted for the two tails of these smoking firebrands,
for the fierce anger of Rezin with Syria, and of the son of
Remaliah . . . Thus saith the Lord God, It shall not stand, neither
shall it come to pass.

Uzziah died in 742. Ahaz came to the throne in 735. Seven years
pass between the vision and the commission, and that's a long
time to nurse a vocation. The situation now is that Jerusalem and
the southern kingdom of Judah are under threat from a confeder-
acy between Rezin King of Syria and Pekah the king of the
northern Hebrew kingdom of Israel/Ephraim, the united kingdom of Israel and Judah having fallen apart after the death of
Solomon two centuries earlier. So how can a small mountain state
survive in the face of its two more powerful northern neighbours?
Now, Ahaz has an answer to that, as you can read in the Second
Book of Kings, from chapter sixteen onwards. His answer was to
our ears scarcely credible: it is, simply, to sacrifice his eldest son,
burning him as an offering to Moloch the god of Moab; and then
to send an appeal for help to an even more powerful monarch,
Tiglath-Pileser III of Assyria. Even more appalling is the fact that,
apparently, it worked. The Assyrians did indeed take the
pressure off Jerusalem by destroying the kingdoms of Rezin and
Pekah, and in gratitude Ahaz installed in the temple of Jerusalem
a replica of a heathen altar which he had seen in Damascus.

That was the king's policy, dramatic and effective, wouldn't
you say? What the prophet has to say is something quite different
from that. He goes out to meet the king with no political
programme, taking with him his own son, a living child, 'a silent
witness at his father's side'. The significance here lies in the boy's

name, Shear-Jashub, A-Remnant-Will-Return. The Jews well understood symbolic actions and significant names; but we don't know what they made of the message which accompanied them. They may have thought that in comparison with the king's incisive course of action the words of the prophet are pretty bland and ineffectual: 'Take care. Be quiet. Don't be afraid. All will be well.' Even though the cities will be desolate, and only a remnant survive? It doesn't make a great deal of sense, by normal standards. But the point is desperately simple: the meeting between the prophet and the king serves purely to emphasize that the people of God have a choice between the king's *realpolitik* on the one hand and God's design on the other. *Tertium non datur.* No other choice is given. And there is a sign to drive the point home.

> Moreover the Lord spake again unto Ahaz, saying, Ask thee a sign of the Lord thy God; ask it either in the depth, or in the height above. But Ahaz said, I will not ask, neither will I tempt the Lord. And he said, Hear ye now, O house of David; is it a small thing for you to weary men, but will ye weary my God also? Therefore the Lord himself shall give you a sign; Behold, a virgin shall conceive, and bear a son, and shall call his name Immanuel. Butter and honey shall he eat, that he may know to refuse the evil, and choose the good. For before the child shall know to refuse the evil, and choose the good, the land that thou abhorrest shall be forsaken of both her kings.

You've heard those words at every carol service you ever attended, but in origin they've nothing to do with the stable of Bethlehem. The message to the beleaguered city is that a young woman conceiving today could reasonably, nine months from now, call her child God-With-Us; and *that* is something she certainly would not do if by then Jerusalem had fallen, because when the enemy arrives pregnant women usually don't survive, or at any rate don't give their children victorious names like God-With-Us. So here, oddly enough, is a sign from God which could have been interpreted as supporting the king's policy. But the king doesn't want a sign. Not because he's modest but because he's stubborn. 'It can be a sign of unbelief to ask for a sign: and it can be a sign of unbelief to refuse a sign.' Ahaz refuses the sign because he wants to keep the initiative for himself. He doesn't want affirmation from the Lord. It doesn't suit the king that the future should be under the hand of God, as this quiet-voiced prophet says it is. And that's why, in this meeting, it is finally Ahaz who comes under judgment and is found wanting.

The Prophet in Action

> Moreover the Lord said unto me, Take thee a great roll, and write in it with a man's pen concerning Maher-shalal-hash-baz. And I took unto me faithful witnesses . . . and I went to the prophetess; and she conceived and bare a son. Then said the Lord to me, Call his name Maher-shalal-hash-baz. For before the child shall have knowledge to cry, My father, and My mother, the riches of Damascus and the spoil of Samaria shall be taken away before the king of Assyria.

Here's symbolic action and no mistake. In God's name Isaiah 'goes in' to a woman colleague, fathers a second child, and gives him the even more outlandish name, Quick-to-Plunder-Swift-to-Spoil. Another silent witness at his father's side. The message is now more specifically directed against Syria and Samaria, but the witness is to his own people:

> I will wait upon the Lord, that hideth his face from the house of Jacob, and I will look for him. Behold, I and the children whom the Lord hath given me are for signs and for wonders in Israel from the Lord of hosts who dwelleth in Zion.

There's poignancy in this family group, standing forlorn in the face of the people, as the prophet's message goes on and on, wrung out of him by his apprehensions of what's to come and by his vision of inundation and violence. But the message has to be given, as the word of God through his prophet. There's to be no resort to witchcraft and necromancy (leave alone human sacrifice) as practised by the neighbouring heathen who 'seek unto them those who have familiar spirits, and wizards that peep and mutter'. It can't be right, he says, to consult the dead on behalf of the living. The word of God may be hard, but it's never arcane. The witness of the prophet is plain and it's public.

The Prophet and his Problems

The Lord spoke to me, when his hand seized me, and he warned me not to walk in the way of this people, saying, 'Do not call difficulty, all that this people call difficulty; and what it fears, do not fear and do not dread.'

That's Otto Kaiser's translation and it goes some way towards making sense of this. The prophet is not to take refuge in obscurities or scaremongering. Nor is he to offer the people some sort of easy way out. Far from it:

> It shall come to pass that when they shall be hungry, they shall fret themselves, and curse their king and their god, and look upward. And they shall look unto the earth; and behold, trouble and darkness, dimness of anguish; and they shall be driven to darkness.

The message may be harsh, but it's plain enough. It has all the realism that you come to expect from Hebrew prophecy. 'The prophets do mourn', and they go in dread of the easy answer which cries 'peace, peace' where there is no peace. From this prophet especially, after what you've learnt of him in these chapters of testimony and self-revelation, you won't expect anything by way of a happy ending. So where does his call lead him, and what's the final content of this witness, this sign to which he and his silent sons are pointing?

The Prophet's End in View

You have to be careful, if you're taking your scriptures seriously, not to slip into a sort of Bible reader's overdrive. The final verses in our study bring us right back to Handel country, the reading that goes with the carol. It's very tempting to find in them the wrong kind of assurance, what used to be misunderstood as Comfortable Words: all shall be well; whatever anxieties or distress may confront you now, there's light at the end of the tunnel, so that you can go home with a blessing. That's how a superficial reading of these words might run:

> The people that walked in darkness have seen a great light: they that dwell in the land of the shadow of death, upon them hath the light shined . . . For unto us a child is born, unto us a son i given: and the government shall be upon his shoulder: and his name shall be called Wonderful, Counsellor, The mighty God, The everlasting Father, The Prince of Peace. Of the increase of his government and peace there shall be no end, upon the throne of

David, and upon his kingdom, to order it, and to establish it with judgment and with justice from henceforth even for ever. The zeal of the Lord of hosts will perform this.

There's no denying the beauty of those words, especially in the language of King James' Bible. They are wonderfully consoling, and they are inseparable, now, from the Christian conviction that in the birth of Christ all prophecy comes to its fulfilment. No doubt there was in the mind of Isaiah something not so different from that. He does indeed point forward; if not to a full-blown expectation of the Messiah, which the Jews weren't yet expecting, at any rate to something much more concrete than mere optimism. Just as there was a specific location for his vision in the temple, so there's a specific location for the future of God's people, and it's the house of David. And just as God's judgment was marked by the birth and naming of the prophet's two sons, so the coming deliverance is to be marked by a birth, a real child. Eastern religions often saw their deliverers as 'adopted' by their gods. That's what lies behind the second psalm, where it's said of the Jewish king 'thou art my son, this day have I begotten thee'. What Isaiah foresees is certainly not some deified manikin in royal robes, but a true manifestation of the reign of the Lord himself. His testimony ends where it began, before the throne of God. It is God's kingdom, God's peace which is to be inaugurated, not some patched-up piece of power politics. As his past mercies are revealed in the glory of the Temple, with its Ark and attendant seraphim, so the future belongs to him, and the kingdom will be his. The initiative lies in God's hands: the zeal of the Lord of hosts will perform this.

5

Three Psalms

The Book of Psalms is also known as the Psalter. It shouldn't be confused with the Psaltery, which is a musical instrument like a zither; nor with the Psalterium, which is part of a cow's stomach. It is a collection of some 150 Hebrew songs and poems, of different kinds and varying dates. Some parts of the collection may indeed go back as far as King David, and although most of it is much later in date the book is often called The Psalms of David; which is misleading but does distinguish this book from other collections of psalms which you can find elsewhere in the Bible and the Apocrypha and the Dead Sea Scrolls and near-eastern literature generally. And while I'm defining terms in this pedestrian way, let me add that when I talk of 'The Psalmist' in the context of any particular poem, I'm referring to the writer of that psalm only; and that Psalmody is a word used to describe the act of writing or of performing psalms. It may be unnecessary to add that Hebrew poetry doesn't look much like the sort of poetry that we've been brought up on: it doesn't rhyme or scan, but makes much use of parallelism (saying the same thing in different ways) and of antithesis (balancing two statements against one another). Hebrew poets were also fond of acrostics – poems in which successive verses begin with successive letters of the alphabet; Psalm 119 is like that, so is most of the book of Lamentations.

I have put down all that, simply to avoid confusion in the words we use. The real value of the Psalms, however, derives from two much more significant facts: they have been used in the worship of God by Jews and Christians, in private and in public, uninterruptedly for two-and-a-half thousand years so that, as one scholar has said, long and active use has created a unique bridge

for us between past and present; secondly, and more importantly, they stand in their own right as the quintessential
expression of Israel's response to God. Another scholar, Gerhard
von Rad, has well said:

> She (Israel) addressed Jahweh in a wholly personal way. She
> offered praise to him, and asked him questions, and complained
> to him about her sufferings, for he had not chosen his people as a
> mere dumb object of his will in history, but for converse with him.

So there, for a start, are two good reasons why the Psalms
command our affection: they remain in use; and they express an
immensely wide range of human feelings.

The three psalms I've chosen for comment are all quite
different. Even so, it's not going to be possible in this chapter to
do any sort of justice to the wealth of material which the Psalter
contains. What follows is intended to be simply a background
sketch.

Many of the psalms are hymns of praise, belonging to festivals
such as Harvest or New Year. Some are associated with royal
celebrations, and may have been part of a re-enactment in
worship of the mighty acts of God, not unlike the 'enthronement
rituals' preserved in ancient poems which celebrate the enthronement of the Babylonian god Marduk. Obviously there was a
close connection between the sacred songs of the Jews and the
worship which they offered in the Temple at Jerusalem, celebrating the majesty of 'him who sitteth upon the cherubim' and is
'clothed in majesty and honour'. We've come across this ceremonial in our study of Isaiah, but in fact we don't know much in
detail about how they actually did worship; so there are different
theories about, for instance, the Songs of Ascent (Psalms 120 to
134). What we can say is that they vividly express the mood of
pilgrimage and holiday in which the people of God 'go up to the
house of the Lord'. Christian worship has taken these poems for
its own use; we're equally familiar with the 'Hallel' psalms with
which the Psalter ends in a ritual chorus to the praise of God.

Then there are psalms of lamentation. These poems too are
very varied. Some of them mirror very precise experiences of
sickness and dereliction. Some of them are apparently written in
response to the taunts of enemies, real or imagined, and may
reflect accusation and counter-accusation in the Temple courts. If
you are under threat, you call upon God to 'give sentence' with

you. However, you can never be sure when the poet, any poet, is speaking literally and when he's not. There's a rather special way in which a Jewish poet can refer back to a shared historical perspective: if he says he is 'sinking in the mire' the likelihood is that he is aligning himself spiritually with Jeremiah who literally did sink in the mud when he was thrown into a cistern in the dungeon of Malchaiah; if he says 'they parted my garments among them' it's likely that he is glancing back at Joseph and his coat of many colours, as surely as we from our standpoint inescapably look ahead to the events of the crucifixion of Jesus. Prayer is a pivot that can tilt you backwards or forwards. Whenever the Jew prays he makes conscious connexions between his own circumstances and specific events in his national history. When Christians pray they do much the same, if with less intensity.

So it's true to say of many of the Psalms that, if we're to understand them, they must be read in the context of 'sacred history', the story of God's activity. There's a lot of narrative in these poems. And yet the very fact that most of the psalms cannot be accurately dated shows how skilfully the psalmists universalize their material, and make it available to successive generations; rather as great musicians can take a sacred text and make of it something that belongs not exclusively to the Bible, nor to the composer's own century, nor even to those who share the beliefs enshrined within the text and the music. In the Psalms, however, there's nothing of the vague religiosity of the Choral Society: the psalmists are deeply committed to the material they enshrine, as they proclaim the name of the Lord, who is Judge, who blesses and curses, who demands loyalty, and who engages with his people in a living and immediate relationship.

This relationship, for Israel, finds its ultimate fulfilment in *Torah*, the Law. Many of the Psalms are songs in praise of Torah, the commandments and ordinances, the statutes and judgments which are bright as a lantern, sweet as honey, worth getting up at night for, inexhaustible in its riches and beauty. This meditative Torah psalmody takes some getting used to; but in the end it's perhaps the most intimate of all, and the most rewarding if you take it into prayer. And if that's what you are in fact trying to do when you use the Psalter, it's not too much to say that whatever you're looking for, whatever you may be trying to articulate, you'll find it somewhere in these poems. You'll find, too, plenty that you don't want to use, that you wouldn't dream of formulating for yourself: a whole literature of vengeance and bloodthirstiness, which you can't conceivably translate into Christian prayer or worship. It's not to be supposed that Israel's experience can be related wholesale to the present day. Your sense of the ludicrous is quite properly aroused if you are invited to stand up and bewail, in public worship, that you are constrained to dwell with Mesech, and have your habitation among the tents of Kedar. So you have to undertake the task, difficult but worth the effort, of treating the Psalms seriously on their own terms, as you find yourself confronted with the stereotypes of a vanished age, wondering exactly who is speaking, and who the enemy is, and why. As you tune in to the rage and lamentations of an ancient people, you can attempt to understand the experience which gave rise to these poems. All the same, you're likely to find, as a recent commentator has said, that there's no need for 'hermeneutical contortions' to make these songs meaningful in our own times.

Two final comments, one from John Calvin writing in sixteenth-century Geneva, the other from Brevard Childs, a present-day scholar from the United States of America:

Here is the anatomy of all parts of the soul, for not an affection will anyone find in himself whose image is not reflected in this mirror. All the griefs, sorrows, fears, misgivings, hopes, cares, anxieties, in short all the disquieting emotions with which the minds of men are wont to be agitated, the Holy Spirit hath here pictured exactly.

The Psalter assured future generations of Israelites that this book spoke the word of God to each of them in their need. It was not only a record of the past, but a living voice speaking to the present human suffering . . . The reader is given an invaluable resource for the care of souls, as the synagogue and the church have always understood the Psalter to be.

Psalm 34

I will alway give thanks unto the Lord: his praise shall ever be in my mouth.

My soul shall make her boast in the Lord: the humble shall hear thereof, and be glad.

O praise the Lord with me: and let us magnify his name together.

An ancient heading associates this psalm with King David's pretended madness when he fled from Saul to the court of the king of Gath. But in the poem there seems to be no connection with those events. Indeed it's a very formal psalm, an acrostic of the kind already mentioned, in which successive verses begin with successive letters of the alphabet. One of the wonders of ancient literature is that artifice of construction so often allows for deep religious and emotional content. This is, anyway, a 'Wisdom Psalm' which means that it is kissing cousin to the books of Proverbs and Job. It is a teaching psalm, about righteousness and its rewards. There's no sacred narrative here, and no direct reference to the Temple and its worship; all of which points to a time late in Jewish history.

One characteristic of the righteous man is the continuity of his prayer. To praise God means to bless him; and if that's an unfamiliar idea to us, who expect God to be doing the blessing, we'll find it again when we look at the beginning of Ephesians. The daily routine of prayer for the Jew was and is still largely a matter of blessing God. Christianity, especially in its monastic form, continues in this idiom. 'Let nothing take precedence over the worship of God', said St Benedict. And the very word-order of that worship emphasizes that precedence. The Latin hymn *Te Deum Laudamus* is a good example: it begins each verse with God's pronoun: 'Thee we praise, O God; Thee we acknowledge to be the Lord; Thee the whole earth worships . . .' You can't do it in English, though the *Alternative Service Book* has a stab at it, but you can in Latin or Hebrew, and Psalm 34 like the Christian hymn starts from the absolute primacy of God.

The primacy of God is the foundation for what the Wisdom Literature of the Old Testament has to say about the humble and meek. Those two words don't ring bells in modern secular English, though a good deal of church-talk at the moment is concerned with God's supposed bias towards the poor. We'll have more to say about that in the chapter on Ezekiel. Poverty, humility and meekness are ideas which fit well into our view of the gospels, and that's fine, so long as our contemporary rhetoric doesn't blind us to what these concepts meant to the biblical writers from whom we derive them.

There are, according to my count, eight different words used in the Old Testament for the humble and meek. The one most commonly found in the Psalms implies 'bowing down'. This attitude may be active, when the humble bow down in modesty and respect for a superior. Or it may be passive, the abjectness of someone bowed down by poverty or misfortune. To our minds, the former may achieve some sort of moral value and dignity, whereas the latter is simply the unfortunate victim of circumstance. But it's not at all clear that the Psalmists or the Evangelists saw things quite like that. What does strike you in both Old and New Testaments is what has been called a 'strange mutuality', which I think we've almost entirely lost, between the humble and the great. 'I will magnify thee,' says the psalmist, 'for thou hast set me up.' And so says the Blessed Virgin in St Luke: 'My soul magnifies the Lord . . . for he that is mighty hath magnified me.' It's a two-way dynamic; and it was easier to make sense of this in the days when the servant took on something of the dignity of his master, and found in the relationship security rather than degradation. If in the search for greater equality we've forfeited that sense of mutual responsibility, then there's loss as well as gain in it.

I sought the Lord, and he heard me: yea, he delivered me out of all my fear.

They had an eye unto him, and were lightened: and their faces were not ashamed.

Lo, the poor crieth, and the Lord heareth him: yea, and saveth him out of all his troubles.

'Seeking' the Lord is a serious matter. Apparently the same word was used in old Hebrew for 'visiting', either in the sense of an excursion to a holy place, or of a search for a holy man. When he loses his livestock, Saul goes to 'seek' the prophet Samuel. When you and your family had something to celebrate, or urgent supplications to make, it was your right and your duty to go up to the house of the Lord, to *visit* his Temple. Pilgrimages played a prominent part in the religion of Israel, as they still do in the Orthodox and the Catholic worlds. But when there are no more prophets, and the holy places are desolate or disreputable, then what do you do? Well, the seeking becomes interiorized. You find there's a shift in your apprehension of the presence of God and you begin to see it in terms of spiritual encounter. I suspect

that the whole story of the Old Testament, and the development
of Western protestantism, could be seen in terms of that shift.
Certainly, the Wisdom Literature, including many of the psalms,
is much concerned with inner illumination.

Seeking the Lord may indeed bring you inner light, but there's
more to it than that. According to this poet it will effect
deliverance from fear, from shame, and from the ignominy of
being poor. 'They had an eye unto him, and were lightened.'
There's another text of about the same date in the third part of
Isaiah which says, 'Lift up your eyes, look and be radiant.' The
transforming effect of seeking God goes well beyond being
simply conscious of interior vision or spiritual experience. As
Gerhard von Rad puts it, 'Man finds that he is beautiful when he
can recognize himself as an object of the divine pleasure, when
God has lifted up his head.' To realize that is to regain not only
your self-respect but your standing in the community, so that
your face is no longer ashamed. As for being poor, there was no
virtue in that: but it did mean that you had a special claim to the
compassion of God, and could expect the protection of his
representatives, earthly and heavenly. What follows in this poem
tells you how this might be manifested.

> The angel of the Lord tarrieth round about them that fear him: and
> delivereth them.
>   O taste, and see, how gracious the Lord is: blessed is the man
> that trusteth in him.
>   O fear the Lord, ye that are his saints: for they that fear him lack
> nothing.
>   The lions do lack, and suffer hunger: but they who seek the Lord
> shall want no manner of thing that is good.

Angels appear in all sorts of roles, as messengers of life or
death. They speak for God through dreams and visions, and
sometimes they stand apparently for the presence of God
himself, as an external sign of the One who may not himself be
seen. But this poet is determined to work in concrete images. To
taste and see, to take and eat, these are actions of profound
intimacy, whether for the Jewish prophet required to devour the
scroll which contains the word of God, or the Christian disciple
challenged to munch the flesh of the Son of Man in order to
receive eternal life. It's easy to see why this psalmody was quickly
commandeered for use in the Eucharist of the first Christians.

However, if Eucharist was in their view the privilege of the initiated, the psalmist has a different outlook. There are two Hebrew words which the older English versions translate as 'saint': *chasid*, which means kindly or pious, and *qadosh*, used here, which has virtually no moral ingredient and simply means those who are set apart, who belong to God's holy people. Their sainthood stems entirely from that belonging. 'You will be for me a kingdom of priests and a holy nation . . . therefore be ye clean . . .' This Old Testament requirement becomes important and does indeed take on an ethical character for New Testament writers as they express a new understanding of church and ministry, but here in the Old Testament the writer stays with his down-to-earth image: the lions suffer hunger, but the Seeker will want for nothing.

At this point most modern Bibles make a new paragraph. The organist prescribes a change of chant. Some scholars have suggested that this psalm wasn't originally a unity, but a sort of anthology of wise sayings. Certainly from verse 11 onwards there's a different feel to the poem.

> Come, ye children, and hearken unto me: I will teach you the fear of the Lord.
> What man is he that lusteth to live: and would fain see good days?
> Keep thy tongue from evil: and thy lips, that they speak no guile.
> Eschew evil, and do good: seek peace, and ensue it.
> The eyes of the Lord are over the righteous: and his ears are open unto their prayers.
> The countenance of the Lord is against them that do evil: to root out the remembrance of them from the earth.

That's not very compelling. Religion as something that children have to be taught, for heaven's sake? Doesn't that carry within it the seeds of its own death? And, anyway, how do you teach anyone fear, in any positive sense of that dodgy word? Don't we all know that there was nothing the malign dwarf Mime could do to teach young Siegfried how to be afraid? that the knowledge of fear came only with the vision of Brünnhilde unarmed and helpless? Yes; but in the Wisdom Literature the fear of the Lord is rather different from what Siegfried felt. It's not basically the response of awe in face of the strange and the numinous. It has more to do with conduct. It goes with understanding, counsel, strength of mind. It seems a very cool quality: 'keep your tongue . . . avoid evil . . . seek peace.' On the other hand, it's not just about being nice people or disdaining to take advantage of the disarmed. It's about 'lusting to live', which is just what Brünnhilde taught Siegfried. 'Relishing life', says the translation in the *Alternative Service Book*, and that's about right. It's not an excessively strong word, but it's a pointer to a quality of life that's worth living, life as it's supposed to be, life enlivened by Torah. And from here, surely, there's a straight line to the Fourth Gospel, with its teaching about eternal life not as a promise of something beyond the grave but as a mark of Christian living here and now. Because when St John speaks of that kind of living, he has in mind the same God as this psalm is on about; one whose eyes and ears are open to us, whose face is against evil. Separation from him, being 'out of remembrance' is for both writers the very worst that can happen to anyone.

> The righteous cry, and the Lord heareth them: and delivereth them out of all their troubles.
>
> The Lord is nigh unto them that are of a contrite heart: and will save such as be of an humble spirit.
>
> Great are the troubles of the righteous: but the Lord delivereth him out of all.
>
> He keepeth all his bones: so that not one of them is broken.
>
> But misfortune shall slay the ungodly: and they that hate the righteous shall be desolate.
>
> The Lord delivereth the souls of his servants: and all they that put their trust in him shall not be destitute.

We are back again with the humble. Some scholars think that the 'righteous' don't really belong in this part of the poem, but have been added by a later hand. 'The Lord hears, not because it is the righteous who call, but simply because those who cry are crying.' It's the broken in heart, the crushed in spirit, who lay claim to God's attention. This is very close to the Beatitudes in St Matthew, and to St Luke's use of the great prophecy of Isaiah 61, where God's promise is for the healing of the broken-hearted. But the commentators remind us to notice what is *not* being promised. You don't escape by being contrite, but you are delivered. And there's a difference. As Mother Julian put it, 'He saith not, Thou shalt not be tempested, but Thou shalt not be overcome.'

I don't understand the bit about broken bones. Perhaps, as we're told, it's merely a 'forcible metaphor for pain', but it doesn't sound like that to me. There are too many pointers back to the Passover ritual and forward to the crucifixion. But there we are: there's always a danger of over-interpreting scripture. You can get to be like those dreadful singers who think they have to interpret Bach, and ruin the St Matthew Passion in the process. Maybe in this psalm there's just a rather strong line of logic at this point: 'evil shall slay the wicked'; the enemy will get his come-uppance and quite right too. And so with the servant of the Lord: when the poet says that the Lord 'redeems' him, you mustn't read into that word the full Christian doctrine of redemption, as it later developed. But what you can read in this psalm is that in God's eyes human life has value and dignity, and human behaviour is to be taken into account for good or ill. Evil brings its own reward. The good man is the blest man, and in being blessed he blesses God, who is not above such tribute from him.

Psalm 51

In pre-Reformation times you could, if you were a clergyman, expect certain privileges at law, and sometimes you could save your skin by claiming the right to be tried by a special court. But you had to provide proof of your ordained status, and one way of doing that was by reciting (in Latin, of course) a verse or two of scripture, thereby showing that you were literate. One of these so-called 'neck verses' was the beginning of this psalm. *Miserere mei Deus* was in fact one of the texts which even the most ignorant cleric could be expected to know by heart. Psalm 51 was in constant use. It was read to the dying. It was recited at public executions, so that Thomas More, Lady Jane Grey, Count Egmont and innumerable others heard it as they went to their deaths. It was and is one of the Seven Penitential Psalms along with 6, 32, 38, 102, 130, 143, which dominate the church's liturgy at appropriate times. During the seventeenth century Gregorio Allegri gave it a beautiful and highly elaborate musical setting which is now one of the Top Pops of sacred music but was kept as a prerogative of the Sistine Choir in Rome, until Mozart after a single hearing wrote it down. All this has made *Miserere* a familiar if daunting text.

For the careful reader there are a number of problems attached
to it. In the Bible it stands as the first of eighteen Psalms of David,
and tradition associated it with the king's remorse over his
adultery with Bathsheba, the death of her husband Uriah and of
the child she bore to the king. But the internal evidence of the
psalm suggests a later date. Just how late depends on how you
read the final verses about sacrifice which seem to imply a time
after the Temple worship had ceased. Some scholars have
suggested that this passage is a later addition to an earlier poem.
And the phrases which describe God as giver of truth and
wisdom seem to belong to a later tradition again.

More puzzling, really, is the question whether this magnificent
psalm is to be seen as an outpouring of individual grief or as a
community lament, an expression of national penitence. The
intensity of the language may strike you as very personal.
However, in the Psalms individual suffering is usually expressed
in very concrete terms (broken bones, suppurations and the like)
and here we find only the faintest hint of physical suffering.
Enemies are hardly in sight. Instead there is much emphasis on
the need for spiritual integrity in public worship, for ritual as well
as spiritual cleansing. This may mean that the psalm was written
as an expression of public, formal lamentation.

What is certain is that this psalm is a deeply felt and forcibly
expressed account of what it was like to be a penitent and a
worshipper in Israel. As one commentator has said, 'the direct-
ness of the life of prayer out of which this psalm has arisen has
also moulded its outward form'. That means that we are
presented with a classical pattern for the Prayer of Contrition
(writers on Prayer always use lots of Capital Letters, have you
noticed?) like this: Invocation, Confession, Prayer for Forgiveness, Prayer for Renewal, Vows, Final Prayer. Indeed, as a model
Psalm 51 could hardly be bettered.

> Have mercy upon me, O God, after thy great goodness: according
> to the multitude of thy mercies do away mine offences.
>   Wash me throughly from my wickedness: and cleanse me from
> my sin.
>   For I acknowledge my faults: and my sin is ever before me.

Penitence is often seen in our time as something degrading, a
grovelling exhibition of self-abasement, mental flagellation and
so on; quite interesting perhaps as a spectacle on Good Friday in

Seville, but otherwise no more than a deplorable survival of unhealthy mediaeval attitudes. This distaste has come about, I believe, because English-speaking people have forgotten the connection between 'mercy' and the French word for thank-you. To 'cry mercy' is to say *merci*. Penitence, properly understood, is an expression of thankfulness.

As so often, we find an almost excessive intensity in the language of the Jews. Classical Hebrew seems to have used an extensive and bright-toned palette to depict the mercies of God. Apart from the term *chanan* found widely and exclusively in the Psalms, they were apt to use the word *rachamim*, meaning 'bowels'; sometimes with startling effect, as in the vigorous complaint of Third Isaiah:

> Look down from heaven, and behold from the habitation of thy holiness and of thy glory: where is thy zeal and thy strength, the sounding of thy bowels and of thy mercies towards me? are they restrained?

No cringing there. Rather, a fierce insistence that God's nature is to be merciful and compassionate, and that's a note to be sounded whenever one feels aggrieved with God. Devotees of Anglican worship will know the fine anthem to those words by the tragic nineteenth-century composer Thomas Battishill, a piece which mustn't be allowed to fall out of repertoire. But the demand for God's mercies aren't something to be left to the choir. It's too deep in the Christian consciousness for that, and with good reason. There's a phrase 'moved with compassion', used regularly in the gospels for Our Lord's response to human suffering, and entirely characteristic of the Lord's response to human need. It depicts that concern for the sufferer which more than anything else brings Christ within our reach, so to speak: and the word in Greek likewise means a stirring of the bowels, what we would call a gut reaction.

There's another Hebrew word, *chesed*, which appears in our Bibles as 'mercy'. To catch the full flavour of that word you have to look carefully at Exodus 34:

> And the Lord descended in the cloud, and stood with Moses there, and proclaimed the name of the Lord. And the Lord passed by before him, and proclaimed, The Lord, The Lord God, merciful

and gracious, long-suffering, and abundant in goodness and truth, keeping mercy for thousands, forgiving iniquity and transgression and sin, and that will by no means clear the guilty; visiting the iniquity of the fathers upon the children, and upon the children's children, unto the third and to the fourth generation. And Moses made haste, and bowed his head toward the earth, and worshipped. And he said, If now I have found grace in thy sight, O Lord, let my Lord, I pray thee, go among us; for it is a stiff-necked people; and pardon our iniquity and our sin, and take us for thine inheritance.

Those verses stand as a kind of compendium or summary of the relationship between God and his people. And there's nothing soft about those tender mercies. D. H. Lawrence spoke of a rich, warm belly-tension between man and woman, and the poets of Israel speak in much the same way of their relationship with Israel's God. He stands with Moses. He goes among his people, as their judge, just and compassionate. That's what they mean by his 'tender mercies'.

Sin, however, does have to be dealt with. You'll notice that there are three things the Psalmist wants done about his sins. First, he wants them done away, blotted out, cancelled like debts in a ledger. Then he asks for a washing away of pollution, as in Islam the faithful wash themselves before prayer. Thirdly, he wants cleansing; and that's a slightly different notion, to do with the healing of the sick rather than the purifying of the unclean. So the psalmist prays for the whole process of restoration to be set in train. It's what you would look for from a therapist or from a lover. And the striking thing is that he can make this prayer because he himself has 'acknowledged' his sin. In Hebrew this acknowledgment is principally an intellectual matter, so the commentary tells us: 'not the fleeting mood of a depressed conscience, but the courage to deal impartially with one's self in the objectivity of knowing one's own limitations.'

Against thee only have I sinned, and done this evil in thy sight: that thou mightest be justified in thy saying and clear [in thy judgment].

Behold, I was shapen in wickedness: and in sin hath my mother conceived me.

But lo, thou requirest truth in the inward parts: and shalt make me to understand wisdom secretly.

Thou shalt purge me with hyssop, and I shall be clean: thou shalt wash me, and I shall be whiter than snow.

Thou shalt make me hear of joy and gladness: that the bones which thou hast broken may rejoice.

There are many difficulties about this, and they are all tied up together. First, there's the statement that sin is (always?) an offence against God. I'm not certain whether or not the Bible distinguishes between sin against God and sin against one's fellow human beings. There are alarming instances, like the death-sentence on Ananias and Sapphira in Acts 5, where an apparently trivial act of human dishonesty is treated as a sin against the Holy Spirit. And when St Paul quotes from this very psalm in the third chapter of Romans his point seems to be that the effect of man's sin is primarily to reveal the righteousness of God. I find it almost impossible to assent to that. It requires a deeper identification with the Jewish view of Law than most of us can attain to. Speaking for myself, I think I am most conscious of the way my sins affect me. Their effect on other people comes next. Only under pressure do I reflect that anything I do may be offensive to the Deity. That does, I suppose, render me liable to St Augustine's charge, 'Thou hast not yet properly considered the weight of thy sinfulness', but that seems to me to be where we are, most of us. So at this verse in Psalm 51 my tongue cleaves to the roof of my mouth.

What follows is harder still, this notion that my conception and birth were in themselves acts of wickedness. That I can't for a moment accept. I have to stand, at this point, outside the tradition of both Jews and Christians. Admittedly, my genes may have landed me with a bias towards certain kinds of wickedness, but the belief that 'all men are conceived and born in sin' is something else. And as you look more closely into the imagery of this psalm you'll see that it is specifically the woman's part in procreation that is seen as not only sinful but actually filthy. This too is part of the tradition: 'Man that is born of woman is of few days, and full of trouble . . . who can bring a clean thing out of an unclean?' asks the book of Job. Time and again the Old Testament and the New reflect the conviction of the ancient world that women are inherently dirty. They bleed, and their blood pollutes. Even virgins. So if you want to stay clean, keep away from women. And if you can't do that, get purged with hyssop, which

will cleanse you from your sins, however scarlet. And so on.
Notice, by the way, that the colour of sin is the colour of blood.
Not black, but red. It's all part of that intense irrational fear which
has from the earliest times marked the man's view of woman.

There's a specially vivid instance of this fear of women in
verse 17 of the last chapter of Isaiah. There you can read an
outburst of horror at certain idolatrous practices. It's about
people who 'go into the garden', and eat a broth made of pork
and reptiles and *mice*, would you believe? And worst of all they
follow 'One in the Midst': and who's that, do you suppose? She's
a female figure, for sure. Can she be . . . ? She must be . . . a
Priestess!

It's from those murky origins that our religious prejudices and
taboos have grown, and our sense of sin developed. The
Christian church is deeply infected and impoverished by this
tradition. And it's only small consolation that when the psalmist
goes on to speak of 'truth in the inward parts' Hebrew grammar
constrains him to use the feminine gender in order to locate the
seat of man's integrity.

So what follows this outburst of abhorrence?

Turn thy face from my sin: and put out all my misdeeds.
      Make me a clean heart, O God: and renew a right spirit within
me.
      Cast me not away from thy presence: and take not thy holy spirit
from me.
      O give me the comfort of thy help again: and stablish me with
thy free spirit.
      Then shall I teach thy ways unto the wicked: and sinners shall be
converted unto thee.

He asks God to turn his face away. Ugh! Don't look. 'Go away',
said St Peter to the Lord, 'for I am a sinful man.' I suppose it's all
to do with bad potty-training in one form or another, this
reluctance to open one's shame to the sympathetic eye of the
healer. But the psalmist does balance his prudishness with a plea
for healing of heart and for a new spirit. One shortcoming in the
new eucharistic liturgies is that we're no longer required to admit
that our sins are an intolerable burden to us, and we no longer ask
leave to serve God in 'newness of life'. Nor does the communi-
cant any longer acknowledge that communion in the Body of the
Lord serves for the cleansing, the healing of our bodies as well as

our souls. There's a great loss of wholeness in our view of things if we don't recognize that we need the face of God to be turned towards and not away from us, even (especially) at our moments of shame and diffidence. There's evidence throughout the Jewish scriptures that it was God's presence, his face turned towards his people that guaranteed to them their corporate and national identity. And so it is, still, or ought to be.

We have to beware of capital letters when we think of 'spirit' in the Old Testament. 'The Holy Spirit' hasn't yet found definition as the Third Person of the Holy Trinity. But the Psalmist in speaking of the spirit shows a very clear sense of the liberation which the presence of God gives to those who know themselves to be forgiven. It may be fanciful to see in these verses a sort of Mannheim crescendo, right spirit → holy spirit → free spirit; but he knows for sure that when sin is properly faced and duly forgiven then you may be able to respond to the call of God as we've seen Isaiah of Jerusalem respond to it. The experience of forgiveness sets you free to become a messenger of God's grace.

Deliver me from blood-guiltiness, O God, thou that art the God of my health: and my tongue shall sing of thy righteousness.

Thou shalt open my lips, O Lord: and my mouth shall shew thy praise.

For thou desirest no sacrifice, else would I give it thee: but thou delightest not in burnt-offerings.

The sacrifice of God is a troubled spirit: a broken and contrite heart, O God, shalt thou not despise.

O be favourable and gracious unto Sion: build thou the walls of Jerusalem.

Then shalt thou be pleased with the sacrifice of righteousness, with the burnt-offerings and oblations: then shall they offer young bullocks upon thine altar.

Blood guilt, again. But perhaps this time there's a new slant to the prayer. If you look at the third chapter of Ezekiel you'll find there that the prophet speaks of the task which God has given him in the same terms as this psalmist has just used to describe his vocation: he is to teach the wicked and convert sinners. And if he fails to do this, says God to Ezekiel, the sinner's blood will be required at his hands. That's an impassioned way of saying that the prayer of the contrite heart and the proclamation of God's forgiveness isn't simply an option for the specially pious: it is in fact a matter of life and death for all God's people. It's that task of warning and converting, of renewal and repentance, which is the ground of meeting between God and the psalmist or the prophet; not precise regulations about sacrifice and burnt offerings. Whatever problems we may have with this psalmist, there can be no doubt of the seriousness with which he treats his subject, nor of his intense absorption in the work of renewal and rebuilding which is achieved through God's grace and forgiveness.

Psalm 107

This psalm is something rather different from the two we've been looking at. It has a stronger narrative ingredient, for one thing, proclaiming the mighty acts of God. And it's comparatively easy to set in context: the reference to 'the redeemed of the Lord' makes it fairly clear that this is a poem about the people of God returning from their exile in Babylon, some time after the Persian king Cyrus had overthrown the Babylonian Empire in 539 BC.

But it's not just a piece of narrative, like the Border Ballad sung to the laird after dinner. It has a liturgical ring to it, in that each section is followed by a refrain or chorus. And, as so often in the Psalms, there's an ambiguity in the poem between the personal element and the corporate. Quite obviously the psalm reflects an intense individual experience of being rescued from desolation. As I read it, I can recognize my own encounters with loneliness and distress. On the other hand, it's ultimately not about derelict individuals, and not about merchants lost in the desert, or storm-tossed sailors, or invalids: it's about the people of God, lost and found, captive and free. It's a song of national deliverance. As such, it needs perhaps less comment than either Psalm 34 or Psalm 51.

> O give thanks unto the Lord, for he is gracious: and his mercy endureth for ever.
> Let them give thanks whom the Lord hath redeemed: and delivered from the hand of the enemy;
> And gathered them out of the lands, from the east, and from the west: from the north, and from the south.

The four points of the compass are not to be taken literally. For a Judaean of the sixth century BC exile from the Promised Land felt like exile to the uttermost parts of the earth: for their descendants in dispersion the feeling has become a fact.

They went astray in the wilderness out of the way: and found no city to dwell in.

Hungry and thirsty: their soul fainted in them.

So they cried unto the Lord in their trouble: and he delivered them from their distress.

He led them forth by the right way: that they might go to the city where they dwelt.

O that men would therefore praise the Lord for his goodness: and declare the wonders that he doeth for the children of men!

For he satisfieth the empty soul: and filleth the hungry soul with goodness.

It's important to keep the imagery crisp. A good deal of nonsense is talked (we've already discussed this) about the desert as the place where one has to go if one is to meet the living God. No doubt the years in the wilderness of Sinai were profoundly formative for the religion of Israel. But this psalm isn't about that at all. It's about the desert as a place of terror, and of separation between the exile and his home. Isn't it an odd thing, when you come to think of it, that from their origins as nomads very much at home in the wilderness, the Jews have grown into an essentially city-dwelling people? Even in present-day Israel, with its remarkable achievements in agriculture, the real prestige belongs to the man who lives in Jerusalem, for whom Galilee is still the pits.

Two small points worth noticing. The first is about poetic language. You'll find in this poem and throughout the Bible, what we shall call 'A of B' constructions: where we might say 'deadly shade', or 'bronze gates', or 'grateful sacrifice', or 'inhabited city', it is more natural in ancient Hebrew to write 'the shadow of death', 'the gates of brass', 'the sacrifice of thanksgiving', 'a city to dwell in'. We shall see how this Hebrew mannerism spills over into New Testament Greek, and indeed it persists in contemporary English to the extent that we hardly notice it. But sometimes it can cloud for us what the writer originally meant, as for instance when 'the appalling idol', which Rome set up in the Temple of Jerusalem, appears in the gospels rather obscurely as 'the abomination of desolation'.

The second point is about the shape of events. You'll notice in this psalm something that we've come across before – Israel's determination to trace a particular pattern in her history: sin → distress → cry → heard → saved → sin again. The pattern isn't quite so insistent in this psalm as it sometimes is, but it's here all right.

So, from the wanderers in the desert we move to a different picture.

> Such as sit in darkness, and in the shadow of death: being fast bound in misery and iron;
> Because they rebelled against the words of the Lord: and lightly regarded the counsel of the most Highest;
> He also brought down their heart through heaviness: they fell down, and there was none to help them.
> So when they cried unto the Lord in their trouble: he delivered them out of their distress.
> For he brought them out of darkness, and out of the shadow of death: and brake their bonds in sunder.
> O that men would therefore praise the Lord for his goodness: and declare the wonders that he doeth for the children of men!
> For he hath broken the gates of brass: and smitten the bars of iron in sunder.

On the day I write this, the Prime Minister of Great Britain has made a spirited appeal through the Press for a return to traditional values, which she identifies as fairness, integrity, honesty and courtesy. Now, I don't want to cavil at that. Not in the least. After all, national renewal by way of reverse gear, through a return to something valuable in the past, is very much what this psalm is about. Sin is rebellion, says the psalmist, and the only hope lies in a return to a former allegiance. You'll find the same in almost every chapter of the Old Testament. But, and here's a surprising thing, you'll find it remarkably absent from the New Testament. The notion of rebellion seems to have disappeared. The moral and ethical demands of the gospel are expressed not as a recall to a past state, but almost entirely in future terms, as requisites of a kingdom that has been inaugurated but which still awaits its fulfilment. It would be a brave politician who made that the subject of a press call.

> Foolish men are plagued for their offence: and because of their wickedness.

Their soul abhorred all manner of meat: and they were even
hard at death's door.

So when they cried unto the Lord in their trouble: he delivered
them out of their distress.

He sent his word and healed them: and they were saved from
their destruction.

O that men would therefore praise the Lord for his goodness:
and declare the wonders that he doeth for the children of men!

That they would offer unto him the sacrifice of thanksgiving:
and tell out his works with gladness!

Here we have a typical Hebrew play-upon-words: the word for
fools differs by only one letter from the word for sick people, and
this whole paragraph is about the connection between folly and
sin and sickness. In the Jewish mind, in the mind of Jesus of
Nazareth and in subsequent Christian tradition, this connection
has remained strong. It torments the sufferer who cries out 'What
have I done to deserve this?' It's at the root of what has come to be
called The Problem of Pain. To say, as I find myself compelled to
say, that this connection can and should no longer be maintained, because we've moved irreversibly away from the world-
view from which it originated, still leaves The Problem unsolved.
But perhaps it reduces the torment, just a little, especially at a
time when the spread of AIDS is adding strength to the view that
disease and sin are two aspects of the same thing. You may want
to resist that view. I hope you do. But it's delicate ground. I
suppose the poet realized it was, and therefore uses a roundabout way of speaking of God's part in the process. He 'sends his
word' to heal, just as in a very similar passage in the book of Job
it's God's messenger, interpreter, agent, who brings relief to the
sufferer. There's bound to be some embarrassment, surely, in
speaking of God himself as both sending the sickness and healing
it.

They that go down to the sea in ships: and occupy their business in
great waters;

These men see the works of the Lord: and his wonders in the
deep.

For at his word the stormy wind ariseth: which lifteth up the
waves thereof.

They are carried up to the heaven, and down again to the deep:
their soul melteth away because of the trouble.

They reel to and fro, and stagger like a drunken man: and are at their wits' end.

So when they cry to the Lord in their trouble: he delivereth them out of their distress.

For he maketh the storm to cease: so that the waves thereof are still.

Then are they glad, because they are at rest: and so he bringeth them unto the haven where they would be.

O that men would therefore praise the Lord for his goodness: and declare the wonders that he doeth for the children of men!

That they would exalt him also in the congregation of the people: and praise him in the seat of the elders.

The island-dweller will read that as a fine piece of nature-poetry, appropriate to a Form of Prayer for Those at Sea. Your Hebrew poet, on the other hand, had little notion of the grandeur of seascape. The ocean was a symbol of chaos, something to be delivered from, like the desert, like folly and sickness. The longed-for harbour, the city, is the place to be. That's where people can properly live. And the place for praising God (by this token) isn't the Cornish cliffs, with the wind in your hair: it's 'in the congregation . . . in the seat of the elders' . . . at the Prime Minister's Press Conference, even.

It's the public aspect of this psalmody, then, which in the end prevails. Scholars say that the final verses are a later addition, a 'general celebration of plenty' which doesn't properly belong to the poet's vision. The refrain disappears; so does the particularity, the concreteness that has marked the rest of the psalm. It ends more like a little Wisdom poem, generalizing the message and drawing a moral for the wise man as he ponder these things.

[He] turneth the floods into a wilderness: and drieth up the water-springs.

A fruitful land maketh he barren: for the wickedness of them that dwell therein.

Again, he maketh the wilderness a standing water: and water-springs of a dry ground.

And there he setteth the hungry: that they may build them a city to dwell in;

That they may sow their land, and plant vineyards: to yield them fruits of increase.

He blesseth them, so that they multiply exceedingly: and suffereth not their cattle to decrease.

And again, when they are minished, and brought low: through oppression, through any plague or trouble;

Though he suffer them to be evil intreated through tyrants: and let them wander out of the way in the wilderness;

Yet helpeth he the poor out of misery: and maketh him households like a flock of sheep,

The righteous will consider this, and rejoice: and the mouth of all wickedness shall be stopped.

Whoso is wise will ponder these things: and they shall understand the loving-kindness of the Lord.

The German scholar Artur Weiser has some enlightening things to say about this psalm. He sees it as the utterance of a community of believers gathered in the house of the Lord to thank him for his mighty acts. They testify that they have seen him at work in their deliverance and return. They make clear the links which are to be made with their earlier history, and proclaim that the same bond between God and his people is still in force. Finally, by giving cultic expression, in their worship, to this understanding of their history, they enable subsequent generations in their turn to identify with it.

The innermost meaning of the community's Thanksgiving Service, which outwardly closes with the sacrifice of thanksgiving, finds its fulfilment in the realization of the presence of God, whereby the religious experience of the individual becomes the concern of the whole congregation.

6

Ezekiel and the Leaders of the Nation

The book of the prophet Ezekiel is one of the longest in the Bible. It is also one of the strangest and least known. And that's a great pity, because if you can get into it you will find yourself in the company of a deeply human and profoundly religious thinker.

It may be just because he is the most religious of the prophets that Ezekiel is hard going today. Amos, Micah, Jeremiah are concerned with religion, true enough; but they are more memorable for their involvement in the social and political life of their people, for what they have to say about justice and the plight of the poor and oppressed. That's what holds our attention. At first sight Ezekiel seems to inhabit a different world and to speak a different language; and in order to grasp what that world was like we need some understanding of the man's personality and of the historical events in which he played his part. We also need to think for a moment about the religious milieu in which he lived.

He was a prophet from a priestly family, and that meant internal conflict and tension for him; to some extent at least, though the polarization between priest and prophet in ancient Israel has been a good deal exaggerated. The priestly caste in Jerusalem, in the later days of the kingdom of Judah, was indeed very important. You can see that power at work if you glance at another strange and little-known part of the Old Testament, the book called Leviticus, with its detailed regulations for public and private religion and its insistence on the holiness of God. And not only there. In many other places, as we've already seen, priestly writers were to have a hand in the formation of sacred scripture. Later on they presided over the editing of Jewish history, and that meant that inevitably they influenced the way the Jewish people thought about themselves. That made them powerful people indeed. Who was it that said, 'I don't care what happens at the meeting, so long as I see the minutes before they go out'? So, with his priestly connections at Jerusalem, Ezekiel was a man of high standing. He could expect to be consulted by the elders of the people. He was quick to condemn idolatry and disobedience among the people, and to demand from his fellow priests a strict attention to ritual cleanness. No less was to be expected by those who served the Temple of the Most High God.

But what would happen when that Temple no longer stood? Earlier prophets had come close to asking that question, though it was almost unthinkable that Zion would in fact be destroyed. And yet that's what happened. The Assyrians had overwhelmed the northern kingdom of Israel in 722 BC. Then for over a century the southern kingdom of Judah, with its capital at Jerusalem, found itself caught up in a deadly game of power politics with Egypt, Syria, Assyria, and finally with Babylon, whose king Nebuchadnezzar in 597 took the holy city, set up Zedekiah as a puppet king in Jerusalem, and carried off a number of influential Jews into captivity. Ezekiel was among them, and some of his prophetic utterances belong to the years immediately after 597. Ten years later Zedekiah in turn rebelled: this time Jerusalem was destroyed, the city and its Temple reduced to rubble. It's in the light of this event that Ezekiel's later prophecies are to be read, though some of them may have been revised later, after Ezekiel's death, when the Persians had resettled a number of Jews in Judaea.

We're listening, then, to a prophet-priest who has to speak to a deeply humiliated people whose centre of gravity has been first threatened and then removed. It's only to be expected that his message is, in the first place, visionary. There are in fact only four formal visions in his book, but his language is often highly coloured and his teaching backed up by symbolic action. Since in exile public expressions of loyalty to God are now restricted, he preaches inward renewal, physically swallowing the scroll on which God's word is written. He warns that God is a jealous God, whose judgments are inescapable: yet those judgments are above all an expression of his covenant with his people. Like other prophets before him, he takes his part in the sufferings of his fellow-countrymen, undergoes his own agony in the loss of his beloved wife, and comes by a hard road to an understanding of God's continuing love for Israel. So close is his self-identification with his fellow-countrymen that he becomes himself a living symbol for his people. And that's what leads him to one of his most startling conclusions. It's the great tragedy itself, the destruction of the Temple and the Holy City, and the subsequent exile that 'releases his prophetic vocation and enables him to proclaim a new offer of salvation', with the astonishing realization that the holiness of God can be proclaimed even among the heathen, and his glory known in the midst of an unclean people.

As examples of his teaching I've chosen two chapters from the later part of the book, where his thinking is perhaps more accessible than in earlier passages. The imagery is on the surface more familiar, the visionary element rather less outré than the earlier chapters: though all the time we have to acknowledge the astonishing sweep of vision that belongs to this most extraordinary man.

Chapter 34

And the word of the Lord came unto me, saying, Son of man, prophesy against the shepherds of Israel, prophesy, and say unto them, Thus saith the Lord God unto the shepherds; Woe be to the shepherds of Israel that do feed themselves! Should not the shepherds feed the flocks? Ye eat the fat, and ye clothe you with the wool, ye kill them that are fed: but ye feed not the flock. The diseased have ye not strengthened, neither have ye healed that which was sick, neither have ye bound up that which was broken, neither have ye brought again that which was driven away, neither have ye sought that which was lost; but with force and cruelty have ye ruled them. And they were scattered, because there is no shepherd: and they became meat to all the beasts of the field, when they were scattered. My sheep wandered through all the mountains, and upon every high hill: yea, my flock was scattered upon all the face of the earth, and none did search or seek after them. Therefore, ye shepherds, hear the word of the Lord; As I live, saith the Lord God, surely because my flock became a prey, and my flock became meat to every beast of the field, because there was no shepherd, neither did my shepherds search for my flock, but the shepherds fed themselves, and fed not my flock; Therefore, O ye shepherds, hear the word of the Lord; Thus saith the Lord God; Behold, I am against the shepherds; and I will require my flock at their hand, and cause them to cease from feeding the flock; neither shall the shepherds feed themselves any more; for I will deliver my flock from their mouth, that they may not be meat for them.

Those of us who have grown up with the picture of Jesus as The Good Shepherd in the tenth chapter of St John may need to be reminded that the figure of the shepherd was at first seen primarily as a model for Kingship. You'll find it so used on the famous Moabite Stone, set up by King Mesa three hundred years before the time of Ezekiel, and in the Code of Hammurabi a thousand years earlier still. And if you're used to hearing preachers expound every detail of St John's parable, with a fine display of what they've read about animal husbandry in the ancient East, you'll certainly notice that this townee Ezekiel isn't at all precise or consistent in the way he paints his picture. He's not concerned to be. He wants to make one simple point: those who should have had the care of God's people have taken the perquisites of power but neglected their responsibilities. The people have therefore been rendered vulnerable – the weak, the sick, the injured, the strays, even the fat and strong. And in saying this, he's in fact making a disturbing comment on one of the favourite clichés of the ancient Near East. Traditionally, the man favoured by God is recognized by his fatness, his prosperity and the size of his flocks and herds: he has a perfect right to devour his sheep if he wants to, and can neglect them if he so pleases. Power in the ancient world was customarily irresponsible and absolute, even when it was exercised in the name of God. We've thought a little, in an earlier chapter, of how our own contemporary clichés have shifted in the other direction. It's now axiomatic for us that God has a bias towards the poor. And if that idea now comes naturally to our minds, it's in part due to this insight of Ezekiel, taken up (as it was to be) in the New Testament.

You'll notice from these verses how very repetitive Ezekiel's style is. He says everything three, four times: 'because . . . because . . . therefore . . .' This is sometimes described as his 'pedagogic manner'; but it may be something more profound than that. Preachers are still taught, 'Tell them what you're going to say, say it, then tell them what you've said.' The prophet, like the preacher or evangelist, repeats himself not because he's pedantic but because his message is so vital. Ezekiel and St John are alike in this respect, that neither of them is concerned with style except insofar as it heightens the effect of what is to be said. To that end they will repeat and repeat the word that comes from God.

> For thus saith the Lord God; Behold I, even I, will both search my sheep and seek them out. As a shepherd seeketh out his flock in the day that he is among his sheep that are scattered, so will I seek out my sheep, and will deliver them out of all places where they have been scattered in the cloudy and dark day. And I will bring them out from the people, and gather them from the countries, and will bring them to their own land, and feed them upon the mountains of Israel by the rivers, and in all the inhabited places of the country. I will feed them in a good pasture, and upon the high mountains of Israel shall their fold be: there shall they lie in a good fold, and in a fat pasture shall they feed upon the mountains of Israel. I will feed my flock, and I will cause them to lie down, saith the Lord God. I will seek that which was lost, and bring again that which was driven away, and will bind up that which was broken, and will strengthen that which was sick: but I will destroy the fat and strong; I will feed them with judgment. And as for you, O my flock, thus saith the Lord God; Behold, I judge between cattle and cattle, between the rams and the he-goats. Seemeth it a small thing to you to have eaten up the good pasture, but ye must tread down with your feet the residue of your pastures? and to have drunk of the deep waters, but ye must foul the residue with your feet? And as for my flock, they eat that which ye have trodden with your feet; and they drink that which ye have fouled with your feet. Therefore thus saith the Lord God unto them; Behold I, even I, will judge between the fat cattle and between the lean cattle. Because ye have thrust with side and with shoulder, and pushed all the diseased with your horns, till ye have scattered them abroad; therefore will I save my flock, and they shall be no more a prey; and I will judge between cattle and cattle.

God himself takes charge of the flock, in a prophecy which forestalls the more famous poem of Isaiah 40, 'He shall feed his flock like a shepherd, and gently gather those that are with young.' Here in Ezekiel he gathers them after disaster has struck on the cloudy and dark day. 'That Day', the day of judgment and of terror, has by this time become a regular part of Hebrew prophecy, as it was later to be a feature in apocalyptic writing.

From Amos onwards the prophets are haunted by the prospect of The Day of the Lord. Ezekiel, however, looks for a happier outcome. Under God's direct protection the flock will have its own land for pasture.

What we have here is no longer just a parable about good government: it's an intervention by God in the history of the nation. However, Ezekiel doesn't leave it at that. He proceeds to stretch his parable beyond what it can properly bear. So far judgment has fallen on the shepherds, but now it's extended to the sheep. Logically it doesn't make a lot of sense: as Walter Eichrodt rather solemnly puts it, 'One cannot stand in judgment upon sheep.' And it's not very sound farming practice to kill your strong cattle in order to prevent the exploitation of the weak. But that's not really the point, is it? What the prophet wants us to see is that it's an affront to God when the violence of the strong against the weak goes uncorrected, and when his people wantonly damage what they cannot use.

The chapter ends with a forecast of peace:

And I will set up one shepherd over them, and he shall feed them, even my servant David; he shall feed them, and he shall be their shepherd. And I the Lord will be their God, and my servant David a prince among them; I the Lord have spoken it. And I will make with them a covenant of peace, and will cause the evil beasts to cease out of the land: and they shall dwell safely in the wilderness, and sleep in the woods. And I will make them and the places round about my hill a blessing; and I will cause the shower to come down in his season; there shall be showers of blessing. And the tree of the field shall yield her fruit, and the earth shall yield her increase, and they shall be safe in their land, and shall know that I am the Lord, when I have broken the bands of their yoke, and delivered them out of the hand of those that served themselves of them. And they shall be no more a prey to the heathen, neither shall the beast of the land devour them; but they shall dwell safely, and none shall make them afraid. And I will raise up for them a plant of renown, and they shall be no more consumed with hunger in the land, neither bear the shame of the heathen any more. Thus shall they know that I the Lord their God am with them, and that they, even the house of Israel, are my people, saith the Lord God. And ye my flock, the flock of my pasture, are men, and I am your God, saith the Lord God.

Of course he could have said it all in about one-tenth of the time. But that's not his way. His message moves slowly and inexorably to its fulfilment, as the shepherding of Israel is handed back to its future ruler, a prince of the house of David. He avoids the word 'king'. Perhaps that's because the Hebrew word *melech* was horribly the same as *Moloch*, the god for whom you burnt your children alive. However that may be, it's hard to tell whether these verses are properly speaking a foretelling of the Messiah, or whether they simply look forward to the restoration of a Jewish monarchy in Palestine. We certainly can't be sure what people five hundred years before Christ had in mind when they looked for the redemption of Israel.

These closing verses reflect something else that figured largely in their minds, and that's the land itself – the Land of Israel. In the creation narratives of Genesis the land is God's gift. In successive covenants, with Noah and Abraham and Moses, the land was secured as Israel's possession for ever. Time and again it had been laid waste, but in Ezekiel's vision it is once again to be blessed as Eden was. The wild beasts themselves fall within the terms of the blessing. Men and women are 'fully reconstituted in the image of God' and Israel is itself again. The words are very like that of another hypersensitive visionary, the poet Christopher Smart: 'At that time malignity ceases, and the devils themselves are at peace.'

Chapter 37

As you read these next verses, bear in mind that Hebrew has one word, *ruach*, where English needs three – breath, spirit, and wind. Yet you can't say that those three English words in fact mean the same thing, can you? And there in a nutshell you have the insoluble problem of translating from one language to another. You'll see what I mean in a moment.

The hand of the Lord was upon me, and carried me out in the spirit of the Lord, and set me down in the midst of the valley which was full of bones, and caused me to pass by them round about: and, behold, there were very many in the open valley; and, lo, they were very dry. And he said unto me, Son of man, can these bones live? And I answered, O Lord God, thou knowest. Again he said unto me, Prophesy upon these bones, and say unto them, O ye dry bones, hear the word of the Lord. Thus saith the Lord God unto these bones, Behold I will cause breath to enter into you, and ye shall live: and I will lay sinews upon you, and will bring up flesh upon you, and cover you with skin, and put breath in you, and ye shall live; and ye shall know that I am the Lord. So I prophesied as I was commanded: and as I prophesied, there was a noise, and behold a shaking, and the bones came together, bone to his bone. And when I beheld, lo, the sinews and flesh came up upon them, and the skin covered them above: but there was no breath in them. Then said he unto me, Prophesy unto the wind, prophesy, son of man, and say to the wind, Thus saith the Lord God; Come from the four winds, O breath, and breathe upon these slain, that they may live. So I prophesied as he commanded me, and the breath came into them, and they lived, and stood up upon their feet, an exceeding great army.

Then he said unto me, Son of man, these bones are the whole house of Israel: behold, they say, Our bones are dried, and our hope is lost: we are [clean cut off]. Therefore prophesy and say unto them, Thus saith the Lord God; Behold, O my people, I will open your graves, and cause you to come up out of your graves, and bring you into the land of Israel. And ye shall know that I am the Lord, when I have opened your graves, O my people, and brought you up out of your graves, and shall put my spirit in you, and ye shall live, and I shall place you in your own land: then shall ye know that I the Lord have spoken it, and performed it, saith the Lord.

It's surely a misunderstanding of Ezekiel to see in this prophecy any hint of a belief in what we've come to call the After Life. No Jew of his day, and only a very few in later times, held any belief in the resurrection of the dead in that sense. This vision is therefore precisely a vision of the impossible. Dry bones do not live, the breath being out. So when the prophet here speaks of new life, it's clear that he is speaking about the future of the nation, in terms of a vision of the impossible being brought about. He doesn't, surely, foresee a personal resurrection for every individual in the community of the faithful, as the New Testament was to proclaim it. His vision is immediate, and restricted to the immediate future. These dry bones will live. This exiled and despondent community, as good as dead, is to come out of exile, as improbably as corpses coming out of their graves. That's the strength of Ezekiel's prophecy, and you only weaken it by attaching to it something that belongs to our Christian tradition but has no place in his.

Once again, there are echoes of the creation narratives of Genesis. There the spirit of God broods upon the waters; his breath is breathed into man's nostrils; he becomes a living soul. Here too the breath of God re-creates his people. They are to be re-made for life in their own land. That's the miracle – stronger, in its own terms, than any individualistic interpretation we may be tempted to impose upon it.

What follows is a symbolic action, the enacted parable of The Two Sticks, showing that God's re-creation of his people has implications which are political and social, as well as religious.

The word of the Lord came again to me, saying, Moreover, thou son of man, take thee one stick, and write upon it, *for Judah*, and for the children of Israel his companions: then take another stick, and write upon it, *for Joseph*, the stick of Ephraim, and for all the house of Israel his companions: and join them one to another into one stick; and they shall become one in thine hand. And when the children of thy people shall speak unto thee, saying, Wilt thou not show us what thou meanest by these? Say unto them, Thus saith the Lord God; Behold, I will take the stick of Joseph, which is in the hand of Ephraim, and the tribes of Israel his fellows, and will put them with him, even with the stick of Judah, and make them one stick, and they shall be one in mine hand. And the sticks whereon thou writest shall be in thine hand before their eyes. And say unto them, Thus saith the Lord God; Behold I will take the children of Israel from among the heathen, whither they be gone, and will gather them on every side, and bring them into their own land: and I will make them one nation in the land upon the mountains of Israel; and one king shall be king to them all: and they shall be no more two nations, neither shall they be divided into two kingdoms any more at all: neither shall they defile themselves any more with their idols, nor with their detestable things, nor with any of their transgressions: but I will save them out of all their dwelling-places, wherein they have sinned, and will cleanse them: so shall they be my people, and I will be their God.

And David my servant shall be king over them; and they all shall have one shepherd: they shall also walk in my judgments, and observe my statutes, and do them. And they shall dwell in the land that I have given unto Jacob my servant, wherein your fathers have dwelt; and they shall dwell therein, even they, and their children, and their children's children for ever: and my servant David shall be their prince for ever. Moreover, I will make a covenant of peace with them; it shall be an everlasting covenant with them: and I will place them, and multiply them, and will set my sanctuary in the midst of them for evermore. My tabernacle also shall be with them: yea, I will be their God, and they shall be my people. And the heathen shall know that I the Lord do sanctify Israel, when my sanctuary shall be in the midst of them for evermore.

What's that all about? It's about one of the great weaknesses of the ancient Jews, which was that like the ancient Greeks they couldn't maintain unity amongst themselves. In an earlier chapter we saw how the House of David managed to rule a united kingdom from Jerusalem for something like seventy years: but when Solomon died in about 922 BC there was a breakaway movement led by Jeroboam the son of Nebat; after which for two hundred years an independent and rather more successful northern kingdom was established at Samaria in the north. As we've already seen, this division between south (the kingdom of Judah) and north (the kingdom of Israel, known also as Joseph or Ephraim) probably had its roots a long way back in Patriarchal pre-history.

By Ezekiel's time there hadn't been a United Kingdom for nearly five hundred years; so his symbolism with the two sticks represents a prophetic vision almost as radical as the re-establishment of the Garden of Eden. It's not just a reunification scheme born out of political necessity. It requires nothing less than a new birth, political and spiritual, for the whole nation. As we read it, the latter part of this chapter may come as something of an anti-climax after the drama of the Dry Bones: but there's no doubt that in Ezekiel's mind the revival of the 'exceeding great army' is no more than a prerequisite for the greater work which the Lord God has in mind with the revival of a united Israel.

And so in these verses, as Eichrodt has pointed out, all six of Ezekiel's great themes come into play as he looks for the restoration of the holy people. First, there's the Call for Purity, the putting away of idols, which has featured strongly in his earlier chapters. This is to prepare the way for the restoration of the Faithful Shepherd from the house of David (kingship being an acceptable idea once more in the context of the Holy Land, the new Eden). In the midst of this is to be set the sanctuary, the tabernacle of the presence of God amongst his people, so that the Heathen will see and acknowledge his glory. Thus a Covenant of Peace will be established between God and his people for all eternity.

Sad to say, Ezekiel's vision was never realized. The internal divisions of Israel persisted throughout her history, finding renewed impetus in the hostility between Jews and Samaritans which is familiar to us through the gospels. None the less, there's something very impressive about the aspirations of this prophet. For all his long-windedness, and the sometimes impenetrable obscurity of his images, here is a man who is stedfast in confronting his own distress and the misfortunes of his fellow-countrymen, and can see beyond them to the possibilities of a future state in which God's creative power is once more acknowledged and experienced. It's true that the prophecies of these final chapters didn't find fulfilment in Ezekiel's own terms: but it's also true that the New Testament understanding of the Kingdom of God owes a great debt to the courage and clear-sightedness of this earlier visionary, called by God to give his witness as 'son of man'.

7

The Wisdom of God

At first sight the Old Testament is a collection of books exclusively concerned with the Jewish people. When other nations figure at all in its pages, they appear with very few exceptions as the adversaries of Israel and of Israel's God. 'O'er heathen lands afar Thick darkness broodeth yet . . .' and there's very little evidence, on the surface, that those who wrote and assembled the Jewish scriptures wanted to encourage contact of any kind between the children of Israel and their neighbours.

Of course life in ancient Palestine can't have been quite as isolationist as that. Trade goes on, regardless of religious and racial differences. And a closer look at the literature shows that indeed there are strong influences coming in to Jewish culture from Mesopotamia, from the Greek world and from Egypt. We've already seen how Israel's understanding of its pre-history was affected by Babylonian mythology. And scholars like J. B. Pritchard have in recent years made available to us a rich variety of other ancient Near-Eastern texts which shed a great deal of light on the biblical writings. Most biblical Introductions and Atlases offer a selection of these texts, and if you follow them up you'll discover how very fascinating they are.

In this chapter we're concerned with the 'Wisdom' books of the Old Testament, especially Proverbs, Ecclesiastes (Qoheleth) and Job. We'll have something to say about two books from the Apocrypha, The Wisdom of Solomon and Ecclesiasticus (also known as Sirach). We'll need to bear in mind that parts of the prophetic books and the Psalms are, properly speaking, 'Wisdom Literature'. It's a rather slippery category, though its characteristics will become clear as we go along. It's not easy to discover its historical origins. But collections of 'Wisdom' texts, even when

they contain earlier material, don't appear until fairly late in
Jewish history, certainly after the Babylonian exile, by which time
the Jews had been obliged to establish closer contact with the
world around them. And that's why a detailed study would show
strong non-Jewish influences, especially from Egyptian books of
courtly etiquette and moral precepts. Many of the ethical maxims
to be found in the Jewish Wisdom Literature can also be found in
Greek literature of the sixth and fifth centuries BC. We'll see
something of this as we look in a little more detail at a chapter
from Proverbs. But first it may be helpful to sketch in the main
characteristics of this literature as a whole, and of the individual
books which comprise it.

Wisdom, in early times, was what enabled you to hold your own
in public debate. Nestor in the Iliad was the archetypal wise man
who held the floor and whose ideas were heard with respect. The
Pharisee Gamaliel, in the book of Acts, stands firmly in this
tradition. But in the Greek world wisdom, *sophia*, could easily
degenerate into sophistry, mere cleverness, which was the
charlatan's weapon for getting his way or attracting a following,
whether as a politician or as a teacher of religion and philosophy;
nevertheless wisdom, skill in argument, familiarity with rhetorical techniques, was not to be despised in societies where public
and private life were less segregated than they are now.

We don't know much about political debate in ancient Israel.
There are glimpses, as when Rehoboam the son of Solomon takes
counsel first with the old men, who advocate a policy of
moderation, then with the young men, who advise the opposite.
On that occasion wisdom did not prevail. But what strikes you as
you read accounts of the public ministry of the prophets before
the exile, and of the priestly leaders after the return, is that in
Israel there was no real distinction between political and religious
controversy. Almost always, as the history of the Jews is
unravelled for us, we seem to be eavesdropping on a theological
debate about right and wrong. Sometimes the context seems to be
public discussion. At other times it's more domestic, belonging to
the classroom or the family circle. In either case it's likely to be
God's reputation which is at stake. Whatever happens to God's
people reflects honour or dishonour upon God himself; and the
Old Testament above all else seeks the honour of God. There's a
technical term, 'theodicy', which describes this determination to
vindicate the justice of God in his dealings with men. And

theodicy is a major ingredient in Jewish Wisdom literature. Oddly enough, God himself is very seldom on stage. His place is taken by the wise man, sometimes even by Wisdom in person (in the feminine gender, strange to say); the opponent is the unrighteous man, or the fool. In this argument the lines are drawn as implacably as the trenches in Flanders: on the one side ignorance, the deceits of the tongue, the seductions of women and of drink, leading to foolish speech and violence and idleness and social decay; on the other side obedience, good learning, reverence for age, wifeliness, the sense of what is fitting and orderly, care of the poor and bereaved. In the outcome of this debate there are no surprises. The cards (to mix the metaphor) are stacked.

But the chief human predicament remains unsolved. If God is good and just, what is to be said about undeserved suffering, and about death?

If you ask whether the Wisdom Literature of the Old Testament has a solution to this age-old problem, the answer is, No, it hasn't. Indeed, I would want to claim that it's to the credit of these writers that they don't claim to have solved the insoluble. What they do offer is a framework within which you can go on engaging in the business of life, and facing its dilemmas without resort to foolish optimism or blind despair. It's true that you'll find entirely missing from these books those great theological concepts which permeate the work of the earlier Hebrew prophets and historians. You'll look in vain for an exposition of God's grace, of his great acts of deliverance. There's nothing about the great figures of the past, and God's covenant with them; not until we get to the very end of the line: and there, in the closing chapters of Ecclesiasticus, we begin to find a saviour-figure in the person of Simon Maccabaeus, and a future hope future to weigh against the greatness of Israel's past. But at that point we find that Wisdom has been overtaken by something quite different, and that's Apocalyptic.

Before looking more closely at one important text, it may be useful to sketch out in broad terms certain characteristics which belong to the individual books in the Wisdom tradition.

Proverbs is made up of several collections of wise sayings. Although the name of Solomon is attached to some sections, it is almost impossible to date them. The proverbs are mostly very short, poetic and antithetical in style, so as to be easily memo-

rized. They emphasize the need for attentiveness and conform-
ity. Be a good boy now, d'you hear? Wisdom is not the same as
cleverness: that is made clear by the weight given to the *love* of
wisdom, as intense in its way as the love of the Law which was so
strong a feature in the later psalms. Love and obedience go
together: they mark the relationship of the wise son and the wise
father. 'God the Father' is a concept not yet in circulation; but
Proverbs points forward to it, describing Wisdom in notably
personal terms. Christian theology was later to identify The
Wisdom of God, *Sancta Sophia*, with the second Person of the
Holy Trinity; but here she is still seen as God's creature, not as a
manifestation of God himself.

Job, for all its narrative brilliance, is really remarkable for its
presentation of an afflicted man answering back. Not that this is
anything new in Hebrew religion. You only have to think of
Abraham at Sodom, or Elijah at Horeb. If you walked with God
you also talked with him, and there was no need to pull your
punches. The same spiritual realism moved St Teresa of Avila to
shake her fist at her Lord and say, 'If this is how you treat your
friends, no wonder you have so few of them.' Job is in this
tradition, though his story is fiction, like that of Ruth, Jonah and
Esther. The story is simply the setting for the dialogue – a formal
debate between Job and his friends, interspersed with psalms
and magnificent descriptive poems about the wonders of God's
creation. In all this dialogue Job 'maintains his integrity'. He will
not forfeit his right to plead with God. He stands, as one scholar
has put it, for 'man's mental agony over the unfathomable face of
God', and it has been suggested that what we have here is a
reflection of some great spiritual crisis in ancient Israel. The
happy ending shows signs of later tampering: the real strength of
the book lies in its refusal to dodge the fundamental problem of
confronting a righteous God in a unjust world.

Ecclesiastes goes further even than Job in its bleak realism about
that world. For this writer ('The Preacher', *Qoheleth*) God doesn't
even reply. The world is vanity. Only the search for pleasure
brings measurable results. It's impossible to know God, leave
alone love him. And death cancels everything. Nowhere in the
Bible do you find such fervent determination to hold on, despite
everything; and in the years which follow the Holocaust this is a
document which you need to read and ponder. You won't find it
easy to answer.

Ecclesiasticus, the Wisdom of Jesus the son of Sirach, like the Wisdom of Solomon, was placed in the Apocrypha because it was thought to exist only in Greek, and clearly belonged to the very last years when the status of 'sacred scripture' could be claimed for any writing. Even though a Hebrew version of Ecclesiasticus has now come to light, it still evidently represents a late stage of Jewish antiquity. It's noticeable that whereas in other Wisdom texts there is no sense of history or of the great traditions of Hebrew prophecy, Ecclesiasticus sees Wisdom as a fulfilment of the Law, of the covenant, of all that gives Israel her true national identity. Consequently, the future for the nation is of prime importance, and the later chapters of the book claim that the future lies with a national leader who will combine in his person the role of both priest and king. It's not hard to see how this search for nationhood prepares the way for the Christian theology of the Kingdom of God and his Christ.

The Wisdom of Solomon also points forwards as well as backwards. It's a compilation from various sources. It appeals to ancient tradition by appropriating the name of Solomon for its title-page. In our study of the Psalms we began to think about writings attributed to people who didn't actually write them, and we'll have more to say about that when we come to the Epistle to the Ephesians. More important in the Wisdom of Solomon are themes which were to attract the attention of New Testament writers: the destiny of mankind, even beyond the grave; and the close identification of Wisdom and Spirit, as something communicable by God to mankind. Chapter 7 of Wisdom is well worth a close look, if you want to understand the thought-world out of which Christian understanding of the Holy Spirit was to develop.

Proverbs 8. 1–31

Doth not wisdom cry? and understanding put forth her voice? She standeth in the top of high places, by the way in the places of the paths. She crieth at the gates, at the entry of the city, at the coming in at the doors.

'Unto you, O men, I call; and my voice is to the sons of man.

O ye simple, understand wisdom: and ye fools, be ye of an understanding heart.

Hear, for I will speak of excellent things: and the opening of my lips shall be right things.

For my mouth shall speak truth: and wickedness is an abomination to my lips.

All the words of my mouth are in righteousness: there is nothing
froward or perverse in them.

They are all plain to him that understandeth: and right to them
that find knowledge.

Receive my instruction, and not silver: and knowledge rather
than choice gold.

For wisdom is better than rubies: and all the things that may be
desired cannot be compared to it.

I, wisdom, dwell with prudence: and find out knowledge of
witty inventions.

The fear of the Lord is to hate evil: pride, and arrogancy, and the
evil way, and the froward mouth, do I hate.

Counsel is mine, and sound wisdom: I am understanding; I
have strength.

By me kings reign: and princes decree justice.

By me princes rule, and nobles: even all the judges of the earth.

I love them that love me: and those that seek me early shall find
me.

Riches and honour are with me: yea, durable riches and
righteousness.

My fruit is better than gold, yea than fine gold: and my revenue
than choice silver.

I lead in the way of righteousness: in the midst of the paths of
judgment;

That I may cause those that love me to inherit substance: and I
will fill their treasures.'

The most striking thing about this poem is, of course, the so-
called Personification of Wisdom. There's more to be said about
that at the end of the next section, but first there are one or two
other striking things about the invitation which wisdom so
beguilingly offers to the sons of men.

The first point is this. All over the ancient world (and our own
world isn't so different) there were groups of people who
believed that religious and spiritual excellence could be achieved
by the pursuit of knowledge, usually of a secret sort. Sometimes
this belief was associated with rites of initiation, as practised in
the Mystery cults of Eleusis or Samothrace, or in that worship of
Mithras which became so popular among the soldiers of the

Roman Empire. (The remains of Mithraic temples are still to be seen in London and in Rome, among other places.) As far as we can judge, there was nothing particularly sinister about these religious rites. Indeed the Mysteries of Samothrace seem to have been admirable both for the high ethical standard required, and for the fact that initiation was open to people of all classes, even slaves. There was also in the Eastern Mediterranean, around the time of Christ, a luxuriant growth of less organized religious sects, some of them apparently within the Christian church itself, which offered salvation through knowledge. The Greek word is *gnosis*, and the movement (if that's not too strong a word; 'tendency' might be better) is known as Gnosticism. Gnostics came in all shapes and sizes, but what seems to be a general characteristic of all these systems is that they were shrouded in secrecy. And here there's a great difference from what we find in the mainstream of Jewish and Christian teaching.

Wisdom cries aloud in the streets. There's never any whispering in the religion of Israel. No omens or auguries. Soothsaying and wizardry were strictly forbidden, and as far as we can tell secret societies never flourished among the Jews, at any rate not until the rise of the Cabbalists in the Middle Ages. Everything has to be open: 'one day telleth another, one night certifieth another . . . their sound has gone out unto all lands.' And if this open-ness is noticeable in Judaism, so it was in Christianity from its very earliest days. So that when, around AD 50, we find St Paul writing 'We speak the wisdom of God in a mystery' the significant thing is that the Christian mystery is not in the modern sense 'mysterious' at all: it is something to be proclaimed aloud, revealed, shared, made known, acknowledged. Those are the words which St Paul uses in connection with the Greek word *mysterion*. So this is no arcane wisdom. And it's difficult to avoid the conclusion that somewhere in the forefront of the apostle's mind as he wrote was this picture from the book of Proverbs of Wisdom crying out at the top of the high places, on the rooftops, at the city gates.

The second point to be noted is the concreteness of what Wisdom puts on offer. This is not a matter for the head, nor even for the heart. It has to do with riches and honour, its treasures are substantial. Moreover, the quest for Wisdom is no mere private pursuit: 'By me kings rule, princes decree justice.' We keep encountering this public and political dimension in the religion of

Israel, even in its later days. 'Keeping politics out of religion' was never an option for the people of Israel.

Thirdly, you'll notice that the concept of Wisdom, which to our minds is essentially intellectual, is for this writer closely associated with the requirement of love. We've already seen in the Psalms how passionately the Jews studied and absorbed their Torah, the Law of the Lord. For us, it's not easy to associate the two notions of love and law. For the Jew they were inseparable: and therefore St Paul was able to sum up his entire moral teaching in the claim that love is indeed the fulfilling of the law. This, too, has its origins in the Wisdom Literature of the Old Testament, and is perhaps most vividly expressed in these verses from Proverbs.

There's something even more vivid to follow:

The Lord possessed me in the beginning of his way: before his works of old.

I was set up from everlasting: from the beginning, or ever the earth was.

When there were no depths, I was brought forth: when there were no fountains abounding with water.

Before the mountains were settled: before the hills was I brought forth;

While as yet he had not made the earth, nor the fields: nor the highest part of the dust of the world.

When he prepared the heavens I was there: when he set a compass on the face of the depth;

When he established the clouds above: when he strengthened the fountains of the deep;

When he gave to the sea his decree, that the waters should not pass his commandment: when he appointed the foundations of the earth;

Then I was by him, as one brought up with him: and I was daily his delight, rejoicing always before him;

Rejoicing in the habitable part of his earth: and my delights were with the sons of men.

It seems that in Egyptian mythology you can find Truth, in quasi-human form, enjoying the caresses of a divine lover. You won't find anything like that in the Hebrew scriptures, but perhaps there was always a tendency for a religion as strictly monotheist as that of the Jews to look over its shoulder at the

possibility of personifying if not God himself at least the attributes of God. There are moments when the Law of the Lord is
so much the object of man's love that it becomes almost a Being
in its own right: and the Word of God, likewise, can appear
almost in bodily form in the ranks of the angels, or (in the
writings of the Egyptian Jew, Philo) as the Divine Logos. Almost, but not quite. Truth, Wisdom, Law, Word – these are, as
Gerhard von Rad reminds us, 'certainly not divine attributes
which have become independent'. To put it more crudely,
there's no question of parts of God splintering off and assuming
independent life. Wisdom is part of God's creation, not a
mythical entity in its own right.

But having said that, we also have to recognize what a short
step it is from these marvellous verses in Proverbs to a Christian
text like the famous christological Hymn in the first chapter of
the Epistle to the Colossians. There, the writer speaks of the pre-
existent Christ, 'the image of the invisible God, the firstborn of
every creature . . . he is before all things and by him all things
consist'. Such claims for the divinity of Christ could hardly have
been made if these verses from Proverbs had not been reverber-
ating in the life of the early church. However, to say that Christ,
like Wisdom, was with God from the beginning; or to say, as
Christian tradition does say, that Christ actually is the Wisdom
of God – this is not at all the same as saying that the writer of
Proverbs had any intention of divinizing wisdom or representing it as some sort of celestial Being at the right hand of God.
That would have seemed blasphemous. Or, more likely, merely
frivolous. Because here again there are two important points to
be made about the language and thought of the Wisdom Literature.

First, the relation between what we might call the world of the
spirit and the visible world of the created universe. In fact
Jewish thought didn't distinguish at all clearly between the two.
To quote von Rad yet again, 'The dualism, familiar to us, of
rules for human society on the one hand and rules for nature on
the other, was unknown.' That's why we find in these verses
such an integrated view of life. We see Wisdom 'set up from
everlasting' as God's daily delight: but we're also shown this
same Wisdom 'rejoicing in the habitable parts of the earth' and
finding her delight among human beings. To talk of incarnation
in this context would be an anachronism: but the way is being

prepared for the moment when God's creative activity is manifested and fulfilled in a human life.

Secondly, it would be a trivialization to see in Proverbs 8 merely a poetical fancy, something to appeal (as the Gnostic systems did) to those who want a short cut to mystical insights and religious enlightenment. The appeal of Wisdom is more serious than that. It is, quite literally, a matter of life and death:

> Now therefore hearken unto me, O ye children: for blessed are they that keep my ways.
>
> Hear instruction, and be wise, and refuse it not.
>
> Blessed is the man that heareth me, watching daily at my gates: waiting at the posts of my doors.
>
> For whoso findeth me findeth life: and shall obtain favour of the Lord,
>
> But he that sinneth against me wrongeth his own soul; all they that hate me love death.

8

Malachi

The prophecy called Malachi isn't a work of major importance, compared with some of the other writings we've been looking at. But you may find it agreeable to end this part of our book with a reading of an Old Testament book in its entirety rather than in snippets. We'll be doing the same with Ephesians when we come to the end of the New Testament section. And in order to do this it's convenient to take as our sample a piece of writing which is not too complex and not too long.

The fact that the word Malachi means 'my messenger' probably signifies that this little prophetic work is anonymous, though there's no reason why the word shouldn't have been used as somebody's name. At all events, even though we know nothing of the author of the book it would be pedantic to call him anything but Malachi. Except for an appendix at the end, this book, unlike most collections of prophecy, appears not to be a compilation from various different hands. And that makes a nice change for the student who has had to wrestle with the authorship problems of the Hexateuch or Isaiah.

It seems fairly clear that Malachi was written after the rebuilding of the Temple in 516 BC, but before 444 when the reforms of Ezra and Nehemiah (which specially affected mixed marriages and the observance of the Law) were complete.

The chief concern of Malachi is the offering of acceptable worship to God. This brings him inevitably into the same priestly world as Ezekiel, but several generations later. He's closer in date to those compilers of the 'Priestly' history which we've had occasion to mention from time to time. Because this author cares about the 'cult' of the Temple, it is often suggested that he is interested in ritual more than prophecy, and therefore doesn't deserve to be reckoned a prophet at all. As you read, you may decide that judgment to be ill-founded, and find there's more to him than meets the eye.

The burden of the word of the Lord to Israel by Malachi.

I have loved you, saith the Lord. Yet ye say, Wherein hast thou loved us? Was not Esau Jacob's brother? saith the Lord, Yet I loved Jacob. And I hated Esau, and laid his mountains and his heritage waste for the dragons of the wilderness. Whereas Edom saith, We are impoverished, but we will return and build the desolate places; thus saith the Lord of hosts, They shall build, but I will throw down; and they shall call them The border of wickedness, and The people against whom the Lord hath indignation for ever. And your eyes shall see, and ye shall say, The Lord will be magnified from the border of Israel.

The word 'burden' is often used of prophetic utterance, even in the religious jargon of today, but it's not clear exactly what the Hebrew word *massa'* means – a load to be borne, or the raising of a voice, or maybe both. English versions often translate the word as 'an oracle', but it's certainly something quite different from the oracles of Delphi or the Cumaean Sybil. There's no mumbo-jumbo about the Hebrew prophets. Malachi begins dramatically, with dialogue. God proclaims his free and arbitrary choice: love to the descendants of Jacob (Israel) and judgment against the descendants of Esau (Edom), even though Jacob and Esau were brothers. The point of the prophecy is to show that the favour of God doesn't depend on your ancestry. There are other criteria. Furthermore, God's glory is to be shown even outside the Jewish community altogether, even among the Gentiles.

So the whole basis of Israel's self-confidence, her relationship with God, and the sacrificial system which was derived from it, is to be called in question in this prophecy:

A son honoureth his father, and a servant his master: if I then be a father, where is mine honour? and if I be a master, where is my fear? saith the Lord of hosts unto you, O priests that despise my name. And ye say, Wherein have we despised thy name? Ye offer polluted bread upon mine altar; and ye say Wherein have we polluted thee? In that ye say, The table of the Lord is contemptible. And if ye offer the blind for sacrifice, is it not evil; and if ye offer the lame and the sick, is it not evil? Offer it now to thy governor; will he be pleased with thee, or accept thy person? saith the Lord of hosts.

And now, I pray you, beseech God that he will be gracious unto us: and [with such gifts] will he regard your persons? saith the Lord of hosts. [Better that you should keep the doors shut than] that you should kindle fire on mine altar in vain; for I have no pleasure in you, saith the Lord of hosts, neither will I accept an offering at your hand. For from the rising of the sun, even unto the going down of the same, my name shall be great among the Gentiles; and in every place incense shall be offered unto me, and a pure offering: for my name shall be great among the heathen, saith the Lord of hosts.

But we have profaned it, in that ye say, The table of the Lord is polluted; and the fruit thereof, even his meat, is contemptible. Ye said also, Behold what a weariness is it! And ye have snuffed at it, saith the Lord of hosts; and ye brought that which was torn, and the lame, and the sick; thus ye brought an offering. Should I accept this of your hand? saith the Lord. But cursed be the deceiver which hath in his flock a male, and voweth, and sacrificeth unto the Lord a corrupt thing: for I am a great king, saith the Lord of hosts, and my name is dreadful among the heathen.

The dialogue continues. Even by secular standards the behaviour of God's people is deplorable. They give him less honour than they would to their parents or their rulers. And therefore it would be better to keep the doors of the Temple closed than to pollute it with unworthy offerings. Malachi has to underline what he means by pollution: it's the pretence that you're giving of your best when in fact you're unloading what you don't want, the sacrificial victim that you can easily spare because it's damaged or sickly or castrated.

It may be difficult for us to feel as strongly as Malachi does about animal sacrifices. We're repelled by the whole idea. But it's even more repulsive, as we can well understand, when religious people become blasé about their religion. And here Malachi scores a bull's-eye. 'They snuff at the Lord's table. What a bore it all is!' And yet even among the heathen you'll find more respect than that for the Lord of hosts.

So far the 'oracle' has been addressed pretty generally to the whole people. Now the prophet becomes more specific.

And now, O ye priests, this commandment is for you.

If ye will not hear, and if ye will not lay it to heart to give glory to my name, saith the Lord of hosts, I will even send a curse upon you, and I will curse your blessings; yea I have cursed them already, because ye do not lay it to heart. Behold, I will corrupt your seed, and spread dung upon your faces, even the dung of your solemn feasts; [and I will put you out of my presence]. And ye shall know that I have sent this commandment unto you, that my covenant might be with Levi, saith the Lord of hosts. My covenant with him was [a covenant] of life and peace; and I gave them to him for the fear wherewith he feared me, and was afraid before my name. The law of truth was in his mouth, and iniquity was not found in his lips: he walked with me in peace and equity, and did turn many away from iniquity. For the priest's lips should keep knowledge, and [the people] should seek the law at his mouth: for he is the messenger of the Lord of hosts. But ye are departed out of the way; ye have caused many to stumble at the law; ye have corrupted the covenant of Levi, saith the Lord of hosts, therefore have I also made you contemptible and base before all the people, according as ye have not kept my ways, but have [shown partiality in your instruction].

I think it's still generally true, even at a time when scandals are widely reported, that people expect a certain standard of morality in the clergy. It comes as a surprise therefore to discover that in many religious systems there has never been any such expectation. We tend to think of priesthood as a vocation: in Israel, as in many other societies, it was an inherited office. In other cultures, too, we find that priesthood goes in families. Sometimes it is associated with political duties. It is commonly exercised within the family by the head of the household. You sometimes hear it said, how truly I don't know, that in Christian marriage it's the bridegroom not the officiating clergyman who is the priest: if that's so, his priesthood is a matter of status; and if you're a priest by reason of status or inheritance or caste there's no reason why your morals should be better or worse than anyone else's.

There were evidently times in Jewish history when the priesthood, because it was restricted to certain families, was seen in this light. Priests were not chosen because they were good men. However, Jewish priests, even though their office was hereditary, were in general expected to behave well; so that when they didn't, like the sons of Eli and what they did at Shiloh when they stole sacrificial offerings and seduced the worshippers, it was an unusual enough matter to cause special comment.

So there are two interesting things about Malachi's attack on the priests. First, he bases it on God's covenant with Levi. Back to the Patriarchs. That's surprising, because it was more usual at this date for the priests to trace their ancestry not from Levi but from Aaron. Perhaps that's a small point, but it may imply that Malachi wants to earth his concept of priesthood as far back in Israel's history as he can. He certainly paints a glowing portrait of Levi walking with God in truth and friendship. And he expects the priests of his own day to follow that example.

The second thing is that the prophet's strictures don't just apply to the way the priests were failing in their cultic duties. That, admittedly, was bad enough. Jane Austen would have agreed with him; if the clergyman is no good at Reading the Prayers, what is he good for? Malachi insists that the priest's work goes deeper than that. He is to maintain the law of truth. God's covenant with him is for life and peace, for justice and equity. He must not abuse the covenant, or scandalize the people, or show favour, or be found treacherous within the brotherhood of the nation. He is above all (and did Malachi adopt the name with this in mind?) God's Messenger.

That's how seriously this writer treats the service of the Lord of hosts. He now has some more precise charges to bring against the priests. The Authorized Version, incidentally, isn't at its best here: where you see square brackets in the text please assume that the sense isn't altered but the meaning has been made a bit clearer.

Judah hath dealt treacherously, and an abomination is committed in Israel and in Jerusalem; for Judah hath profaned the [sanctuary] of the Lord which he loved, and hath married the daughter of a strange god. The Lord will cut off the man that doeth this, the master and the scholar, out of the tabernacles of Jacob, and him that offereth an offering unto the Lord of hosts. [And this again you do]: you cover the altar of the Lord with tears, weeping and crying [because] he no longer regardeth your offering any more, nor receiveth it at your hand. [And why does he not receive it?] Because the Lord hath been witness between thee and the wife of thy youth, against whom thou hast dealt treacherously: yet she is thy companion, and the wife of thy covenant. [Has not God made us one, and sustained for us a living spirit? And why? Because he desires godfearing children.] Therefore take heed to your spirit, and let none deal treacherously against the wife of his youth. For the Lord God of Israel saith that he hateth putting away, and [concealed violence]. Therefore take heed to your spirit, that ye deal not treacherously.

It isn't altogether easy to see what's going on. Mixed marriages, presumably: they were a problem for Israel in the fifth century BC, and both Ezra and Nehemiah were to deal fiercely with them. It seems in this instance as though Malachi has someone in mind, unless he's taking the individual as a symbol of the whole nation. Perhaps some priest has divorced his wife in order to marry outside the covenant. And that, says the prophet, is not only disloyal but cruel. It's an offence against the spiritual vocation of Israel. And more explicitly in the case of the priest it's a profanation of the sanctuary, and therefore offensive to the holiness of God.

Ye have wearied the Lord with your words. Yet ye say, Wherewith have we wearied him? When ye say, Everyone that doeth evil is good in the sight of the Lord, and he delighteth in them; or, Where is the God of judgment.

Behold, I will send my messenger, and he shall prepare the way before me: and the Lord whom ye seek shall suddenly come to his temple, even the messenger of the covenant whom ye delight in: behold, he shall come, saith the Lord of hosts. But who may abide the day of his coming, and who shall stand when he appeareth? For he is like a refiner's fire, and like fuller's soap: and he shall sit as a refiner and purifier of silver: and he shall purify the sons of Levi, and purge them as gold and silver, that they may offer unto the Lord an offering in righteousness. Then shall the offering of Judah and Jerusalem be pleasant unto the Lord, as in the days of old, and as in former years.

And I will come near to you to judgment; and I will be a swift witness against the sorcerers, and against the adulterers, and against false swearers, and against those that oppress the hireling in his wages, the widow, and the fatherless, and that turn aside the stranger from his right, and fear not me, saith the Lord of hosts.

For I am the Lord, I change not: therefore ye sons of Jacob are not consumed.

I don't know if this is really, as it seems to me, the climax of Malachi's message; or whether it's the Messiah Factor again. Once the words have become familiar in a different setting you can't any longer be entirely objective about them. Even so, I think we have here something very powerful in its own right. These aren't the words of some churchy fusspot looking for a tidying-up of the liturgy. In his call for renewal Malachi may start with the worship of the Temple, but he goes as far beyond that, as Ezekiel did when he saw the waters of life issuing from underneath the doors of the Temple and bringing new life to all the country round about.

Malachi's vision has to do, not with rituals and structures, but with the imminent appearance of the Lord of hosts himself. It's his temple, and he'll be there when the Day of the Lord comes. Ever since the time of Amos, the Day of the Lord had been firmly written into the calendar of Jewish expectation: it was to be the Day when God vindicated himself and his people in the sight of the Nations. And as the Jews' visionary writing (Apocalyptic) developed, so their understanding of how things were going to end (Eschatology) became more detailed and colourful. Malachi stands at a fairly early point in this development, compared with the later prophecies of Daniel or the Book of Revelation. What's striking about his message is that God is not only going to purge his Temple, with fire and astringents, but is proposing an audit of social conditions in Israel. The Lord Who Comes, either in his own person or through the agency of his Messenger, will concern himself with the way the nation worships, certainly: he will require a pure offering, 'as in the days of old'. But he will also look into the treatment of the underprivileged and the alien: because decline in religious observance is essentially a symptom of something worse. Dishonesty, and falsehood, and unscrupulous manipulation of the truth: these are the real sins of the community.

It's hardly necessary to underline the relevance of that message to the present situation in a country like Great Britain. We don't know how Malachi's warning was received, or what the influential people of his day thought about it. But we know from recent experience that governments react negatively when religious leaders speak out about social matters, about poor people and aliens and the treatment of the disadvantaged. I daresay it was much the same in Jerusalem in 450 BC. It's all too tempting to dissociate the Temple from public life. But here we have a prophet insisting above all on the integrity of his message, calling with equal passion both for social justice and for pure worship. The two cannot be separated.

It's a message to be taken seriously, and at the close of his prophecy Malachi takes up his dialogue again.

> Even from the days of your fathers ye are gone away from mine ordinances, and have not kept them. Return unto me, and I will return unto you, saith the Lord of hosts.

> But ye said, Wherein shall we return? Will a man rob God? Yet ye have robbed me. But ye say, Wherein have we robbed thee? In tithes and offerings. Ye are cursed with a curse: for ye have robbed me, even this whole nation.

> Bring ye all the tithes into the storehouse, that there may be [food] in mine house, says the Lord of hosts; [test] me and see if I will not open for you the windows of heaven, and pour out [such] a blessing that there shall not be room enough to receive it. And I will rebuke the devourer for your sakes, and he shall not destroy the fruits of your ground; neither shall your vine cast her fruit before her time in the field, saith the Lord of hosts. And all nations shall call you blessed: for ye shall be a delightsome land, saith the Lord of hosts.

This is all about cheating. Priests didn't actually have to pay tithes. But they administered them, and they fall within the condemnation of those who rob God. From time to time in this book we've made reference to the story of Ananias and Sapphira in the fifth chapter of Acts: that's because their gruesome fate is the most extreme comment on something that seems trivial enough until you think of its implications, which are the same as here. Dishonesty in the face of God; a fraudulent gift to the Lord of hosts. St Luke and Malachi are at one in seeing this as a lethal corruption, a denial of that relationship which should be like the opening of the doors of heaven. If the grapes rot and drop before harvest, there's no wine for the kingdom. But God is poised to wipe away the curse, to save his people from the destroyer, and to make them a delight to all the nations.

It's on that note that the collection of books which we call the Old Testament draws to its end. Malachi was not of course the last, chronologically speaking, of the canonical writers. After his time there was to be another two hundred years of prophecy and historical writing, of psalmody and lawmaking, before this collection of books, later to be designated sacred scripture, was complete. And indeed in our Bibles there's a later addition to Malachi, from chapter 3 verse 13 to the end of chapter 4, which has apparently been tacked on as a tailpiece not only to Malachi but to the prophetic books as a whole. For completeness we ought to look at these verses. We'll come back finally to Anonymous Malachi himself, but meanwhile there are in these attached verses some general comments on what East Anglians would call the awkwardness of the people of God, both the good and the bad.

Your words have been stout against me, said the Lord. Yet ye say, What have we spoken so much against thee? Ye have said, It is vain to serve God: and what profit is it that we have kept his ordinance, and that we have walked in black before the Lord of hosts? And now we call the proud happy; yea, they that work wickedness are set up; yea, they that tempt God are even delivered.

Then they that feared the Lord spake often one to another: and the Lord hearkened and heard it, and a book of remembrance was written before him for them that feared the Lord, and that thought upon his name. And they shall be mine, saith the Lord of hosts, in that day when I make up my jewels; and I will spare them, as a man spareth his own son that serveth him. Then shall ye return, and discern between the righteous and the wicked, between him that serveth God and him that serveth him not.

For behold, the day cometh that shall burn as an oven; and all the proud, yea, and all that do wickedly, shall be stubble: and the day that cometh shall burn them up, saith the Lord of hosts, that it shall leave them neither root nor branch.

But unto you that fear my name shall the Sun of Righteousness arise with healing in his wings; and ye shall go forth, and grow up as calves of the stall. And ye shall tread down the wicked; for they shall be ashes under the soles of your feet in the day that I shall do this, saith the Lord of hosts.

Remember ye the law of Moses my servant, which I commanded unto him in Horeb for all Israel, with the statutes and judgments.

Behold, I will send you Elijah the prophet before the coming of the great and dreadful day of the Lord; and he shall turn the heart of the fathers to the children, and the heart of the children to their fathers, lest I come and smite the earth with a curse.

It does less than justice to the genuine prophecy of Malachi when people say that his book, and therefore the entire Old Testament, ends with a curse, whereas the Book of Revelation, and therefore the entire New Testament, ends with a blessing. And that is a preacher's cliché. Malachi Proper, as we've seen, ends with a message of reconciliation; with a theology that ranks with *Magnificat* in its concern for the poor and its promise of a blessing to come.

These concluding verses are a later addition, but important all the same. They are typical of the dialectic of Jewish prophecy, the struggle between good and evil, loyalty and rebellion, choice and rejection, which characterizes the Old Testament from start to finish. The fire is laid; the Book of Life ready to be inscribed. And as a tailpiece to the tailpiece, so to speak, there's a glance over the shoulder, back to Moses and Elijah, those two great figures of Israel's past who were expected to appear again when the promises of God came to fulfilment, and who (in the Christian interpretation of that moment) were to be glimpsed for a moment on the Mount of Transfiguration.

But we end with Malachi himself. There's a very definite context to his prophecy. He doesn't peddle generalities. He speaks to particular people at a particular time. And what sort of people were they? One commentator has pointed out that they were not the self-satisfied folk against whom the earlier prophets took their stand. These latter-day Jews, according to Malachi, are loveless, irreverent, listless, ignorant, heartless, faithless and contemptuous. Those are the exact words he uses of them, and it's hard to think of a nastier set of characteristics for any group of people. Yet these are the people of the covenant, the beloved of the Lord. And there lies one of the great mysteries of both the Old Testament and the New. In this stark contrast between a loving God and a debased people we are confronted with the realities of our situation. Under the law, and under the gospel, we find ourselves in the presence of the Lord of hosts who is both our judge and our saviour.

9

Speaking in Parables

Mark 4. 21–35

The academic study of the New Testament is becoming more technical day by day. This is all to the good, as the tools for scholarship, and the technology of communicating knowledge, become more and more sophisticated. But specialism brings disadvantages with it. For instance, in recent publications from the United States you're likely to find individual writers described no longer simply as specialists in the New Testament, but as 'Luke scholars' or 'Pauline experts'. I daresay there are 'parable pundits', come to that.

It's doubtful if such a narrowing of range is the surest way of deepening our understanding of the New Testament and the world in and for which its books were written. The most illuminating ideas often come from the non-specialist. On the other hand, it's foolish to belittle the strict disciplines of biblical scholarship, and it's a sad business when words like 'academic' or 'specialist' are used in a derogatory sense. Scholarly precision, not least in the field of biblical studies, has over the past two hundred years yielded remarkable results. And the strange consequence is that if you're able to follow these results through the learned journals and the libraries and museums, you have access to more information about the ancient world than did the people who actually lived in it.

If you know where to look. That's the problem. Very often the findings of scholars remain inaccessible except to other scholars, if only because of the highly technical way in which they are communicated. Inevitably so. We've thought a little about that in the Introduction to this book. To take one instance, now we've come to the New Testament, there has been in very recent years a great upsurge of interest in the actual forms of language and the speech-patterns which are to be found in the New Testament documents. The study of metaphor, parable, rhetorical figures of speech of all kinds, has become a significant element in the study of all kinds of literature, secular as well as sacred. Structuralism is, I suppose, the best-known form this interest takes. And all this is now part and parcel of New Testament Studies. Results, as the news-readers say, are still coming in.

This means that an apparently straightforward passage like the first one we're going to look at, from the fourth chapter of St Mark, because it's concerned with parables and what they are for, has become one of the key texts for discussion of a number of extremely important questions. They are questions not only for experts in the field of scholarly interpretation, but for anyone who sets out to read the gospels attentively. Different people formulate the questions differently; the ones I want to ask go something like this:

How did Jesus actually think and speak?
In what shape did traditions about Jesus' thought and speech reach the gospel-writers of the next generation?
How did those gospel-writers use this material when it reached them?
How is our understanding of the message of Jesus affected by the form in which we have received it?

That seems a fairly logical sequence, though we'll see in a moment that in looking for answers you sometimes have to tackle them in a different order. In any case, neither this nor the following chapters presume to offer neat solutions. But please keep those questions in mind. If you think they are the right ones (or something like), you'll want to go on asking them when you read the gospels for yourself, or have them expounded to you in sermons or films or tapes, or in the context of private and public worship.

At the beginning of the fourth chapter of his gospel, then, St Mark sets for us a scene which is apparently characteristic of the teaching of Jesus.

And he began to teach by the sea side: and there was gathered unto him a great multitude, so that he entered into a ship, and sat in the sea; and the whole multitude was by the sea on the land. And he taught them many things by parables.

There follows the Parable of the Sower.

And when he was alone, they that were about him with the twelve asked of him the parable. And he said unto them, Unto you it is given to know the mystery of the kingdom of God: but unto them that are without, all things are done in parables: that 'seeing they may see, and not perceive; and hearing they may hear, and not understand; lest at any time they should be converted, and their sins should be forgiven them.'

(The words in quotation marks are already familiar to us: they're a quotation, slightly garbled, from chapter 6 of Isaiah.)

St Mark proceeds with an interpretation, on allegorical lines, of the Parable of the Sower, evidently meant only for the inner circle of his followers.

This is followed by two short sayings about hearing. That sounds a bit odd, but you'll see what it means. Then come two short parables about growth, and a final comment by the evangelist. Both the short sayings and both the short parables are introduced by 'and he said' or 'and he said unto them', not specifying whether he's speaking to the multitude or to the narrower circle. Like this:

And he said unto them, Is a candle brought to be put under a bushel, or under a bed? and not to be set on a candlestick? For there is nothing hid, which shall not be manifested; neither was anything kept secret, but that it should come abroad. If any man have ears to hear, let him hear.

And he said unto them, Take heed what ye hear: with what measure ye mete, it shall be measured to you: and unto you that hear shall more be given. For he that hath, to him shall be given: and he that hath not, from him shall be taken even that which he hath.

And he said, So is the kingdom of God, as if a man should cast seed into the ground; and should sleep, and rise night and day, and the seed should spring and grow up, he knoweth not how. For the earth bringeth forth fruit of herself; first the blade, then the ear, after that the full corn in the ear. But when the fruit is brought forth, immediately he putteth in the sickle, because the harvest is come.

And he said, Whereunto shall we liken the kingdom of God? or with what comparison shall we compare it? It is like a grain of mustard seed, which, when it is sown in the earth, is less than all the seeds that be in the earth: but when it is sown, it groweth up, and becometh greater than all herbs, and shooteth out great branches; so that the fowls of the air may lodge under the shadow of it.

And with many such parables spake he the word unto them, as they were able to hear it. But without a parable speak he not unto them: and when they were alone, he expounded all things to his disciples.

If those words are very familiar to you, you'll have to make an effort to see how puzzling they are. Did Jesus want to get his message across to the crowds, or did he not? That's a rather bald question. The straight answer seems to be, On this evidence, no, he didn't. And if that doesn't make you scratch your head, nothing will. What on earth was he up to?

It's exactly at this point that we have to look at subsidiary questions before we can get back to the main one. What did St Mark understand this teaching to be about? When he transmitted it to his readers, why did he do it like this? And why, in his writing of the gospel, did he put it in precisely here?

Let's look at the context, first of all. Perhaps even this exercise may be surprising, if you were brought up (as I was) to think that the gospel narratives are written in the way they are, simply because that's how it all happened. That would be fine if all the gospels said the same thing. But they don't. So: either they're all wrong; or some of them are wrong; or they all arranged their material in the way they did because they wanted to make a point by arranging it just like that. There may be other explanations; but I'm happy to settle for that last one. And I want to know why chapter 4 of St Mark follows chapter 3 and comes before chapter 5, and why its contents are what they are. Chapter divisions, by the way, don't usually signify anything: they were added for convenience, long after the books were written.

So we need to take note, for a start, of the shape of St Mark's Gospel, and where chapter 4 fits in.

There's no birth-narrative. Jesus makes his début in the
wilderness when he is baptized by John. After forty days in the
wilderness he proclaims the arrival of the kingdom, chooses four
followers, goes into the synagogue of Capernaum, teaches, and
casts out an unclean spirit. The people are astonished: some of
them go and bring their sick folk to him, and there are more
healings, though Jesus tries to keep himself apart and tells his
'patients' to keep quiet about him. But news spreads, the
healings continue. He moves freely among disreputable people,
he sits lightly to sabbath observance, so opposition mounts
among the scribes and Pharisees. His teaching, recorded in
fragments by St Mark, mainly takes the form of controversy with
these opponents: topics include sin and forgiveness, keeping bad
company, fasting, the sabbath, the new and the old. Then there's
a threat against his life, and he withdraws to the sea, hoping still
that those he heals 'should not make him known'. Up in the hill
country he appoints the Twelve and returns home to encounter
further hostility from opponents who have come, this time, from
Jerusalem itself: the argument now is about good and bad spirits.
Finally there's conflict, apparently, with his own family: he turns
from them, identifying himself with those who 'do the will of
God'.

And that's the point, in the fourth chapter, where St Mark
gives us this substantial collection of parables.

Immediately afterwards Jesus crosses the water, stills a storm,
and encounters the madman in Gadara. Back in Galilee he raises a
dead child to life. He heals a sick woman, still commanding
secrecy, and goes about the villages teaching. He sends out the
Twelve to preach; the death of John the Baptist is recorded; on
their return the Twelve are involved with the feeding of the five
thousand and with another mysterious event on the water.
There's a long passage of controversy with the Pharisees; more
excursions, this time to Tyre and Sidon and the Decapolis; further
healings, and the feeding of the four thousand, and yet more
controversy. At Caesarea Philippi he evokes from Peter an
avowal that he is the Christ; he then begins to foretell his own
death, and is glorified on the Mount of Transfiguration. After
more acts of healing and exorcism he sets off on the road to
Jerusalem: while on the road there is more teaching, more
conflict, as St Mark unfolds the story of Jesus' passion, and then,
elliptically, his resurrection.

There, crudely put, you have the shape of the second gospel and the context of its principal collection of parables.

In his commentary on St Mark, D. E. Nineham argues that the sayings attributed to Jesus in this parable chapter aren't likely to have been uttered all at one time. He also maintains that the evangelist isn't concerned to offer a representative selection of parables to illustrate the Lord's teaching, but that all the parables and the sayings recorded here 'are connected in one way or another with the question of the nature and purpose of parables themselves'. If he's right, then what concerns St Mark at this point in his gospel is not only what Jesus taught, but how his words were received, and why he spoke as he did.

Now, there's no doubt that most people, if you asked them why Jesus taught in parables, would say that it was to make his message easily understood by simple people. Yes, surely; in some instances that seems to be how it is. The Lost Coin, the Good Samaritan, taken at face value, as earthly stories with a heavenly meaning, carry a message which can't easily be missed, even if there are hidden depths which you need to look into. Indeed, you'll find that some preachers and commentators will tell you that all the parables of Jesus are of that kind; that there's one main point to them, and that the details are only there to embellish it. You'll be told that a parable is to be defined as a simple story with one point; it is different from an allegory, in which every detail stands for something and has a symbolic significance. You may even be warned of the dangers of treating parables as though they were allegories, as people used to do with the story of the Good Samaritan, interpreting the inn as the church, the wine and oil as the sacraments, the ass as the clergy . . . That kind of allegorical interpretation, we're told, just won't do.

But you soon discover that the parables of Jesus as the gospels recount them aren't all simple one-point stories by any means. As we learn more about the way Jewish rabbis taught it becomes clear that they used a great many different techniques. You find just this variety in the parables of Jesus. Some were simple maxims, more like proverbs: 'a little yeast leaveneth the whole lump'. Some were elaborated to make a strong point stronger: 'a certain man had two sons . . .' and may indeed carry allegorical meanings. Some were more like riddles: 'new wine for new bottles'. And, most confusingly, there are some which are clearly there to tease, to make you think, and not to give you an answer at all: 'make friends with the filthy rich' is an exact translation of Luke 16.9. There a good deal of this kind of irony in the teaching of Jesus. It is full of paradox and exaggeration: 'if your hand hurts cut it off'. Many of the parables are open to divergent interpretations: the parable of the Sheep and the Goats, or the Great Assize, is it a 'Christian Aid' story, or is it a warning about the treatment of missionaries?

This great variety highlights, I suggest, the four questions which I posed a moment ago. Can we be sure as we read the parables that this is what Jesus really thought and said, or are his actual words in fact lost beyond recall? There he is, talking Aramaic in rural Galilee: so what happens to the story by the time it re-appears in Greek on the Evangelist's desk in urban Antioch? And what about the context? The parable of the Great Supper for instance, as it's told both in St Matthew and in St Luke, has clearly become the property of an established Christian community: it is addressed to one of the problems which a rapidly increasing church always has to face – who's in and who's out? Which suggests that very early in their transmission, perhaps even before they were written down, the sayings of Jesus must have become 'Gospel Readings' and used in church worship. If that's so, then church use will have distanced these sayings from their original setting, which must now be impossible to recover.

So, in this collection of parables assembled by St Mark in chapter 4, particularly the parable of the Sower, it's possible that we have before us sayings of Jesus which have been re-set like old jewels and used in a new 'churchy' context, as Nineham suggests, to explain the whole process of teaching-in-parables. In which case the meaning would be something like this: some parables fall on good ground and produce the desired effect; but many of them don't, either because of their literally throw-away character, or because people can't or won't hear them. If that's what the evangelist is doing in his use and perhaps re-shaping of this parable, is he moving away from what Jesus originally said? Or is he in fact preserving for us an important clue to the mind of Jesus as teacher?

Is it possible that Jesus did in fact expect the greater part of his message to bear no fruit at all? Is that why he chose to speak in parables, specifically so that most people should not understand and turn and be converted? As we've seen, that's the plain sense of the quotation from Isaiah chapter 6. If that's so, why, for goodness' sake, did he opt for such an oblique, contrary, hit-or-miss way of proclaiming Good News? Nobody, of course, can be sure of finding the right answer to those questions. But St Mark elsewhere gives us a good many hints, thirty years after the event, how he at any rate understood the message of Jesus to have been originally proclaimed. What he tells us is still surprising, even shocking.

As we go deeper into this, try thinking of St Mark's Gospel in terms of pairs of opposites, the positive and negative aspects, so to speak, of the ministry of Jesus. You'll have noticed in the outline I've given you a regular alternation between public discourse and private instruction; between disclosure and concealment; between suffering and glory. These opposites aren't as obvious in St Mark as they are in St John, but plain enough all the same. It's one way, perhaps the only way, of communicating the mystery of the kingdom. The mystery is made plain through contradiction. In the end, we come to understand that the mystery is in fact Jesus himself. Let me see if I can unwrap that for you.

In 1901 a German theologian, Wilhelm Wrede, drew attention to the fact that at many points in the gospels, and especially in St Mark, we come up against what he calls the Messianic Secret. Even in our very sketchy outline we've seen that in his healing work Jesus is continually enjoining silence, either on the person healed, or sometimes on the spiritual beings that he has exorcised. He 'suffered not the devils to speak'. And why? 'Because they knew him'! He wasn't telling people to be quiet because he wasn't sure of his ground. Far from it. Even the devils knew who he was. But for one reason or another, and I think the reasons are very hard to understand, he wanted his true nature and vocation kept quiet. You might think this was simply a matter of concealing it from the crowds, so that he could the better teach the inner circle of his followers. Certainly, Peter's avowal at Caesarea Philippi, and the Transfiguration which followed it, might seem to support that view. On the other hand, if you want to keep a low profile do you undertake a miraculous feeding of thousands of people on the mountainside? And what do you make of the little parable of the lamp and the lampstand? It seems to me that like most theories about Jesus, that of the Messianic Secret doesn't quite account for all the facts. Of course those bits of evidence which don't match the theory can be explained as later additions; but that's a two-edged argument. Better, I think, to hold on to the contradictions of the gospel, and to acknowledge that in his teaching Jesus is quite likely to say one thing at one moment ('He that is not with me is against me') and another thing at another ('He that is not against us is on our part'). Interpreters have gone to excruciating lengths to reconcile or harmonize the incongruities of scripture. You have to decide on your own account whether any resolution is possible in the light of the gospels themselves, and St Mark's in particular.

Look again at one of those short parables. This is an entirely subjective judgment, but I can't help feeling that if anywhere in the gospels we can hear the authentic voice of Jesus, it's here:

> So is the kingdom of God, as if a man should cast seed into the ground; and should sleep and rise, night and day, and the seed should spring and grow up, he knoweth not how. For the earth bringeth forth fruit of herself; first the blade, then the ear, after that the full corn in the ear. But when the fruit is [ripe], immediately he putteth in the sickle, because the harvest is come.

The point, if there is a single 'point', is surely that the kingdom of God, which is the content of Jesus' preaching, is to be brought about not by man's activity but through its own inherent growing-power. You'll remember that in the Genesis creation story God creates 'grass, the herb yielding seed, and the fruit tree yielding fruit after his kind, whose seed is in itself, upon the earth'. I don't know how that strikes the botanist, but the theological point is clear: God's creation has within itself a potential for growth. And here in the gospel, in his new work in the kingdom, that same inherent creative process is at work. The mystery consists in the hidden-ness by which the potential of growth is contained in the seed.

In the Gospel of St John this mystery is linked explicitly with the death and resurrection of the Lord, and with the dying-and-rising principle which is the mark of the Christian disciples:

> Except a corn of wheat fall into the ground and die, it abideth alone: but if it die, it bringeth forth much fruit. He that loveth his life shall lose it; and he that hateth his life in this world shall keep it unto life eternal . . .

You can't, of course, interpret Mark through John; but it does seem likely that both are teasing out the same strand in Jesus' teaching. Mark doesn't, to be sure, link the parable of the sower with the crucifixion and resurrection: but he does introduce the figure of the harvester. And who's he, then? In terms of the parable there's no doubt that it's God who creates and gives the increase: but who is this figure, at the end of things, who decides when the time is ripe, and the sickle ready to be put in? Surely, in the light of St Mark's teaching on the Son of Man, this consummation is the final work of Jesus, the Christ. Jesus himself is the mystery. The word is sown haphazard, the seed grows secretly, the whole process goes forward in equipoise between disclosure and concealment: if there's any resolution to be found, then it has to be sought nowhere else but in the person of the teacher himself. That, surely, is why he said to his disciples,

> Unto you it is given to know the mystery of the kingdom of God: but unto them that are without, all these things are done in parables.

10

Clean and Dirty

Mark 7. 1–23

This section of our book and the one which follows will be concerned with the whole of the seventh chapter of St Mark. I've chosen this chapter, rather perversely you may think, because there are things in it which, left to ourselves, we'd rather not look at.

There's no denying that there are discordant moments in the life of Jesus, and hard sayings among his teachings. Indeed, you may come to feel that one of the striking things about the four gospels is that they don't always portray Jesus in what we should see as the most favourable light. If the piety of later ages tended to turn gospel into panegyric, the evangelists themselves were not always so careful of his reputation. For instance, a clear-eyed reading of chapters 8 and 9 of St John shows us, surely, a man under great pressure, ill-at-ease, even tetchy. And though Matthew and Luke are inclined to soften the focus from time to time, Mark more than once shines a harsh light on his subject. Therefore it seems to me our plain duty to maintain a steady gaze when we're confronted in scripture with things we don't much like. It goes with our freedom as students of the New Testament.

The first part of chapter 7, then, is a controversy about defilement and cleansing. To make the argument clearer, we'll be using the Revised Standard Version for these verses. The second part, which we'll consider in our next chapter, and for which we'll revert to the Authorized Version, tells of two acts of healing, and is specially informative about Jesus' reaction to the people involved.

Now when the Pharisees gathered together to him, with some of the scribes, who had come from Jerusalem, they saw that some of his disciples ate with hands defiled, that is, unwashed. (For the Pharisees, and all the Jews, do not eat unless they wash their hands [. . .] observing the traditions of the elders; and when they come from the market place, they do not eat unless they purify themselves; and there are many other traditions which they observe, the washing of cups and pots and vessels of bronze.) And the Pharisees and the scribes asked him, 'Why do your disciples not live according to the tradition of the elders, but eat with hands defiled?' And he said to them, 'Well did Isaiah prophesy of you hypocrites, as it is written,

> "This people honours me with their lips,
> but their heart is far from me;
> in vain do they worship me,
> teaching as doctrines the precepts of men."

You leave the commandment of God, and hold fast the tradition of men.'

As St Mark tells it, this is what the form critics call a pronouncement story. That's to say, it's a slice of narrative presented so as to lead up to a verdict on a matter of principle. St Matthew handles the event in much the same way, but alters the order: St Luke treats the story quite differently. For all the synoptics (i.e. the three gospels of Mark and Matthew and Luke, which share a common outlook and background substantially different from John) this is an important debate because it describes the attitude of Jesus to questions of ritual purity. These questions may not seem important to us, but in the early church consciences were very tender in this respect, as you can judge from the debate of the Jerusalem Council in the book of Acts. That Council had to take extremely seriously those matters on which the early church found itself most painfully divided: 'pollutions of idols, fornication, things strangled, and blood'. St Paul himself was obliged to devote a large part of his Corinthian epistles to just these same topics; and if in our day we're disposed to think them not really central to our Christian concerns, we need to remember that in a different context they are still very serious matters in many parts of the world today, where the work of famine relief has to take careful account of just such susceptibilities. So we can't pass over this controversy as though it's of no consequence.

To begin with, we need to consider St Mark's vocabulary, because there are some individual words which need to be explained.

The first thing to notice is that there's a collision between the Pharisees and 'the disciples of Jesus'. In a later chapter we shall have to consider just who these disciples were. At this stage it's worth noticing what the New Testament word *mathētēs* means. It isn't found in the Greek Old Testament: 'the Old Testament prophets have servants but not disciples', we're told. In papyrus fragments contemporary with the New Testament the word is used for apprentices of various kinds. So it's not a grand word or a holy word for a privileged group. These are therefore likely to be people who were loosely attached to Jesus as students might be to a rabbi. 'the Twelve', as we'll see, are something else again.

Then there's the word which appears as 'defiled' in most English versions. The Greek word is *koinos* and its basic meaning is something shared, common in the sense of Common Prayer, or a common language. The Koinē is in fact the phrase used for that 'vulgar' Greek in which the New Testament is written, and very good it is too. It also underlies the word used for fellowship, 'koinonia', and for communion in the eucharist. So it doesn't necessarily mean dirty, though here as elsewhere it has to do duty for a Hebrew word which does. This debate therefore isn't about insanitary habits. Nobody is suggesting that the disciples were unhygienic. The question revolves around ritual uncleanness. Unfortunately we can't actually tell what the niceties of the argument were, because there's a crucial word, which I've represented by [. . .], that's otherwise unknown. The RSV doesn't attempt to translate it. Nobody knows what it means. So there's a hole in the middle of the argument. But the drift is plain enough. Why do the disciples disregard the traditions of the elders?

Here, once again, we need to know what the words mean. From where we stand, the traditions of the elders smell a bit musty and suggest something faded and obsolete. But that certainly wasn't the case then. It's worth quoting at length what Nineham has to say about this 'honoured teaching' and about the question which underlies this controversy:

> To the earliest Jewish Christians, this must indeed have been a live question. They believed, as all Jews believed, that the written

Law, found in the Pentateuch, was absolutely binding. But over
the years an oral code had grown up alongside the written Law;
essentially it was designed to ensure the full observance of the
written Law by prescribing for its detailed application, settling
disputed points of interpretation, reconciling apparent inconsis-
tencies, and the like. This oral tradition . . . is here described as
'the tradition of the elders'. The conservative among the Jewish
leaders [the Sadducees] would have nothing to do with this
oral tradition, but the increasingly powerful and popular
[Pharisees] . . . regarded it as of at least equal importance with the
written Law itself. Where was Christianity to take its stand in this
matter?

That last sentence exactly pinpoints what was bothering St Mark
and his readers. Clearly, the tradition of the elders was not
something Christianity could casually brush aside, though, as it
happens, it's not clear that the ritual washings which occasion
this discussion actually did apply to 'all the Jews' or even to the
Pharisees: according to the later teaching of the Talmud it was the
priests who had to undergo these elaborate ablutions. No one
else. That, perhaps, is why Jesus doesn't at first give a direct
answer to the question about clean hands, but addresses himself
to the wider matter of the tradition.

You may think that he dodges the question altogether. What
sort of an answer is it that he gives? A text from Isaiah. And even
that is a bit suspect, because it's only in the Greek version of
Isaiah, in the Septuagint, that the people are accused of substitut-
ing tradition for God's commandment. The Hebrew text says
'their fear of me is a commandment of men learned by rote . . .'
which is a rather different thing. Surely Jesus didn't quote from
the Greek Bible? However that may be, it's not unusual to find
Jesus resorting, as the rabbis commonly did, to a clinching
quotation as the last word in the discussion; that's common
practice in the theological debates of the first century even if, on a
twentieth century view, we feel that the matter is left in mid-air.

Anyhow, what follows in St Mark carries the argument into
another court. In these next verses we're faced not with questions
of purity (though we come back to them in a moment) but with
this discrepancy between Torah and Tradition:

And he said to them, 'You have a fine way of rejecting the
commandment of God, in order to keep your tradition! For Moses

said, "Honour your father and your mother"; and "He who speaks
evil of father or mother, let him surely die"; but you say, "If a man
tell his father or his mother, 'What you would have gained from
me is Corban' (that is, Given to God) – then you no longer permit
him to do anything for his father or his mother, thus making void the
word of God through your tradition which you hand on. And
many such things you do."'

Jesus accuses the Pharisees of teaching people to use the oral
tradition as a cop-out, to avoid the responsibility of keeping the
Law. But there is a real puzzle here, because apparently there's
no trace of any such tendency anywhere in the Jewish records.
Indeed, such behaviour is almost unthinkable at any level of
Jewish life, let alone among highly-motivated people like the
Pharisees. So where does this dispute spring from? Nobody
knows. It has been described as 'scripture in a vacuum':
conceivably there may have been an individual case to which
Jesus was referring, but the context is now lost. We're reduced, it
seems, to assenting to a very general principle, that you don't
look for loopholes for evading the plain commandments of God.

St Mark now returns to the question of the clean and the
unclean. But the argument has moved on a stage:

And he called the people to him again, and said to them, 'Hear me,
all of you, and understand: there is nothing outside a man which
by going into him can defile him; but the things which come out of
a man are what defile him.'

If this is a statement about food, there's no great problem. Give
me fried clams, and they may disagree with me. With reasonable
care I can survive the after-effects without fouling myself. If I am
sick over my shoes, it's reasonable to say that it's what has come
out of me, the vomiting not the eating, which has defiled me.

However, that's a pretty superficial way of taking this saying.
Evidently the disciples felt there must be more to it than that, so
in private they ask him to explain what he meant.

And he said to them, 'Then are you also without understanding?
Do you not see that whatever goes into a man from outside cannot
defile him, since it enters not his heart but his stomach, and so is
evacuated.' (Thus he declared all foods clean.)

That's pretty well what we were saying about the clams. The comment in brackets, by St Mark or some later commentator, anchors the saying to the question whether certain kinds of food are ritually clean or unclean. That question, which is not in fact the question he was originally asked, is now solved, as it were, by one stroke of the pen. And if that was all, there'd be no great problem. St Luke indeed doesn't pursue it any further, but St Mark (followed by St Matthew) does.

> And he said, 'What comes out of a man is what defiles a man. For from within, out of the heart of man, come evil thoughts, fornication, theft, murder, adultery, coveting, wickedness, deceit, licentiousness, envy, slander, pride, foolishness. All these evil things come from within, and they defile a man.'

That's a very different matter. Vincent Taylor says that if the previous passage represents 'a cycle of catechetical tradition formed before the Gospel was written . . . [these two verses] may be an exegetical comment which arose in the course of catechetical praxis.' A prime piece of theological jargon, that; what it means is that somebody other than Jesus, later on, in some classroom or other, added these words, and turned a discussion about food into a general principle of morality.

Well, I suppose that may be so; though we should be chary of dismissing awkward verses as later additions. Interpolations are more often put in to make things easier, not more difficult. Besides, the evangelists do sometimes use the device of underlining the so-called stupidity of the disciples, as they do here, in order to draw attention to a particularly difficult saying of Jesus. If that's the case there are important questions to be faced. Is it true to say that all these wicked things which may hurt and corrupt you come from inside you? Is it true that nothing external can pollute you? You may think that, even if you can make sense of what was being said earlier about food, this later statement is wide open to question. Aren't there lots of outside things that come at you and leave you contaminated? What about gossip, lies, bad memories, unfair treatment, pornography, violence, being burgled, mugged or raped? You can't, surely, say that all defilement comes from inside yourself. All right, then: where does it come from?

I should love to be able to settle for you the age-old problem of the origin of evil. I don't expect to be able to do that; but I do think these verses in St Mark point us in the right general direction. You see, if you resist the idea of evil springing up, so to speak, from within yourself, you're on the way to saying that it must have some kind of independent, extrinsic existence. If you say that, you may find yourself having to introduce Old Nick, in one form or another, to explain things. That may be all right, but where does Old Nick come from? Is he part of God's creation? in which case the origin of evil lies ultimately within God himself. Or is he independent? in which case creation is no longer totally within God's control. We've looked briefly at this horny old dilemma in an earlier chapter, and we'll have to come back to it again. Traditional theology has tended to sit on the fence, suggesting that God has an opponent to whom he has given some kind of provisional independence, so that evil will have its day, but that all will be sorted out in the end. I must say that has never seemed to me a very good answer, though I think it's the one which most New Testament writers come up with. So, does the text we're looking at offer anything better? Perhaps it does.

The twentieth-century Jewish theologian Claude Josef Goldsmit Montefiore had many illuminating things to say about the New Testament. Here, italics and block capitals and all, is one of them, à propos the seventh chapter of St Mark:

> THINGS cannot be *religiously* either clean or unclean; only PERSONS. And *persons* cannot be defiled by *things*, they can only be defiled by themselves, by acting irreligiously.

I'm not keen on his use of the term 'religious', but he does help us carry the argument a step further. Instead of talking about what goes in and what comes out he speaks of THINGS and PERSONS, and claims that evil, or defilement at any rate, is of personal not impersonal origin. All right, so long as you don't have to personalize evil into the shape of Old Nick or someone like him. For evil to be personal, if I understand him right, it does have to come from within. In that case I can see clearly enough that theft, fornication, and anything else that defiles, must indeed come from within someone. But not, of course, necessarily from within the victim, the person who is being desecrated by it. And that really is quite important, because you oughtn't to allow yourself to believe that everything bad that happens to you is the result of your own obliquity. It's not. It's very often somebody else's.

I wonder what you've made of St Mark's story so far. It's certainly not one of those favourite parts of the gospel to which you return time and again for edification. You wouldn't want it whispered to you as you lie a-dying. You may have found much of it obscure, obsolete perhaps. This business of clean and unclean food, in the ritual sense, doesn't matter very much to me, even if it is still important to my Jewish neighbour. But once the argument moves beyond that particular point to the field of general moral dilemma, I find myself listening more intently. In either case I think there's something important we have to bear in mind. And it's this. I believe we are free to sit lightly to some of the things which were momentous to people in Jesus' time. Amongst these things I would number Old Nick, the eating of pork, and the need for ceremonial washing. If this is so, then it's because you and I are occupying ground which has been won for us in old battles long ago. The disciples, and the early church, had to come to terms with a new world in which all meats were declared clean, and religion was declared to concern the hearts of men and women. That was no easy matter for them, but they did it. And if we are free to inhabit that new world, it's because they discovered it for us.

11

Children and Dogs

Mark 7. 24–37

And from thence he arose, and went into the borders of Tyre and Sidon, and entered into an house, and would have no man know it: but he could not be hid. For a certain woman, whose young daughter had an unclean spirit, heard of him, and came and fell at his feet: the woman was a Greek, a Syrophenician by nation; and she besought him that he would cast forth the devil out of her daughter. But Jesus said unto her, Let the children first be filled: for it is not meet to take the children's bread, and to cast it unto the dogs. And she answered and said unto him, Yes, Lord: yet the dogs under the table eat of the children's crumbs. And he said unto her, For this saying go thy way; the devil is gone out of thy daughter. And when she was come to her house, she found the devil gone out, and her daughter laid upon the bed.

It looks as though St Mark is introducing a new topic as well as giving us a change of scene. Quite often he punctuates his gospel by telling us how Jesus goes into the hill country, or takes a boat across the water. There's constant movement throughout his ministry: which is natural enough, because Galilee was always, and still is, a place where people travel around a good deal. Before the days of air travel it was on the main highway for travellers from the sea coast to the interior, and from Africa to the Middle East. It wasn't the rural backwater that people sometimes suggest it was. In the first century Galileans may have lived in a countrified style, compared with the people of Jerusalem or Damascus, but it was an international sort of countryside, 'Galilee of the Gentiles', where people of different races and religions had to rub along together. So when we read that Jesus goes into the territory of Tyre and Sidon, the Phoenician trading cities which bordered on Palestine to the north, we don't have to suppose that he was making a great journey into strange country. It's an open question whether St Mark saw this move as 'the initiation of a Gentile Mission', as it's sometimes rather grandly described. We'll come to that question at the end of this chapter.

Nothing in St Mark can be safely dismissed as merely incidental. His is a closely wrought book, and his sequence of events is never haphazard. So it's probably no accident that Jesus' discussion about purity is immediately followed by a visit to more specifically Gentile surroundings. By the way, St Matthew, who has a very Jewish sense of propriety, misses out St Mark's preliminary statement that Jesus 'entered into a house', perhaps because if it was a Gentile house this would certainly have entailed religious defilement. It looks, then, as though some of the vibrations of the previous controversy are going to follow us over the border, so to say.

We're not told why Jesus 'would have no man know it'. Perhaps St Mark is simply reiterating his intimation of the Messianic Secret. Vincent Taylor's comment that 'the purpose of the retirement is not missionary . . . it may be conjectured that He desired to reflect upon the scope and course of His ministry' is conjecture indeed. We're not told, either, why the secrecy could not be maintained. The Authorized Version seems to imply that it was the woman's intrusion which blew the gaff; but the Greek doesn't actually say so. Not in St Mark's narrative. But here St Mark and St Matthew are noticeably different. (St Luke doesn't have the story at all, and that's quite significant too.) It's worth taking a little time to look more closely at the differences between the two accounts.

St Mark	St Matthew
went away to coasts of Tyre [and Sidon]	withdrew to the parts of Tyre and S.
went into a house	—
wanted secrecy; couldn't be hid	—
a woman . . . Greek/ Syrophenician	a Canaanite woman from those parts
—	shouted 'have pity Lord Son of David'

her daughter possessed by unclean spirit	'my daughter tormented by a devil'
—	He answered not a word.
—	Disciples say 'send her away . . .
—	. . . she is shouting after us'
—	'I am sent only to the lost sheep of the house of Israel'
fell at his feet	venerated him
asked him to cast out the demon	saying, 'Lord, help me'
'Let the children first be satisfied . . .	—
. . . it's not good to take children's bread and throw it to dogs'	'It's not good to take children's bread and throw it to dogs'
'Yes, Lord, even the dogs under the table eat the children's crumbs'	'Yes, Lord, even the dogs eat the crumbs from the lord's table'
—	'Woman, you have great faith . . .
'For this saying, go your way, the demon has left your daughter'	. . . be it as you wish'
going home, she found the child laid on the bed, and the demon gone out	and her daughter was healed from that hour

As you read the New Testament you may find yourself irritated by lots of small discrepancies in the wording of the different English versions. After all, you want to know what Jesus did and said; why worry about little differences between the gospels? Does it matter whether it was an unclean spirit or a demon that was bothering the child? How much of all this is mere nit-picking? Well, you have to decide for yourself what is important and what is not. Small is not necessarily trivial. And I believe that very often, and not least in this incident, the minute particulars hold a special significance for us, so that it's well worth keeping an eye on them.

In what follows I'm going to assume, though this can't be proved, that St Matthew used and adapted St Mark's version of the story. Most commentators think that's what happened. There are some who think it was the other way round, and maintain the primacy of St Matthew. If they are right my interpretation would have to be turned on its head. But the discrepancies would still have to be accounted for.

How does St Matthew tell it? We've already looked at the context, and the setting of the story in the country just north of Galilee, and how St Mark brings in his theme of the Messianic

Secret. St Matthew isn't interested in that, but he does have a good deal to say about the woman. He calls her a Canaanite, the only place in the New Testament where we meet this word. (The apostle Simon is a Cananaean, or zealot, which is a different thing altogether.) Canaanites were 'the ancient pre-Israelite occupiers of Palestine', aborigines. And this one makes her presence felt. She shouts aloud, for her wretched daughter's sake. Even though her address is highly respectful, 'Lord, Son of David, have mercy', she doesn't get an answer from Jesus; and her shouting annoys the disciples. 'Get rid of her', they say. Jesus then speaks, to the disciples presumably, though the text doesn't say so: 'I am sent only to the lost sheep of the house of Israel.' A technical point, almost; a theological one, certainly, and an important one. Always, in the religious tradition of the Jews, people wanted to know, Who is God's word being addressed to? Here, apparently, the child's condition is quite a secondary matter. So the woman comes nearer and becomes more than just respectful. She does obeisance: 'Lord, help me.' Lord, or Sir, there's no exact English for *Kyrie*, which can swing between Sir and Sire, but it's very polite. So Jesus' next words come as a shock. Again, it's not absolutely clear who he's talking to, but the message is plain enough. What he says, and the woman's reply, are virtually identical in St Matthew and St Mark, except that St Matthew omits the bit about satisfying the children's needs and records that Jesus does then address the woman directly, commends her faith, and does what she wants. The child is immediately healed.

St Mark's account is even more bleak and uncompromising. He calls her Greek, probably meaning non-Jewish by religion, as Syrophenician means non-Jewish by race. She doesn't make a nuisance of herself, simply falls down and makes her request for her child. Jesus addresses her directly, with those same daunting words, and receives the same answer. There's nothing about her faith. She is simply dismissed, request granted, goes home and finds the child recovering in bed. You could hardly have a less cordial encounter, and one can see why St Matthew might have wanted to embellish the story.

If that's what St Matthew did, others have gone further, doubtless feeling that as it stands the account shows Jesus in a less than favourable light. For instance, you'll find commentators saying that he didn't really make that disagreeable remark about dogs: the Greek word *kynaria* is a diminutive, puppies rather than dogs; household puppy-dogs too, otherwise they'd not be under the table. Well, now. Even if that's what the gospels mean, and I doubt it, does it make Jesus' remark any less offensive? For offensive it is. Parallels from the rabbis make that quite clear. Gentiles were commonly called dogs. 'He who eats with an idolator is like unto one who eats with a dog.' That's the background. And the Syrophenician woman wouldn't have failed to understand what was being said to her.

Another scholar suggests that the bit about dogs has been 'thrown back into Jesus's words from the woman's reply', whatever that's supposed to mean.

Another emollient which you'll hear especially from preachers is that the whole exchange was intended to test out the woman's faith. St Matthew seems to point tentatively in that direction, St Mark not at all. But suppose that is the case: doesn't it make the whole exchange even more chilling? I wonder if the gospels ever suggest that Jesus tested out people's faith when they came to him in need, or equated his response accordingly. I think not. Certainly he commends people for their faith, but he doesn't make it a pre-requisite.

Even more distasteful, to my mind, is the suggestion of one commentator (and you do hear this from the pulpit sometimes) that the child's healing was the result of 'the woman's witty reply, and the pleasure it gave Jesus'. It may just be conceivable that the power of God's healing depends on faith; but not, surely, on quickness of repartee.

What does all this add up to? It suggests that from very early days there has been unease among the followers of Jesus about certain aspects of his recorded life. Did he behave well to his family? Was his teaching always strictly consistent? And, in this case, were his feelings about foreigners, especially foreign women, exactly what one would wish them to be? These are questions which many people, out of a very proper sense of reverence, want to avoid. And you can, of course, avoid such questions altogether. There's one sure-fire way of doing so: you can appeal to the doctrine of the sinlessness of Christ. If Jesus was without sin, he couldn't have done or said anything reprehensible, to this Gentile woman or anyone else – end of argument. Except that you then either have to find a way of reinterpreting the awkward passages, so that Jesus comes out with his reputation undamaged; or else you say that somehow the evidence has got confused, and our understanding is imperfect.

It's my belief that such reasoning does not in fact do justice to the truthfulness of the gospels, or indeed to the integrity of Jesus himself. The notion of Jesus as sinless, without spot, rests uneasily on a verse in the Epistle to the Hebrews, and on the imagery of animal sacrifice where a spotless offering was required. But may I ask you to consider what sinlessness, as a human quality, really might mean? Since there's no other person to whom it applies, you'll have trouble in defining it. It's certainly not an ordinary human characteristic. Does that mean, then, that you have to use extra-ordinary categories to account for the behaviour of Jesus? Maybe you do: perhaps that's what the writers of the gospels are doing when they record his miracles. But the effect must be to put a distance between him and us which, if one dare say it, runs counter to that other New Testament emphasis on Jesus as fully human. Fully human? What's a fully-human being? You can't define that, either; because there's never been a partly-human being, apart from Centaurs and Minotaurs and such. So we're in some kind of a logical bind, and I don't see the way out of it. Which makes me all the more disposed to take the gospels as they stand, rather than re-vamp them, especially at moments when they show their subject in a less than sympathetic light.

The story of the Syrophenician woman is emphatically such a moment. It shows Jesus reacting just as you would expect a Jewish man of his day to react to an encounter with a Gentile woman. Such behaviour today would be described as both racist and sexist; but you can't apply such anachronistic words to this event. I would want to say, even at risk of pretention or sanctimoniousness, that these verses in St Mark show there's no area of human experience which was beyond the scope of Jesus' life, not even those areas where prejudice stands revealed as racial and sexual discrimination. He lived and thought as a first-century Galilean Jew; and if, through his submission to the will of God, the outcome of that life was salvation for men and women of all times and races, we can hardly doubt that it was achieved by overcoming those antipathies and limitations which would have been entirely natural to him. That, I suggest, is at least part of the meaning of this incident. It is also the story of a child made whole.

And again, departing from the coasts of Tyre and Sidon, he came

unto the sea of Galilee, through the midst of the coasts of
Decapolis. And they bring unto him one that was deaf, and had an
impediment in his speech; and they beseech him to put his hand
upon him. And he took him aside from the multitude, and put his
fingers into his ears, and he spit, and touched his tongue; and
looking up to heaven, he sighed, and saith unto him, Ephphatha,
that is, Be opened. And straightway his ears were opened, and the
string of his tongue was loosed, and he spake plain. And he
charged them that they should tell no man: but the more he
charged them, so much the more a great deal they published it;
and were beyond measure astonished, saying, He hath done all
things well: he maketh both the deaf to hear, and the dumb to
speak.

This appears to be a simpler story than the previous one. And
in many ways it is. There's apparently no complexity in the
relationship between the healer and the healed of the sort we've
just been examining. However, as always in the New Testament,
when you look closely at the details there are interesting things
below the surface.

The geography doesn't make sense, for one thing. As the map
shows, you don't go through the Decapolis to get from Tyre to the
Sea of Galilee. This could mean that St Mark has rather awk-
wardly fitted into his narrative framework a story which originally belonged somewhere else. Or perhaps somebody else did.
That's why some scholars want to discard the first and last
sentences as later additions. But if we take the section as it stands,
we may come to see very cogent reasons why St Mark should
have put it where it is. It's not in the other gospels, but here it
stands as a kind of tailpiece to the encounter with the Syrophenician. Does it, do you think, make sense as an intensification
of the point made during that encounter?

What we have here is presumably another Gentile; and for him
the way of healing is 'opened', not simply through the word
spoken, 'Ephphatha', but by physical contact of a specific and
intimate kind. In the woman's case there was no touch. Her child
was healed at a distance. The deaf and dumb man, on the other
hand, is the recipient of a whole series of carefully-described
actions. We need to examine these actions, and see the contrast
with the previous healing.

First 'they' bring the man to Jesus: the woman had to make her

own way. Then they ask Jesus to put his hand on him, which by
itself needn't be significant, since laying-on hands 'comes to be
used as a metaphor for healing': but it would have been less likely
if the patient had been female. Jesus takes the man aside
privately: again, a contrast with the public humiliation of the
woman. The next three actions certainly go beyond the formal
laying-on of hands: the insertion of the fingers, the spitting, and
the smearing of the man's tongue with spittle (if that's how it was
done), all this is much more elaborate than most of his healing
acts. So is what follows: groaning and looking up to heaven were
apparently recommended in contemporary books of magic, but
they were frowned on by the rabbis later on, and they're not
usually in the repertoire of Jesus.

If the actions are remarkable, what about the words? The use of
Aramaic, Ephphatha, may not have been unusual. In one sense
obviously not, as Jesus spoke Aramaic all the time. But when
St Mark takes pains to reproduce the foreign word and translate
it for Greek readers, it adds a certain emphasis. And that makes
one wonder exactly what is being emphasized. I've suggested
that he may be wanting to show that the healing power of the
gospel is now opened up to Gentiles, in a way not unlike the
opening up of food that had hitherto been forbidden as unclean,
in the earlier part of the chapter, and of doors which for the
Syrophenician seemed for a moment to be tight shut. The
significance is perhaps further underlined by what comes in the
following chapter, where the earlier feeding of the five thousand
with its Jewish overtones is paralleled by a feeding of four
thousand with a seemingly Gentile background.

This idea of an opening-up of the gospel may be too fanciful.
But there are other things beneath the surface of this story which
suggest that St Mark is indicating to us a critical moment in his
narrative. There's the re-iteration of the demand for secrecy.
There's also an implied reference to Messianic texts from the Old
Testament: 'he maketh the deaf to hear and the dumb to speak'
points you to Isaiah 25:

> Then shall the eyes of the blind be opened, and the ears of the deaf
> shall be unstopped. Then shall the lame man leap as an hart, and
> the tongue of the dumb sing.

Furthermore, St Mark uses a very unusual word *mogilalos* for the
man's speech impediment, a word found nowhere else in the

Greek Bible except for that passage from Isaiah. So the reference back to the prophet must surely be intentional. In which case there's a definite heightening of the Messianic significance of this healing.

Even more striking, if the final verse is not to be cropped from the story, is the hyper-hyper-amazement of the crowd. St Mark is so determined to stress this that he invents a word not found anywhere else in the whole of Greek literature. And why, do you suppose, does he do that? The event in itself wasn't any more astonishing than many other of Jesus' acts of healing. So is this account of the flabbergasting of the crowd cumulative, so to speak, as would be appropriate if this verse originally stood at the end of a whole succession of healing miracles. That's one possibility. Or are we witnessing the wonder of a Gentile crowd, of strangers aghast at finding themselves at last included in the community of the redeemed?

12

The Finger of God

Luke 11. 14–36

And he was casting out a devil, and it was dumb. And it came to pass, when the devil was gone out, the dumb spake; and the people wondered. But some of them said, He casteth out devils through Beelzebub the chief of the devils. And others, tempting him, sought of him a sign from heaven. But he, knowing their thoughts, said unto them, Every kingdom divided against itself is brought to desolation; and a house divided against a house falleth. If Satan also be divided against himself, how shall his kingdom stand? because ye say that I cast out devils through Beelzebub. And if I by Beelzebub cast out devils, by whom do your sons cast them out? therefore shall they be your judges. But if I with the finger of God cast out devils, no doubt the kingdom of God is come upon you.

Most experts think that St Mark's Gospel was the first of the four to be written; that if there were other written records before his they are now lost; that much of St Matthew and St Luke is based on St Mark, and that they seem to have had his book in their hands; but that there are other parts of St Matthew and St Luke which apparently derive from a common source which is not St Mark. If that source was another written document, it hasn't survived; so its existence can be no more than a hypothesis, and as such it has been given the name of Q. Some scholars think it was a collection of sayings, others that it never existed as a document at all. But at all events there remain these places where St Matthew and St Luke agree and St Mark is silent, and the name Q is as good as any other for identifying those passages.

We're going to look at some Q material as it appears in St Luke at what he evidently thought was an important moment in the ministry of Jesus. He has included it in a section of his gospel which is usually called the Lucan Travel Narrative, or the Greater Interpolation. It's in this section that he makes his most individual contribution to what has become the traditional picture of Jesus. So much so, that if you were to ask people in a Bible Study Group to say what sort of a person Jesus was, and what his teaching was like, I think you'd get answers based very largely on St Luke 9.51–18.14. That's where everybody's favourite bits are to be found. And it's specially interesting to notice that there's practically nothing in those chapters which is based on St Mark. It's almost all either Q material, or else it's St Luke's very own. One exception, and I think it's an important exception, is found at the beginning of the verses we're to look at, the passage known as The Beelzebub Controversy. Here St Luke starts from the same place as St Mark, though later on he goes his own way.

Let's see how St Mark tells it. Strikingly, his account comes immediately after another controversy. 'His people' (the friends of Jesus, or his family?) had heard about his behaviour, and 'went out to lay hold of him; for they were saying "he is beside himself"' And then what happens?

> The scribes which came down from Jerusalem said, He hath Beelzebub, and by the prince of devils casteth he out devils. And he called them unto him, and said unto them in parables, How can Satan cast out Satan? And if a kingdom be divided against itself, that kingdom cannot stand. And if a house be divided against itself, that house cannot stand. And if Satan rise up against himself, and be divided, he cannot stand, but hath an end. No man can enter into a strong man's house, and spoil his goods, except he will first bind the strong man; and then he will spoil his house.

There are strong insinuations here, from friends and opponents alike, that Jesus himself is possessed by the devil. And St Mark continues immediately with one of the most puzzling of all the sayings recorded in the gospels:

> Verily I say unto you, All sins shall be forgiven unto the sons of men, and blasphemies wherewith soever they shall blaspheme:

but he that shall blaspheme against the Holy Spirit hath never forgiveness, but is in danger of eternal damnation: because they said, He hath an unclean spirit.

Whatever that means, and we should ignore the capital letters attached to holy spirit, St Mark has anchored it firmly in the setting of this slur on the sanity of Jesus. To St Matthew and St Luke such an association is altogether too shocking: they preserve the saying about blasphemy against the holy spirit, but put it into an altogether less disturbing context.

Well, that is all very enigmatic. It comes down to this: St Luke takes material from St Mark, separates it from the personal attack on Jesus, associates it with the otherwise non-controversial healing of the dumb man, combines it with other material from Q and from his own sources, and out of this amalgam creates the carefully-constructed unit which we've referred to as the Beelzebub Controversy, within the larger unit known as the Travel Narrative. Now, if you read through that larger unit, you'll see that it is much concerned with prayer, with watchfulness and repentance, with discipleship. That's typical of St Luke, who keeps firmly in mind the needs of the emerging Christian communities for whom he is writing. In these chapters too you'll find those great parables special to his gospel: The Good Samaritan, the Friend at Midnight, the Rich Fool, the Prodigal Son, the Unjust Steward, Dives and Lazarus, the Reluctant Judge, the Pharisee and the Publican. And I would think that those parables have lodged in the imagination of his followers more firmly than anything else in his whole ministry and teaching. If that's so, then it's here in St Luke that we find what we most easily recognize as The Jesus of the gospels, the normal Jesus, so to speak. Consequently other accounts, St Mark's in particular, are going to strike us as perplexing and odd. In other words if, God forbid, you were to expunge St Luke's version from your mind, you'd be left with a very different Jesus, wilder and more intractable; just the sort of man, indeed, whose associates might describe as being beside himself.

However, that goes well beyond the scope of the present study. It's time we looked more closely at the Beelzebub controversy as St Luke tells it.

Very little is said about the dumb man. This is an exorcism of a dumb spirit. Out comes the demon, the man speaks, the bystanders are amazed. St Matthew adds a Messianic touch, 'surely this must be the Son of David?'; St Matthew and St Mark then introduce bigwigs from Jerusalem to lead the attack on Jesus; St Luke simply says, 'Some of them said . . .' not quite that Jesus is in the power of Beelzebub for only St Mark goes that far, but at least that he is in league with the prince of the demons. The name Beelzebub, or Beelzebul, is interesting. It means either Lord of Flies or Lord of Dung, and it's probably a derisive distortion of the name of a Phoenician god, Lord of the House or some such. Anyway, the gospels soon turn our attention away from this bogey to a more serious personage, the Satan, the Adversary who looms so large in the pages of the New Testament. But not before St Luke's bystanders have said, in effect, that exorcisms are all very well, but please can they have a sign from heaven? To that request St Luke returns later, and so shall we.

Meanwhile, how is Jesus to answer the charge of collusion with Beelzebub? In St Luke it's a crisp reply (St Mark is more expansive) incorporating, perhaps, a folk-saying: a divided house can't stand. On a larger scale, nor can a divided kingdom; and from this point the debate is no longer about exorcism but about authority. If it is acknowledged that Satan does have a kingdom, it follows that the prince of demons isn't likely to authorize anyone to commit sabotage in that kingdom. That's the first answer, 'in parables', as St Mark says.

The second answer turns the tables. Jesus calls 'your sons' to witness: if there are recognized exorcists working in Israel, what's their authority?

Thirdly, and now Jesus takes the argument a stage further, if it's by the finger of God that he does this, what's the consequence? Perhaps we shouldn't be distracted by the lovely image of God's finger, which may be just a figure of speech to avoid claiming to collude with God as one might with Satan, since Jews don't like making such direct comparisons on behalf of the Almighty: but when you've once seen Michelangelo's picture in the Sistine Chapel where God reaches out to Adam, it's tempting to let your mind dwell on the power of that divine finger-tip. St Luke's point, anyway, is that if God is at work in all this, then no doubt The Kingdom has come. The whole event is thus set in the framework of Messianic expectation. Jesus, according to St Luke, has seen his ministry in these terms from the outset, when he read in the synagogue of Nazareth those words of Isaiah:

The Spirit of the Lord is upon me, because he hath anointed me to preach the gospel to the poor; he hath sent me to heal the broken-hearted, to preach deliverance to the captives, and recovering of sight to the blind, to set at liberty them that are bruised, to proclaim the acceptable year of the Lord.

adding, without qualification,

This day is this scripture fulfilled in your ears.

And now that claim is reiterated, and Jesus not only affirms his power to exorcise but proclaims that the Messianic Kingdom has arrived. It has come, not only upon the man who was dumb, but 'in your ears'.

St Luke and St Matthew now have three further sayings:

When a strong man armed keepeth his palace, his goods are in peace: but when a stronger than he shall come upon him, and overcome him, he taketh from him all his armour wherein he trusted, and divideth his spoils.

He that is not with me is against me: and he that gathereth not with me scattereth.

When the unclean spirit is gone out of a man, he walketh through dry places, seeking rest; and finding none, he saith, I will return unto my house whence I came out. And when he cometh, he findeth it swept and garnished. Then goeth he, and taketh to him seven other spirits more wicked than himself; and they enter in, and dwell there: and the last state of that man is worse than the first.

The first of these proverbs, if that's the right word for them, uses a metaphor of military victory, very much along the lines which are now becoming familiar to us from the Dead Sea Scrolls. The kingdom is the scene of God's triumph. If there's conflict between God and Satan, the kingdom has indeed been won by the Strong Man. We'll come back to this in a moment. The second saying, about gathering and scattering, sits less comfortably here: perhaps it simply adds an agricultural metaphor to the military one. The third, about the seven other devils, can be interpreted in a number of ways, and it needs a closer look.

In one sense, it may be a straightforward nugget of medical wisdom. Health is more than simply being put to rights; you need to substitute something positive for the negative preoccupations of the invalid.

Alternatively, you can see it as a piece of guidance for your spiritual life. I don't recommend this. My own experience as a growing boy was one of extreme anxiety, preachers having suggested to me that not only did I have to get the devil out from my perfectly deplorable inner life, which seemed pretty well impossible as far as I could see, but if I subsequently relaxed for a single moment, whoosh, back he would come, with all his friends . . .

I really don't think that young people should be taught that sort of thing, do you? So perhaps we can find more edification in a slightly different interpretation. I think this saying may be a warning to those who see healing, specifically exorcism, as an end in itself, but don't 'follow through', as the golfers say. It's short-sighted, after all, to limit your view of Jesus' ministry and see it simply as a struggle with Satan, or as the career of a successful healer, or even as a victory over the forces which imprison people in the chains of dumbness or blindness or mental disturbance. That victory must surely be a sign of the kingdom: but you have to follow on. You have to go on from there and take possession of the freedom which has been won for you. And that's much more than the purely negative freedom of the house swept and garnished: it's much more a matter of sharing with the Lord in what Edward Schillebeeckx calls 'his marvellous freedom to do good'.

This brings us back, I think, to the question we shelved a moment ago. Is it true that the struggle with Satan is over and done with? More precisely, did St Luke think it was? After all, his second volume, the book of Acts, is the story of how the early church measured its strength against the powers of evil which confronted it. He lived in a world of demons. Although the Roman Empire was not usually as oppressive as Christian tradition has made out, the Powers That Be were often seen as hostile, even diabolical. So it can't be supposed that St Luke believed that the struggle against evil was at an end. However, he still has more to say on the subject. He tucks in the strange little dialogue with one of the onlookers:

And it came to pass, as he spake these things, a certain woman of the company lifted up her voice, and said unto him, Blessed is the womb that bare thee, and the paps which thou hast sucked. But he said, Yea rather, blessed are they that hear the word of God, and keep it.

This encounter is mentioned only by St Luke. So is another incident later in the gospel when some women in the crowd cry out in sympathy with Jesus on the way to Calvary. On that second occasion he counters with some words which sound like a bitter echo of this earlier event:

Behold, the days are coming, in the which they shall say, Blessed are the barren, and the wombs that never bare, and the paps which never gave suck.

The parallel can't be accidental, but its significance isn't easy to grasp. It may simply be that Jesus brushes aside extravagance either in praise or lamentation; but doesn't that sort of disapproval strike you as a rather nineteenth-century attitude? It doesn't fit, for instance, with St Luke's account of the woman with the alabaster box, where an even more extravagant gesture is accepted with the utmost grace. So you're left to interpret this incident simply in terms of the blessing which Jesus gives to those who hear the word and keep it. As distinct from whom? Emotional women? Surely not. From what follows isn't it clear that Jesus is re-engaging with those who earlier in the controversy were seeking for a sign? He continues:

And when the people were gathered thick together, he began to say, This is an evil generation: they seek a sign; and there shall no sign be given it, but the sign of Jonas the prophet. For as Jonas was a sign unto the Ninevites, so shall also the Son of man be to this generation. The queen of the south shall rise up in the judgment with the men of this generation, and condemn them: for she came from the utmost parts of the earth to hear the wisdom of Solomon; and, behold, a greater than Solomon is here. The men of Nineve shall rise up in the judgment with this generation, and shall condemn it: for they repented at the preaching of Jonas; and behold, a greater than Jonas is here.

This is a real old jumble of allusions and cross-references. St Matthew makes different use of this same Q material, addressing it to the scribes and Pharisees, and making direct reference to the resurrection of Jesus: for him the Sign of Jonas was that he was three days in the belly of the whale and was then delivered, and likewise the Son of man will be three days and three nights in the heart of the earth. St Luke doesn't make that connexion. As far as the Sign of Jonas is concerned, he contents himself with the fact that the Ninevites repented. Repentance, *metanoia*, change of heart, is a recurrent theme in his gospel. And if you follow the clues provided in the book of Jonah itself (when did you last read it?) you'll find that the people of Nineveh repented at the word of God proclaimed by Jonah, whereas for the prophet himself the word was not enough; he had to be convinced by signs, the fish, the gourd and the worm.

But what's the Queen of Sheba doing here? The link seems to be that she came to Solomon 'to test him with hard questions', as the present bystanders want to test Jesus. As for signs, she saw everything there was to see in Solomon's treasury, and it took her breath away. But there's nothing about repentance in her story. So it looks as though two Old Testament references have been cobbled together, and have somehow become associated with a variety of ideas which were important in early Christianity: the search for signs, especially those which pointed to the resurrection; the testing of Jesus; the call to repentance; the conversion of the Gentiles; the appearance of the Son of Man; the judgment at the Last Day. All these elements are present here, but it's difficult to see how they help us understand what is still the main question, the conflict between good and evil, between Satan and the Son of Man.

Perhaps the final words of this section will illuminate things for us:

No man, when he hath lighted a candle, putteth it in a secret place, neither under a bushel, but on a candlestick, that they which come in may see the light.

The light of the body is the eye: therefore when thine eye is single, thy whole body also is full of light; but when thine eye is evil, thy body also is full of darkness. Take heed therefore that the light which is in thee be not darkness.

If thy whole body therefore be full of light, having no part dark, the whole shall be full of light, as when the bright shining of a candle doth give thee light.

Here we have a number of precepts about light and darkness. Two of them are familiar in a different setting, because St Matthew places them in that great collection of sayings which we call The Sermon on the Mount, where the metaphor of the candlestick is attached to the words 'Ye are the light of the world . . .' and the second saying is included in teaching about treasure in heaven. The third belongs only to St Luke, and is simply an expansion of the second. But why does St Luke place this collection at just this point in his gospel?

I can't see any obvious answer to that. Unless, perhaps, something like this makes sense to you: the collection of sayings which both St Matthew and St Luke were using must have been arranged in some sort of order, however haphazard. That order could have linked these light-and-darkness verses with other sayings about hypocrisy, corruption and so on; and that may have suggested to St Matthew his placing of them in the Sermon on the Mount, and to St Luke a similar context just before the discourse against the Pharisees which is to follow. That's as may be. In any case what we've been looking for, a final verdict on the Beelzebub controversy, still escapes us. On reflection, you may think that such a final verdict was hardly to be expected.

Is there, in fact, any more to be said? I think there is.

The more carefully you listen to the New Testament, the more you become aware that you are in a strange world. If you become a regular listener, so to speak, a number of things may happen. Some things about that world may be elucidated for you by commentaries and sermons, so that you start to feel almost at home in it and can begin to come to terms with its strangeness. Or you can export your own values into that world, like the English taking their fish-and-chip shops to the Costa Brava, and alleviate the oddities of the ancient world by turning it into a version of your own. Or you may, on the contrary, try to import exotic elements from that world into yours, and lay on a bull fight at the church fete.

In particular, you can't go very far in this New Testament world without finding that those who lived there believed themselves surrounded by a whole host of spiritual beings, good and bad, demons and angels doing battle with one another. But then, once that's been explained to you, you can quite easily accommodate yourself to that point of view, and actually disregard its strangeness. Or you can export your own world-view on the matter, and 'explain' these supernatural manifestations in terms of hysteria or manic-depressive illness or psychosis, installing a psychiatrist next door to your fish-and-chip shop by the Sea of Galilee. Or you can settle for a wholesale importation of first-century notions into your own world of ideas and actions: and if you think that's even more fanciful than bull-fighting at the church fete, believe me, it's not.

I suppose that in every age people have been absorbed by an interest in the paranormal. The middle ages, in the West at any rate, saw demons at every turn. So did the England of James I and the France of Louis XIV. And we all know about the Witches of Salem. What is more surprising is to find Old Nick still alive in the so-called mainstream churches of the twentieth century. And yet I can tell you that I've seen an Anglican clergyman approach a patient with terminal cancer of the liver and wrestle, shaking and grunting, with an unseen adversary: 'thou foul and disobedient Spirit of Cancer', he said, 'in the name of Jesus Christ I command thee to come out of him . . .' I've known otherwise intelligent undergraduates pray all night round the bed of a friend with infective hepatitis to prevent the doctors from getting at him. I've been told in all seriousness of the discomfort felt by a blind man who discovered that as a result of the prayers of his friends new eyeballs were beginning to grow beneath his glass ones. We're all too polite to mock, but *really*! The trouble is, of course, that this kind of importation is not only foolish but dangerous. Charismatic renewal is all very well, but not when it's accompanied by nonsense of this sort.

No doubt there will always be those who hold on to a belief in a personal devil of some sort. It's a convenient way of accounting for the continuance of evil in a redeemed world. And of course it's not easy to counter the argument, 'Well, Jesus believed in him, so we ought to.' But I'm sure that argument does have to be resisted. I'm sure that illness, physical or mental, is no longer to be explained in terms of demonic possession. I'm convinced that spiritual maturity is severely hampered, as it always has been, by the search for signs and wonders. And it depresses me that when Christian groups get together for prayer, they so easily become obsessed by the idea that intercession is predominantly a technique for healing, for procuring signs from God.

The question seems to me to boil down to this: can we accept the gospels as the Word of God without at the same time giving credence to a whole array of notions which in any other context we should dismiss as ludicrous? In the specific instance we've been studying, does your study of St Luke lead you to the conclusion that Satan's kingdom still stands? Or are you to see the crucified and risen Christ as having won a victory, once and for all, over those malign forces with which St Luke shows him in conflict? It is in fact my profound if paradoxical belief that the gospel delivers us from many of the things which it proclaims. Even from death, though goodness knows how that deliverance works. I don't think the seventh chapter of this gospel on its own would lead me to that conclusion. I see it, rather, as part of the whole struggle of the early church to account for sin and death and evil in God's world. I suspect that St Luke ended up in two minds as to whether the fight against Satan was over or not. Maybe it wasn't all that clear to Jesus himself. The short-term outcome of the struggle may have been unclear. The long-term victory is incontestable.

13

Jesus at Bethany

Luke 10. 38–42
Mark 14. 3–9 = Matthew 26. 6–13 = Luke 7. 36–50
John 11. 1–2; 12. 1–8

E. M. Forster used to say that there were two things about Jesus of Nazareth which he found unattractive: that he seemed to welcome pain, and that he liked to be surrounded by disciples. People with disciples, said Forster, were always disagreeable.

I don't think the first of those charges will stick. But the second might, at any rate from the viewpoint of the twentieth century. In politics and in the arts, as well as in religion, we've suffered a good deal in our time from cadres, masters and followers, ideological bully-boys of one sort and another; and if Jesus was in that category, it would be hard to defend him. On the other hand it must be admitted that Forster lived his life in circumstances where teaching was invariably laid on for him, where newspapers and books were easily available, where there was free exchange of ideas. First-century Palestine wasn't like that at all. In a largely illiterate society your only hope of enlightenment lay in finding a teacher and attaching yourself to him as his disciple. And that, you may think, puts Jesus and his disciples in a rather different perspective from that of Edwardian England.

There are various traditions about the companions of Jesus. None of them tell us as much as we should like to know about his family, about his closest friends, about 'the Twelve' or about the women in his life. If that last phrase carries for you overtones from the gutter press, so much the better: innuendo surrounded the person of Jesus from the outset.

We can gather some idea of his family circle from the narratives of his birth and childhood, but these are interwoven with legend and hard facts are mostly out of reach. There are hints elsewhere in the gospels. Jesus is described as the son of Mary, which may or may not be offensive. He's also called the son of the craftsman; though by the time of his adult ministry the family group seems to have consisted only of 'his mother and his brethren'. And clearly, at some early point in that ministry, he found himself required to make a choice between his family on the one hand, and a group or groups of associates on the other. Dramatically, he chose the second, as we find in the third chapter of St Mark:

> There came then his brethren and his mother, and, standing without, sent unto him, calling him. And the multitude sat about him, and they said unto him, Behold, thy mother and thy brethren without seek for thee. And he answered them, saying, Who is my mother, or my brethren? And he looked round about on them which sat about him, and said, Behold my mother and my brethren!

Dramatic, and poignant. Although we shouldn't read into that incident family sentiments which belong to our own time, it seems that the evangelist himself was uncomfortable with it and felt the need to soften the impact of those words by adding:

> For whosoever shall do the will of God, the same is my brother, and my sister, and mother.

Almost certainly, by the time St Mark wrote, the mother of Jesus had become a revered figure in Christian circles; if so, it's only to be expected that the account of this rejection should have attracted that sort of 'rider' at an early stage.

Jesus, it seems, chose to live amongst those who sought to do the will of God. The three years of his public ministry were very public indeed. He was constantly surrounded by crowds. The words which we've just considered suggest that this was from choice. On the other hand we've seen earlier how often in St Mark he tries to withdraw from those crowds, and how consistently he tries to maintain secrecy, 'but he could not be hid'. Evidently he was pulled both ways. We've seen, too, how the evangelists record his teaching in two contexts, at two levels: the parable is first offered to the multitude; later it is expounded privately to the disciples. What's not clear is who, precisely, these disciples were. No doubt the membership, if one can use such a word, of these smaller groupings varied from time to time. I think that's evident from the way the gospels speak of them; and we'll need to consider this in some detail.

The three synoptic gospels agree that Jesus called twelve men. However, they don't agree about their names, nor about their function. St Mark says they were 'to be with him', and also that 'he might send them out to preach and to have authority over the demons'. St Mark doesn't at this point call them the Apostles, as St Matthew and St Luke do, but all the synoptists refer to a sending-out of the Twelve during the ministry of Jesus. St John, for his part, doesn't use the word Apostles at all, though he does refer to the Twelve. And St Luke speaks also of the Seventy who go out as forerunners. In other words, the New Testament writers never unequivocally identify the Apostles with the Twelve. St Paul for instance, before the gospels were composed, is writing regularly about apostles, but only once does he mention the Twelve. Yet it's clear that the number twelve is richly symbolic. And it's for that very reason that some scholars say categorically 'the circle [of the Twelve] arose only after the resurrection of Jesus', when such symbolism was only to be expected. You can see what they mean; but in that case the inclusion of Judas Iscariot among the number, about which all four gospels agree, is inexplicable, don't you think?

I don't see how you can reconcile all those different traditions, or draw up a definitive list of the Twelve Apostles. It's much the same when we're confronted with another group, a sort of inner-inner circle to which all the gospels testify. The synoptic gospels identify Peter, James and John as a particularly close group within the Twelve. St John never does that; his inner circle, apart from the unnamed 'disciple whom Jesus loved' who doesn't appear under that description in the synoptic gospels, is made up at first of four men whom he names in his first chapter as Simon Peter (a disciple of John the Baptist), his brother Andrew, a fellow villager named Philip, and a friend called Nathanael who doesn't figure elsewhere in the New Testament at all. Later in St John, as we shall see, there's another company of close friends. Various attempts have been made to harmonize this nominal roll with what the other evangelists say: we are told that Nathanael may have been 'the same person as Bartholomew' who appears in the other gospels, but that's mere speculation. The problem, such as it is, remains insoluble.

You'll also find a good deal of confusion about the individual names which we encounter in the gospels. It may be rather a tedious process, but perhaps we should spend a bit of time sorting out some of them. The name of John, first.

There's John the Baptist, son of Zacharias. His mother Elizabeth is described by St Luke as a cousin of the mother of Jesus. This John is known in the Orthodox Churches as The Prodromos, the fore-runner. He preached repentance and baptism, and was beheaded by order of Herod at some point during the three years of Jesus' ministry. John the Baptist is a figure of great importance in all four gospels and in the history of the early church.

There's John the son of Zebedee, brother of James. Peter, James and John belong together, as we've seen, in a special grouping in the first three Gospels. Neither James nor John is mentioned by name in the Fourth Gospel. There is, to be sure, mention of the Sons of Zebedee in chapter 21 of that gospel, but that chapter is very probably an addition to the original text.

There's the author of what we call the Gospel according to St John. The Fourth Gospel is, properly speaking, anonymous; but the appended Chapter 21 implies that the entire gospel was written by the unnamed 'disciple whom Jesus loved'. Traditionally this person has been identified with John the Son of Zebedee: but there's no hard evidence for this. Tradition goes further, and says that John the Beloved Disciple, having taken the mother of Jesus into his household, went with her to live at Ephesus, and survived there to a great age. But this takes us way beyond anything the New Testament has to say to us.

There's the author of the Book of Revelation. He identifies himself as John, and is often known as John the Divine or, as we would say, John the Theologian. He says of himself that he was on the island of Patmos 'on account of the word of God' which could certainly mean that he was an exile from Ephesus. Tradition, once again, has identified this John with the author of the Fourth Gospel: but this identification seems to most scholars now to be a very unlikely indeed, as the style is totally dissimilar and the historical background doesn't fit.

After that digression let's return to the question, Who were the disciples of Jesus? What we have to envisage, I think, is that if you were a disciple of Jesus you might, like Nicodemus for instance, be fairly loosely attached to him; or you might find yourself in some sense representing him in missionary work, without belonging to the most intimate circle. That inner circle may well have included the Twelve, though it's not certain exactly what their names were. And there was a still smaller group of three or four very close associates. There was also the household at Bethany, two women and one man.

The women in Jesus' life are every bit as elusive as the men. Even his mother. The synoptic gospels and Acts call her Mary, and although she is never actually named in St John's Gospel (why, do you suppose?) or any of the other books of the New Testament, there are no serious questions about her identity. Legends galore, of course, surround her; but they can't concern us here. We have to notice, though, that in the New Testament mention is made of no fewer than six women called Mary, apart from the mother of Jesus. So we have to do a little more sorting:

Mary of Magdala, also called Mary Magdalene, appears in all four gospels; but apart from a mention in St Luke's eighth chapter, where she is listed among other women who had been healed by Jesus, she doesn't appear in the gospel narratives until the crucifixion. She plays an important part in the resurrection stories.

Mary the mother of James and Joses is mentioned in the synoptic gospels but not in St John.

Mary the wife of Cleopas is mentioned in St John but not in the synoptic gospels.

Mary of Bethany plays a considerable part in St John's Gospel with her sister Martha and her brother Lazarus. St Luke more briefly mentions the sisters, but not the brother.

Mary the mother of John Mark appears in the Acts of the Apostles.

Mary is commended at the end of St Paul's Epistle to the Romans as a worker in the Roman church.

There's nothing to suggest that the last two women in this list were associated with the inner circle of disciples, but the others evidently were. Whether the wife of Cleopas is the same as the mother of James and Joses, we just don't know. Nor can we tell whether Mary of Magdala is identical with Mary of Bethany. Writers of fiction find it tempting to make the identification, and tell us it was the Magdalene who anointed Jesus for his burial; but the gospels don't say so. There's a further temptation to adorn these friendships, particularly the household at Bethany, with a high emotional gloss. Not surprisingly, since it's in these surroundings that Jesus gives some of his most vivid teaching about sin, forgiveness and love, life and death. They are, as preachers are apt to say, precious glimpses of Our Lord at ease within the circle of those whom he loved and who loved him best.

For that reason we need to look more closely at the texts in which those glimpses are enshrined. One is special to St Luke, one is common in one form or another to all four gospels, but is handled in a special way by St John.

We start with a passage from the tenth chapter of St Luke:

> Now it came to pass, as they went, that he entered into a certain village: and a certain woman named Martha received him into her house. And she had a sister called Mary, which also sat at Jesus' feet, and heard his word. But Martha was cumbered about much serving, and came to him, and said, Lord, dost thou not care that my sister hath left me to serve alone? Bid her therefore that she help me. And Jesus answered and said unto her, Martha, Martha, thou art careful and troubled about many things: but one thing is needful: and Mary hath chosen that good part, which shall not be taken away from her.

St Luke's geography is unspecific. He doesn't here mention Bethany, which was for him the scene of the Lord's ascension. St Mark and St Matthew do specify Bethany as the place where Jesus was anointed by a woman with a jar of perfume, but they say it was in the house of Simon the leper. Only in St John do we find this house of friends located firmly in the village of Bethany and the anointing taking place in that household.

This incident in St Luke, then, is quite detached from the story of the anointing, which that gospel places in a quite different setting. What we have here is a charming vignette of domestic life. You can't resist the humanity with which the story is told, and the translation in the Authorized Version is surely as near perfection as anything in the English language. Until the day before yesterday this story was part of the common stock. Everybody knew it. So we're not surprised to find it used in apparently contradictory ways as a model for Christian discipleship. Advocates of the contemplative life see in Mary a nun in the making, while those who come every Friday to dust the pews proudly call themselves the Marthas. So I suppose that when one scholar says St Luke is interpreting the incident 'in a spiritual way' he means that we can find here in the gospel the sort of pattern-story on which 'spiritual' writers so heavily depend. But, then, another commentator sees it as 'an instruction for those entertaining missionaries' which conjures up for the irreverent mind a wholly different picture, with cucumber sandwiches.

St Luke, now, puts it in a rather precise setting. In his gospel it follows immediately after the parable of the Good Samaritan. A lawyer, you'll remember, asks him 'What shall I do to inherit eternal life?' Jesus answers that he must keep the two great commandments in the Law: love God, and love your neighbour. But who, asks the lawyer, is my neighbour? The parable answers that question. What's to be said, then, about loving God? That question wasn't asked; but the answer is given in this dialogue with Martha. And it's quite uncompromising, really: the love of God requires total attention. There's no room for distractions; not even in the cause of entertaining missionaries.

One detail, in passing. What, do you think, is the 'good part' that Mary has? To our ears it sounds like a rôle in a play, but I don't think it means that in Greek. It can mean a share in an inheritance; but that's not something you can choose, is it? The word is more commonly used for your portion at table: and that might indeed be something you choose for yourself, or it may be what is sent to you from your host's dish. 'Sending portions', 'being a partaker', are phrases commonly found in the Old Testament which came to be used in a wider moral sense, so that the wicked man in the Psalms is described as having been partaker with the adulterers, literally messing with them. When St Paul asks what portion can the believer have with the unbeliever, I suppose he has at the back of his mind the whole question of Table Fellowship which underlies so much of his correspondence with the church at Corinth. We've already seen how the matter of who's allowed to eat with whom remains a vexed question throughout the New Testament, not least in St Luke. So I think we can take it that here in the story of Martha and Mary, which immediately follows that subversive parable of the Samaritan, we have a clear message that the best portion belongs not to those who think they are entitled to it, or can earn a right to it by diligent service, but to anyone who will simply sit at the feet of Jesus and hear his word. That's a verdict as radical as the parable which precedes it.

Who can you sit down with? Who can you allow to touch you? Those aren't academic questions for the gospel writers, and no doubt they are present in the incident of the anointing of Jesus, which all four gospels tell in their different ways. Take the version in the twenty-sixth chapter of St Matthew:

> Now when Jesus was at Bethany, in the house of Simon the leper, there came unto him a woman having an alabaster box of very precious ointment, and poured it on his head, as he sat at meat. But when his disciples saw it, they had indignation, saying, To what purpose is this waste? for this ointment might have been sold for much, and given to the poor. When Jesus understood it, he said unto them, Why trouble ye the woman? for she hath wrought a good work upon me. For ye have the poor always with you; but me ye have not always. For in that she hath poured this ointment on my body, she did it for my burial. Verily I say unto you, Wheresoever this gospel shall be preached in the whole world, there shall also this, that this woman hath done, be told for a memorial of her.

St Matthew follows St Mark closely, with only very small differences of detail. For both writers the setting is in the house of Simon the leper. It's part of the story of the Passion of Jesus; immediately afterwards Judas goes out and sells him to the priests. Nothing is said about the woman. She simply anoints Jesus' head. The disciples object to the waste. Jesus defends her act as a preparation for his burial, and promises her a memorial in the gospel.

St Luke relocates the incident entirely. It takes place early in his gospel, in chapter 7. Bethany is not mentioned. It's a Pharisee, not a leper, who invites Jesus to eat in his house. The woman is described as 'a woman in the city which was a sinner'. She weeps, washes with her tears not Jesus' head but his feet, wipes them with her hair, kisses them, anoints them. It's the householder not the disciples who takes offence, not because of the waste but because of the defilement. How can he let her touch him? Jesus reads his thoughts and replies, not by accepting the anointing for burial, but with a parable about two debtors, about sin and forgiveness and love. He contrasts the woman's generosity with the Pharisee's scant hospitality. Her love and her faith bring forgiveness of her sins. She is told to go in peace.

St John's setting is characteristically complex. At the beginning of chapter 11 he introduces the Bethany household and gives advance notice of the anointing which is to follow:

> Now a certain man was sick, named Lazarus, of Bethany, the town of Mary and her sister Martha. (It was that Mary which anointed the Lord with ointment, and wiped his feet with her hair, whose brother Lazarus was sick.)

The scene is set, but the anointing has to wait: first Lazarus must be raised from death, the Jews have to be engaged in the subsequent controversy, and at the council of priests and Pharisees Caiaphas must 'prophesy' that one man must die for the people. The decision is taken for his arrest, and only then do we find Jesus again at Bethany, six days before the passover. The feast is in Lazarus' house. Martha serves. And it's Mary who takes the precious ointment, anoints Jesus' feet, and wipes them with her hair. There are no tears. It's Judas Iscariot who objects at the waste, 'not because he cared for the poor; but because he was a thief, and had the bag, and bare what was put therein'. And what are we to make of Jesus' answer, which seems to have been 'Let her keep it for the day of my burial'?

St John has evidently made use of the same material as the synoptic writers, but he has made it very much his own. Most noticeable is the fact that St Mark and St Matthew (who perhaps belong to that part of the early church associated with St Peter) show no interest at all in the family group at Bethany. St Luke affords us a glimpse, but only in passing. St John, however, gives high prominence to these friends. Indeed, it has been pointed out that, apart from the passion narrative itself, the scene at Bethany in chapter 11 is the longest single unit in the Fourth Gospel, even without the anointing which follows in chapter 12. There's not an extended discourse of the kind you expect from St John. It's more dramatic than that. The story is told in great detail interwoven with dialogue. No fewer than seven different protagonists take part. I don't think we can doubt that St John's Gospel sees this company, this household, as the setting in which the ministry of Jesus finds its consummation.

For St John it was the raising of Lazarus, not the cleansing of the Temple, which finally brought Jesus into conflict with the chief priests. Earlier, as we can read in chapter 5, he had entered into controversy with 'the Jews'. At the heart of that argument was his claim to speak authoritatively for God:

> Verily, verily, I say unto you, He that heareth my word, and believeth on him that sent me, hath everlasting life, and shall not come into condemnation; but is passed from death unto life. Verily, verily I say unto you, The hour is coming, and now is, when the dead shall hear the voice of the Son of God: and they that hear shall live.

And now, at Bethany, that claim is vindicated by the greatest of all the signs of the gospel round which the gospel narrative is woven, and by the highest of all the claims which Jesus makes for himself. 'I am Resurrection, and I am Life', he says; not only for the Last Day, but in this company, here and now. And the word of life is at once proclaimed: 'Lazarus, come forth!'

The raising of Lazarus is not only a sign of God's power in Jesus. It is, as one scholar says, the 'first instalment of the promised gift of eternal life'. It becomes also the immediate prelude to his own death: one man must die for the people. All this is set by the evangelist in that intimate band of close friends, men and women, of whom it is simply said

> Now Jesus loved Martha, and her sister, and Lazarus.

He stands at the centre of this group, not only as master but as life-giver. Whether this relationship is really of the kind that Forster so much disliked, you must decide for yourself.

14

God is Glad

Luke 15. 11–32

A certain man had two sons: and the younger of them said to his father, Father, give me the portion of goods that falleth to me. And he divided to them his living. And not many days after the younger son gathered all together, and took his journey into a far country, and there wasted his substance with riotous living. And when he had spent all, there arose a mighty famine in that land; and he began to be in want. And he went and joined himself to a citizen of that country; and he sent him into his fields to feed swine. And he would fain have filled his belly with the husks that the swine did eat: and no man gave unto him. And when he came to himself, he said, How many hired servants of my father's have bread enough and to spare, and I perish with hunger! I will arise and go to my father, and will say unto him, Father, I have sinned against heaven and before thee, and am no more worthy to be called thy son: make me as one of thy hired servants. And he arose, and came to his father. But when he was yet a great way off, his father saw him, and had compassion, and ran, and fell on his neck, and kissed him. And the son said unto him, Father, I have sinned against heaven, and in thy sight, and am no more worthy to be called thy son. But the father said to his servants, bring forth the best robe, and put it on him; and put a ring on his hand, and shoes on his feet: and bring hither the fatted calf, and kill it; and let us eat, and be merry: for this my son was dead, and is alive again; he was lost, and is found. And they began to be merry. Now his elder son was in the field: and as he came and drew nigh to the house, he heard musick and dancing. And he called one of the servants, and asked what these things meant. And he said unto him, Thy brother is come; and thy father hath killed the fatted calf, because he hath received him safe and sound. And he was angry, and would not go in: therefore came his father out, and intreated him. And he answering said to his father, Lo, these many years do I serve thee, neither transgressed I at any time thy commandment: and yet thou never gavest me a kid, that I might make merry with my friends: but as soon as this thy son was come, which hath devoured thy living with harlots, thou hast killed for him the fatted calf. And he said unto him, Son, thou art ever with me, and all that I have is thine. It was meet that we should make merry, and be glad: for this thy brother was dead, and is alive again; and was lost, and is found.

C. H. Dodd said that there are three special characteristics of the parables of Jesus:

they arrest attention by their strangeness,
they leave you in some doubt about their meaning,
they tease you into active thought.

It's remarkable that a scholar who spent a long life in the study of these stories should have continued to find them strange. Most of them, and the Prodigal Son more than most, are so familiar, even to those who don't read the Bible any more, that you'd think they were no longer in the least startling. What's more, the parables more than other texts attract the attention of preachers, so that you might suppose that over the centuries every last drop of significance had been wrung out of them. Their meaning, surely, can't be any longer in doubt; active thought hardly seems called for.

The trouble with preaching is that when you have to do a lot of it you can fall into a number of traps. One of them is to think you're always obliged to say something new about the text you're handling. I remember with shame preaching for the umpteenth time about the Feeding of the Five Thousand, and basing my sermon on the words 'Make the men sit down', as though that was what mattered, and investing that detail with an entirely spurious significance. On the other hand, it's not much better when the expositor finds one interpretation and sticks to it through thick and thin; there's a deadliness on the tongue of the one who says 'I always thought it meant . . .' Yet again, one may feel a compulsion to make every word of scripture in some way relevant to the contemporary scene; or to extract a moralistic or spiritualizing message from it. There are many such allurements for those who handle the scriptures, and particularly the parables, and the effects must be an endless source of irritation and confusion in the mind of the listener.

Another factor which could affect your understanding of the scriptures, the parables especially, is that you may have become familiar with them by hearing them read aloud in church services. A particular passage may be put before you because someone has chosen to preach about it, and your view of the text will be to a greater or less extent influenced by how it's preached. Or it may be on the agenda because it has come round as a prescribed Lectionary Reading for that Sunday; and if, as is fashionable, the services for that Sunday are given a theme, then you'll be encouraged to see the parable in the light of that theme. For instance, in the Church of England lectionary the story of the Labourers in the Vineyard is now read on a Sunday devoted to the theme of 'The Serving Community': is that, then, what the parable is about? I don't think so. And I'm afraid that this piecemeal encounter with sacred texts out of context leaves people with a badly dislocated view of what the gospels are saying. It's therefore well worth trying to relocate these stories in the context in which the writers of the gospels first set them.

Here we need to pause while I tell you about canonical criticism, which is a formidably technical name for something quite simple. Briefly, there has for a long time been a tendency for students of the Bible to study texts by breaking them down into the smallest possible units, getting behind, discounting, even undoing the work of the editors who assembled those units in their present form. This tendency came to the fore in what's called form criticism and source criticism, which we've briefly looked at. But more recently scholars have found it valuable to study their material in the actual form in which it has come down to us in the canonical scriptures. The assumption is that if the evangelist, or the compiler of a prophetic book, has arranged his texts in a particular way, he probably had a very good reason for doing so; in which case we need to discover what that reason was. In the case of the Prodigal Son, for instance, it may very well be that the story was originally rather simpler. The part which concerns the elder brother may have been added later. Well and good, but it's none the less important to pause and reflect why, in the gospel as we have it, that story in that form should be placed precisely where it is. If we look at that question, we may well discover new insights, or rediscover old ones, into the meaning of the story.

The Prodigal Son is part of St Luke's Travel Narrative, or Great Interpolation, about which we've already had something to say. As you look at that part of the third gospel, you're bound to notice how much of the teaching of Jesus was concerned with, or illustrated by, the very basic activities of social living. You hear about a wage claim, a mugging, a troublesome neighbour, an anxious housewife, a dishonest employee, an absent landlord. There's a row about a will. There's a great deal about farming. As usual, in the circle which surrounds Jesus, there's a lot about food and drink. Altogether, you feel you're listening to just those memories which you'd expect to be circulating among the second-generation followers of Jesus, in much the same way as the early chapters of St Mark give us a very clear view of the Galilean surroundings of his ministry. On the face of it, that's what you'd expect: after all, the ministry of Jesus took place mostly in the countryside of northern Palestine, and of course the gospels reflect that fact. On the other hand, when you think a bit more about it, it's quite surprising that the evangelists (or three of them, at any rate) should have been so careful to preserve this rural element in their gospels. Especially if it's true that St Mark wrote for the church in Rome and had links with Alexandria; that St Matthew and St Luke were based in Antioch; and that St John's Gospel is associated both with the high-priestly circle at Jerusalem and with the church at Ephesus. All these centres of early Christianity were essentially urban. Rome, Ephesus, Antioch and Alexandria were the four greatest cities of the Roman world. The churches for which the gospels were written, and out of which they grew, were cosmopolitan. Furthermore, it's a mistake to suppose that their members were exclusively poor folk and slaves: although St Paul, himself a townee if ever there was one, says that not many of them were powerful or highly born, by the end of the century they included merchants and people from the imperial court. And what has this got to do with the Prodigal Son? Well, I suggest that it's important as you read the gospels to remember the background of those who wrote them and those who first read them; because many of us have grown up with the romanticized view that the origins of Christianity are somehow to be found

In simple trust like theirs who heard
Beside the Syrian sea
The gracious calling of the Lord . . .

and that can be quite misleading. When present-day travellers in
the Holy Land are encouraged to search for their spiritual roots
among the simplicities of the Galilean scene they may indeed find
themselves close to their Lord among those hills, even if
Nazareth comes as rather a nasty shock to the susceptibilities. But
in all this there's more than a touch of what an American
sociologist called 'the nostalgia for agrarian innocence'. The
cradle of Christianity may have been rural Palestine, but its
growing years were spent in very different surroundings, in the
stinking tenements of the great cities of Imperial Rome.

I have laboured that point because I think we'll find it
significant when we consider how the evangelists used their
material. So let's get back to the fifteenth chapter of St Luke, or
rather to the chapter before it.

In chapter 14 we have the magnificent story of the Great
Supper, common to St Matthew and St Luke. In St Matthew it's
told in a Jerusalem setting, as part of Jesus' confrontation with the
priests and Pharisees as they plot his death. St Luke sets the
scene earlier. Jesus is actually sharing a meal with Pharisees who
are friendly enough to warn him to beware of Herod, and the
events of the Passion are still some way off. The immediate
pretext for the parable is the behaviour of his fellow-guests as
they struggle for the best seats. The point of the parable, in
St Luke's version, is that at the great feast of the kingdom of God
the invited guests will forfeit their places to the poor, the
crippled, the blind and the lame. Have we, then, moved away
from the controversy which formed the original setting of the
parable? And do you become even more removed from it when
you hear that parable read in a church service in Great Britain or
the United States, and reflect on the discrepancy between that
vision of the Great Supper and the actual make-up of the
congregation in which you're worshipping? I want to go further
still, and ask if you think St Luke himself was aware of just such a
discontinuity between the Galilean scene he describes and the
church in which and for which he himself was writing. I think he
probably was, and that the way he treats the parables in the next
chapter reflects that awareness.

The Pharisees murmur, because they don't like the company Jesus keeps. That's not because they were self-righteous people: on the whole they weren't, but they thought certain people ought to repent, mend their ways, before one sat down to eat and drink with them. So, says St Luke, Jesus answers them with a parable. With three, in fact. The first two go like this:

> What man of you, having an hundred sheep, if he lose one of them, doth not leave the ninety and nine in the wilderness, and go after that which is lost, until he find it? And when he hath found it, he layeth it on his shoulders, rejoicing. And when he cometh home, he calleth together his friends and neighbours, saying unto them, Rejoice with me; for I have found my sheep which was lost. I say unto you, that likewise joy shall be in heaven over one sinner that repenteth, more than over ninety and nine just persons, which need no repentance.

> Either what woman having ten pieces of silver, if she lose one piece, doth not light a candle, and sweep the house, and seek diligently till she find it? And when she hath found it, she calleth her friends and her neighbours together, saying, Rejoice with me; for I have found the piece which I had lost. Likewise, I say unto you, there is joy in the presence of the angels of God over one sinner that repenteth.

The third is the parable of the Prodigal Son, the story of the man who had two sons and wouldn't give up either of them, even though they both turned their backs on him.

Do these stories in any way affect you as Dodd suggested they should? Do they 'arrest your attention by their strangeness'? Do they 'leave you in some doubt about their meaning'? Do they 'tease you into active thought'? I wonder. If they don't, I suggest it may be because St Luke has adapted them to fit in with his particular concerns, spiritualizing the stories and presenting them in terms which would be of interest to a settled Christian community in a busy town. Under St Luke's pen they have, partly at least, lost their roots in Galilee and have become stories about repentance and forgiveness, taking on a general religious significance which no longer challenges us. But is that what they really are?

The first two certainly aren't. It's nonsense to talk about forgiving sheep or coins which you've been careless enough to mislay. The prodigal son, admittedly, 'comes to himself' and is received back into favour, so forgiveness does come into the reckoning. But it's not really what he's looking for, as you see when you scrutinize his motives: he remembers how many of his father's servants have bread enough and to spare, while he's dying of hunger, and that's what drives him home, and it's not penitence. I don't think it's a story about gratitude and ingratitude, either: 'when I think of all the sacrifices your mother and I have made for you children . . .' It's not like that. Nor is it in essence a comparison between the good boy and the bad boy, one being more precious than the other. We're not, after all, asked to believe that the poor and the lame and the blind were, as such, more welcome in the kingdom than the Pharisees or the invited guests. We may find that there are some quite disturbing implications in St Luke's Gospel at this point, especially as he enrols our sympathies against the elder brother: as a representive of 'the underside of rigid morality' that young man is, and is meant to be, decidedly unattractive.

How then are we to discover what St Luke saw in these parables of Jesus? The trouble is that we're conditioned to expect from religious story-telling some kind of moral content. But the stories of Jesus are very often not moral stories at all. They are sometimes deliberately and teasingly anti-moralistic. 'Make friends with rich crooks' is a bit of advice we've considered in an earlier chapter. It's no less outrageous for being ironic; and indeed the people with whom Jesus ate were sometimes rich and sometimes crooks and sometimes both, and that seems to be exactly what the Pharisees are grumbling about at the beginning of chapter 15. But it does seem that St Luke likes to have morals for his stories. He wants to suffuse them with good ethical significance. He's always interested in prayer and in penitence. He's disposed, from his urbane Greekish standpoint, to take his Galilean raw material and transform it into something appropriate to the religious circumstances of his companions and contemporaries, whether in Antioch or wherever it was that the most excellent Theophilus lived. I rather think that's what he did with the Prodigal Son, but that he hasn't quite succeeded, because the story itself is very strong and resists his interpretation of it.

I suspect that in essence the story speaks simply of the gladness of God. 'Joy in the presence of the angels of God' is a periphrasis, a reverent and roundabout way of saying what the parable is really about. It's God who's rejoicing. What, then is God glad about?

I don't think that he's particularly glad that the stuffed-shirt elder brother decides to scowl in the shadows. Not that. 'Son, thou art ever with me, and all that I have is thine . . .'

Is he, then, glad because the bad boy has been brought to heel, has realized the error of his ways and come home again, like a reformed and less bouncy Tigger? Not that, either.

Is he glad because he himself can stand revealed as a gloriously loving father, generous and outgoing and inexhaustible in his determination to love? Is this divine delight simply the proper attitude of the Heavenly Father witnessing the repentance of the sinner? That, I think, is closer to what St Luke wanted to portray for us. But it's not quite what the story says, especially when we take it together with the two shorter parables of the coin and the sheep.

Ultimately the Prodigal Son is not a story about attitudes. It's not even about reconciliation. Both these things come into it, but the gladness of God is in the end simpler than that. 'It was meet that we should make merry, and be glad: for this thy brother was dead, and is alive again; and was lost, and is found.' So it's a story about life and death, about extinction and resurrection. You look to free yourself from God, and you find you are perishing. You go back to him, even if everyone else disapproves, and you guess that some daunting excess of fatherly love is waiting to stifle you. And you are met simply by the gladness of God, who makes merry over you, whatever you may feel about it.

And that, perhaps, may tease the sleepiest of us into some kind of active thought.

15

Who Then Can Be Saved?

Luke 17 and 18

And the apostles said unto the Lord, Increase our faith. And the Lord said, If ye had faith as a grain of mustard seed, ye might say unto this sycamine tree, Be thou plucked up by the root, and be thou planted in the sea; and it should obey you.

But which of you, having a servant plowing or feeding cattle, will say unto him by and by, when he is come from the field, Go and sit down to meat? and will not rather say unto him, make ready wherewith I may sup, and gird thyself, and serve me, till I have eaten and drunken; and afterward thou shalt eat and drink? Doth he thank that servant because he did the things that were commanded him? I trow not. So likewise ye, when ye shall have done all those things which are commanded you, say, We are unprofitable servants: we have done that which was our duty to do.

There we have two brief snatches of gospel. We're told what Jesus said, and a bit about the circumstances in which he said it. The technical word for this kind of snippet is a 'logion', and it's likely that the very earliest records of the life of Jesus were simply collections of these logia. The achievement of the first three gospels was that each of them took this material and made out of it an orderly account of the life of Jesus. The Fourth Gospel went about it rather differently, basing its narrative on a number of 'signs' and weaving round those signs a substantial fabric of theological discourse.

The middle part of St Luke consists largely of such logia. There's not much narrative, but a great many parables and pithy sayings. Many of them are 'peculiar to Luke' which means that they don't appear in the other gospels, and St Luke assembles them in such a way as makes it convenient for scholars to talk about The Great Interpolation or the Lucan Travel Narrative, but there's no way of knowing whether these sayings of Jesus originally belonged together in a coherent and systematic course of teaching, or whether they were originally quite separate from one another. Most scholars think that in the Travel Narrative, like St Matthew in the Sermon on the Mount, St Luke assembled his material without much regard for its original setting. Admittedly there are times when successive logia deal with same topic; the Lost Sheep and the Lost Coin, for example, or sayings in St Matthew about yeast and salt, or about the old law and the new. But it's never safe to assume that because one saying follows another in the gospel there was originally any link between the two sayings in the teaching of Jesus. What is certain is that the evangelist, deliberately or at random, and you can't always tell which, has put those two sayings together. That's the point from which we have to start. We can look for connections in the mind of St Luke, sometimes perhaps where he himself wasn't conscious of them; but we mustn't assume that those connections existed in the mind of Jesus.

After all those qualifications let me say that I think there is in fact a thread running through the sayings in the two chapters of St Luke which we're now going to look at. They are, I think, largely concerned with faith. From a variety of angles, certainly; but this very diversity may be a positive help to us as we try to understand St Luke and his interpretation of the message of Jesus.

The first of these two 'faith logia' exists in two forms. In St Luke faith can remove trees, and the saying comes to us after a rather unfocussed challenge from the apostles: 'Lord, increase our faith.' St Mark and St Matthew by contrast tell us that it can remove mountains, and both of those evangelists link the saying with the mysterious cursing of a barren fig-tree. St Matthew moreover has already introduced the saying earlier in his gospel in connection with the healing of an epileptic child.

All this suggests that what we have here is a proverbial tag which Jesus may have used in more than one context. We know of some other uses, too. 'Moving mountains' was a phrase used by Jewish teachers to describe difficult or impossible tasks. The

rabbis used the phrase to describe the interpretation of troublesome texts in scripture. They also, incidentally, expected the two
mountains Horeb and Sinai to be moved to Jerusalem when
Messiah came, but I doubt if that was to the fore in the mind of
St Luke who, as we've noticed, modifies the imagery; faith
uproots trees instead of moving mountains. It's an impossible
thing all the same. Even though St Luke has detached it from any
particular instance of healing or miracle-working, it remains a
starkly provocative statement. Teaching by hyperbole seems to
have been characteristic of the teaching of Jesus. It's not
surprising that interpreters are so often ill-at-ease with it.

G. B. Caird, for one, suggests that St Luke is offering us 'a
spiritual message'. As distinct from what? one might ask.
Perhaps Caird has in mind the way this saying of Jesus has come
to be used out of context as a Spiritual Instruction for people
struggling to grow in the life of faith and of prayer. You know the
kind of thing. If you pray hard enough, they tell you, God will do
miracles for you, move mountains, as it were. Ah, you may say,
but I don't think that's true: I prayed long and hard for my child
and my prayers remain unanswered; the miracle didn't happen,
so how do you account for that? Well, it must mean that you just
don't have enough faith: if you really believed . . .

You may want to resist that conclusion. I hope you do. But then
you have to say either that the word of Jesus is untrue, or that the
truth of it lies elsewhere. I must say that I find both St Matthew
and St Mark obscure in the way they handle this proverb. But
St Luke, if you look again more closely, does offer a clue. Scholars
have said that St Luke's context, the apostles coming to Jesus and
asking for more faith, is simply an editorial introduction to the
logion. I wonder if it is. Or could it be that he has faithfully given
us a setting in which Jesus might well have applied such a
disconcerting proverb. The apostles come with their request,
'Lord, increase our faith.' Why do the apostles want more faith,
do you suppose? Is there some sort of competition going on? If so,
it wouldn't be the first or the last time. In religious circles there are
always people who want more faith than other people. And they
are very ready to believe that the more faith you have, the more
likely you are to get results. That's nasty; but I'm afraid it's a
commonly-held point of view, and thought to be perfectly
respectable. And if it's that sort of hankering ambition which
prompted the apostles' question, you may feel that they needed a

proper put-down for an answer, and that according to St Luke that's exactly what they got. A foolish question invites a ludicrous, ironic answer: Oh yes, move mountains, uproot trees by all means; and I'll give you the wherewithal – a grain of mustard seed.

Behind the irony, if that's what it is, lies absolute seriousness. Faith is like mustard, or like anchovy relish. You don't need much. And you're a fool if you think you can quantify it, and reckon that large amounts of it entitle you to better rewards than small amounts of it. If St Luke intended, and you can't be sure whether he did or not, to make a connection between this saying and the one that follows, about the servant and his master, then we may have found an important clue to understanding him. 'All our righteousness,' said Third Isaiah, 'is filthy rags': all our earning potential and our devoted service to the Lord and our great reserves of faith add up to this, that we are unprofitable servants. And if we think that's a depressing conclusion, it's only because we've been encouraged to measure discipleship, and prayer especially, by results instead of taking delight in the presence and the service of the master for its own sake.

> And it came to pass, as he went to Jerusalem, that he went through the midst of Samaria and Galilee. And as he entered into a certain village, there met him ten men that were lepers, which stood afar off: and they lifted up their voices, and said, Jesus, Master, have mercy on us. And when he saw them, he said unto them, Go shew yourselves unto the priests. And it came to pass, that, as they went, they were cleansed. And one of them, when he saw that he was healed, turned back, and with a loud voice glorified God, and fell down on his face at his feet, giving him thanks: and he was a Samaritan. And Jesus answering said, Were there not ten cleansed? but where are the nine? There are not found that returned to give glory to God, save this stranger. And he said unto him, Arise, go thy way: thy faith hath made thee whole.

There are several layers to that story. You're confronted first by the predicament of the lepers, standing far off. That's something to arouse sympathy in the reader, and Jesus responds immediately to their appeal. Then comes a strange course of events: they are told to present themselves to the priest before any healing has taken place; they have the confidence to do so, and they are healed as they go. Then there's the contrast between the one who returns to give thanks and the nine who don't, and the added piquancy of the fact that the odd man out was a Samaritan. We have Jesus' comment on this contrast before he dismisses him. Finally there's the important rider, 'Thy faith hath made thee whole.'

It's those final words which suggest a link between the healing and the dialogue on faith which precedes it. Indeed, when you look again you see that it's a rather contrived connection. The healing of the ten isn't effected by their faith, but by the Master's command. Obedience, yes, but that's not quite the same thing. I think I want to reiterate my suspicion, which I voiced in the chapter on the Syrophenician woman, that the healing work of Jesus seldom if ever depends on the faith of the recipient. It certainly doesn't here. The situation is quite clear: ten were obedient, only one was 'faithful', but all ten were healed. Incidentally, one comment you sometimes hear is that there's a difference between healing and wholeness; healing, we're told, is merely an outward manifestation, but wholeness is a spiritual and much more important condition which may or may not be accompanied by physical cure. I don't think I believe a word of that. It sounds to me like another wheeze for getting God off the hook when your prayers don't work. But I do think that in the particular case we're looking at we can see, once again, a sort of faith which isn't avid for results. The tenth leper didn't come back for more. Faith, in him, wasn't a search for an even richer gift but the response to what he'd been given.

> And when he was demanded of the Pharisees, when the kingdom of God should come, he answered them and said, The kingdom of God cometh not with observation: neither shall they say, Lo here! or, lo there! for, behold, the kingdom of God is within you.

This saying of Jesus is special to St Luke, but he follows it with an extended passage, in apocalyptic language, about the coming of the Son of Man, which is also found in St Matthew and St Mark in different contexts. It's not easy to discover why St Luke stresses the 'end of time' ingredient at just this point in his story. Maybe he's leading up to a question which he puts into the mouth of Jesus in the next chapter:

> When the Son of Man cometh, shall he find faith on the earth?

Why this talk about the End Time, when it's faith for the present that's under consideration? Well, it could very well be that St Luke is doing what we see St Matthew doing at the end of his gospel – projecting back into the teaching of Jesus a topic which must have caused anxious concern to a later generation of Christian believers, as the delay of the Lord's return became more and more of a problem for them. When he did come, would he find his followers still in that state of expectation which had characterized his disciples forty years earlier?

St Luke, you see, can't quite separate his discussion of faith from the question of future expectations. But it's hard to see what exactly is the point at issue here between Jesus and the Pharisees, unless we can get a clearer view of the meaning of the word observation.

Observation can mean a correct interpretation of omens and portents. In the ancient world people hoped to learn what was coming to them by observing the flight of birds or the disposition of sacrificial entrails. It was like reading the tea-leaves, only more serious. You had to look carefully for signs. And even though Hebrew religion disapproved of that kind of divination, Jewish apocalyptic is still full of signs and wonders as men and women looked forward to the End. In the gospels you quite often find hints that some people thought that faith in Jesus consisted in knowing how to discern the signs of the coming of the Son of Man. Something of the kind seems to lie behind this saying of Jesus that the kingdom does not come with observation.

The Greek word can also mean proper observance of festivals and other religious rituals. It's tempting to apply that meaning here, and argue that Jesus meant to say that the discharge of religious formalities won't bring in the kingdom. But unfortunately the word never carries this meaning in the New Testament; so that argument won't work.

It does look, then, as though the saying means that there can be no forecasting the coming of the kingdom of God, not even by means of orthodox religious expectations. For the kingdom of God is within you. Or among you. But which? Here again, and much more critically, the Greek phrase is ambiguous; *entos humôn* can mean either 'within you' or 'among you'.

It could mean that the kingdom of God is inside you; that it's an interior disposition of the soul, and that's why its coming doesn't depend upon observation. You can't see it. It has no objective reality. 'The kingdom of heaven is within you' has very often been taken in this sense, and conscripted to support the view that Christians should not concern themselves with political or social issues. In a more sophisticated way, some traditions within the church, notably in the East, have maintained that by this saying Jesus gives weight to the idea that the image of God is implanted in each individual at birth, and that to speak of the kingdom of God 'within you' is to proclaim his sovereignty in this inner core of the human personality. Against this it has to be said that in the New Testament the kingdom is not usually interiorized in this way. Some of the parables (the Sower, the Seed Growing Secretly) certainly come quite close to it, but in general the proclamation of the kingdom clearly implies a challenge to men and women in their common daily living. 'Jesus speaks of men entering the kingdom, but not of the kingdom entering men', says one commentator, and that sounds right. The gospels also speak of the kingdom 'coming upon you', creeping up on you, almost. And that implies something much more external and objective than anything we've looked at so far.

Are we then to assume that Jesus meant that the kingdom of God is among you? that it's not a frame of mind or a part of the mysterious inner workings of God in the human soul, but a programme to be implemented, in concrete real-life terms, so that the people of God can become what they truly are, and God's creation be restored to what it was meant to be? that this programme has been inaugurated by the saving death and exaltation of Jesus Christ, but its fulfilment is yet to come, and has to be worked for? that it is in essence social, and in the proper sense political, because the kingdom is among you?

Now that view, which to many of us is immensely attractive, can certainly be maintained with plenty of support from other parts of the New Testament. But it must be admitted that in the present context, in the seventeenth and eighteenth chapters of St Luke, this strongly corporate interpretation of the text doesn't really fit. It looks as if we're going to be forced to the conclusion that this evangelist is at this point concerned to explore the nature of faith as an interior quality, in contrast with the search for external manifestations of divine power. We may be able to see in a moment if that's so or not.

Meanwhile, I think there's no way of deciding which of those two translations, 'within you' or 'among you', is the better. But there is another possible interpretation, a sidelong view which I find attractive. From papyrus fragments of the first century AD we can discover a lot about how 'ordinary' people used the Greek language; and these fragments, scraps of letters and notes from the wastepaper basket, suggest that *entos humôn* could mean something like 'in your house', 'under your control'. On this reading, the kingdom of God could be that to which you have access, something to which you can lay claim, as God's gift to you. In chapter 12 of St Luke there's some support for this:

> Seek ye the kingdom of God; and all these [other] things will be added unto you. Fear not, little flock; for it is the Father's good pleasure to give you the kingdom. Sell that ye have, and give alms . . .

This comes close to saying that the kingdom is there for the asking, at your disposal through the generosity of God. I wonder if you'll agree, as we go further in our present study, that St Luke has something like this in mind here when he says that the kingdom of God is within/among us. That it's this givenness, this availability of the kingdom which escapes the Pharisee the more he looks for it.

We're now going to jump ahead, missing out not only the apocalyptic passage at the end of chapter 17, but two parables at the beginning of chapter 18. One of them is about a plaintiff who won't take no for an answer; the other is about the Pharisee and the Publican at prayer. The first parable carries the rider we've already mentioned: 'When the Son of man cometh, will he find faith on the earth?' The second is summed up in the proverbial saying, 'Every one that exalteth himself shall be abased; and he that humbleth himself shall be exalted.' We should bear those stories in mind as St Luke, still concerned with the question of faith, directs our attention to the moral requirements of the kingdom, in particular simplicity and humility. He's beginning to sharpen up for us this all-important question, 'Who then can be saved?' Who gets in?

> And they brought unto him also infants, that he would touch them: but when his disciples saw it, they rebuked them. But Jesus called them unto him, and said, Suffer little children to come unto me, and forbid them not: for of such is the kingdom of God. Verily

I say unto you, Whosoever shall not receive the kingdom of God as a little child shall in no wise enter therein.

Here's a text that has been bandied around more than most.

Churches which baptize infants find it theologically hard to justify the practice and pastorally impossible to abandon it. The difficulty is that faith is required of those to be baptized, and infants don't have faith – impasse. So some kind of biblical precedent has to be looked for, and the nearest we get is the baptism of the gaoler 'and his household' at Philippi, which is far from conclusive. But there's also this passage from the synoptic gospels about Jesus taking the children in his arms and blessing them, and this has become a standard part of our baptismal liturgies. It is of course critical for the pastoral care of children, but it says nothing about baptism, and nothing explicit about faith.

Nothing explicit. But by now, in St Luke's Gospel, we have reached a point where the question of how you get into the kingdom is becoming acute. In his second volume, the Acts of the Apostles, that question is explicitly answered, 'Repent and be baptized.' In the gospel nothing is said about the baptism of Christian believers: but a good deal is implied, as we've already seen, about what's required of the Christian convert. Not least in this passage, which is apparently concerned with small children, do we find that the real point is a challenge to adult belief and behaviour, of the kind that would have certainly have been put to people in the early church as they prepared for Christian initiation. But that's speculative. Better that we should look a bit harder at the text as it stands.

There are lots of small points of difference between the three synoptic accounts of Jesus and the children. St Luke alone describes them as infants, and he's not concerned about the annoyance of Jesus when the disciples interfere. More significantly, perhaps, he doesn't speak of Jesus taking the infants into his arms and blessing them. This, says one commentator, 'enables Luke to generalize the story and make it suitable for adults', which sounds pretty silly but is probably true: if we're reading it right, this is indeed a story for grown-ups.

What then does it mean for an adult to become like a little child? Plenty of answers have been put forward: that Jesus requires not childishness but child-likeness; that of course you can't recover lost innocence but you can cultivate child-like qualities of

obedience, humility and a sense of wonder and joyful depen-
dence. Joachim Jeremias says it's a matter of being able to say
'Abba, Father'. All of which may be true. But St Luke, if we're
right in our sidelong view of an earlier verse, may already have
given us another clue. If the kingdom 'within/among you' means
the kingdom within reach, on offer, waiting to be claimed, or
something like that, then we should reflect that one glaringly
obvious quality of children is that they love to get presents – and
to give them. Adults find this harder, as we are about to see.

> And a certain ruler asked him, saying, Good Master, what shall I
> do to inherit eternal life? And Jesus said unto him, Why callest
> thou me good? None is good, save one, that is, God. Thou knowest
> the commandments, Do not commit adultery, Do not kill, Do not
> steal, Do not bear false witness, Honour thy father and thy
> mother. And he said, All these have I kept from my youth up.
> Now when Jesus heard these things, he said unto him, Yet lackest
> thou one thing: sell all that thou hast, and distribute unto the poor,
> and thou shalt have treasure in heaven: and come, follow me. And
> when he heard this, he was very sorrowful: for he was very rich.

> And when Jesus saw that [the man] was very sorrowful, he said,
> How hardly shall they that have riches enter into the kingdom of
> God! For it is easier for a camel to go through a needle's eye, than
> for a rich man to enter into the kingdom of God. And they that
> heard it said, Who then can be saved? And he said, The things
> which are impossible with men are possible with God.

This character is often called the Rich Young Ruler, though
only St Luke calls him a ruler and only St Matthew says he's
young. St Mark says that Jesus looked at him and loved him,
since when a good deal of sentiment has gathered round the
story, together with a wealth of detail in the dialogue which it
would be good to examine. But the point of it, the heart of it, is
another of those hard sayings of Jesus. It is easier for a camel to go
through the eye of a needle than for a rich man to enter the
kingdom of God. Teaching by hyperbole, the impossible demand, pigs can't fly. This man (any man?) will get into the
kingdom only if he gets rid of absolutely everything he possesses.
No compromise is offered. Not to him, nor subsequently to the
bystanders. The whole thing is so startling that in St Mark's
version Jesus says it twice.

I wonder if this absolute demand is just a little less shocking to us than it was to them. There have been, after all, men and women in the Christian tradition who have taken Jesus at his word and chosen to live in extreme poverty. We can't talk about absolute poverty in this connexion, because when poverty is a matter of choice it's not total poverty. All the same, we've come to accept the cliché that the poor, the voluntarily poor at any rate, are blessed; in spite of what we've also seen, in an earlier chapter, of what the Old Testament has to say about the rich and the poor. In that earlier tradition it's the rich man, not the poor man, who stands out as the one God has blessed. Consider Job. Of course rich people have a duty not to oppress the poor: the prophets say so repeatedly. And the Psalmist says 'Blessed is he that considereth the poor and needy', but that's because he's the one who will prosper and be able to withstand his enemies. Not until we reach the Sermon on the Mount do we find the poor unequivocally blessed just because they are poor; and even there it's not as unequivocal as it looks, because there are a lot of rewards around, which somehow take the sting out of poverty. And when we look at what Jesus did, rather than what he said, we find that Jesus' preference for the poor isn't as unambiguous as we might wish: publicans and sinners, social and religious outcasts, yes; but that's not quite the same thing. Whores and extortioners sometimes get very rich. No wonder, then, that this bald statement about the rich man and the kingdom so astonished his contemporaries. Even those closest to him needed to be reassured that their ears had not deceived them:

> Then Peter said, Lo, we have left all, and followed thee. And he said to them, Verily I say unto you, There is no man that hath left house, or parents, or brethren, or wife, or children, for the kingdom of God's sake, who shall not receive manifold more in this present time, and in the world to come life everlasting.

It looks as though permanent, total absolute poverty isn't after all required. Only for now. There are rewards to come. Once you've squeezed through the eye of the needle, you will be rich again, much richer than you are now.

Is that what St Luke wants to say to us? Well, yes, I rather think it is. Not that he's altogether happy about it. It seems that both he and St Matthew have had to take liberties with what they found in St Mark's tenth chapter. In St Matthew Jesus tells Peter that 'in the resurrection' his disciples will sit as judges on twelve thrones and have all their possessions restored to them. This puts the whole matter safely into the future. St Luke is less grandiose, but he too substantially alters St Mark's version, which is so extraordinary that we need to quote it in full:

> Verily I say unto you, There is no man that hath left house, or brethren, or sisters, or father, or mother, or wife, or children, or lands, for my sake, and the gospel's, but he shall receive an hundredfold now in this time, houses, and brethren, and sisters, and mothers, and children, and lands, with persecutions; and in the world to come eternal life.

That's St Mark's forecast: now, in this life, a hundred mothers . . . He can't be serious, can he? But there it is, that's what he says, and St Luke has to do what he can with it. Not a hundred perhaps, but you'll get much more than you give.

When you get this sort of synoptic muddle it's usually a sign that something important is lurking under the surface. And in this case I wonder if each of the evangelists in their different ways may have preserved for us fragments of Jesus' talk which, pieced together, could offer a clue to this whole puzzling business. St Matthew, you see, says that Peter doesn't merely point to what he and his colleagues have given up; he specifically asks, 'What shall we have then?' He wants to know what are to be the returns on this investment. Is it perhaps that question which gets its answer in St Mark, even though in St Mark Peter doesn't ask it? What a way to expound scripture, St Mark answering St Matthew's questions indeed! It won't do, of course; we can't get back to the authentic words of Jesus by jumbling up what the individual evangelists say. But it's with some reluctance that I abandon the idea that Jesus, faced with a stupid question, would typically have given an exceedingly paradoxical answer. It would be very much in keeping with Jesus' irony to offer a hundred mothers, in this life and in the next, to the disciple who wants a reward for his discipleship, who isn't child-like enough either to give unreservedly, or to accept without further ado what is offered to him, even when what's on offer is a place in the kingdom of God.

I don't think we can expect from the gospels a final, exclusive answer to the question 'Who then can be saved?' But if we've read

these chapters of St Luke at all accurately we'll have come to one
or two conclusions. It's people like this, apparently, who will take
their place in the kingdom of God:

  those with a mustard-seed of faith
  those who don't look for it (but keep awake)
  those who find it within reach
  those who won't take no for an answer
  those who don't exalt themselves
  child-like people
  the poor
  those who can give up everything
  those who can take what they are given.

16

Go and Make Disciples

Matthew 28. 16–20

This chapter could be subtitled 'After Billy Graham'. It arose from discussion which took place in a pub after a visit to hear that evangelist speak in the City Football Ground at Bristol. We were all feeling a bit battered by that experience. It seemed to most of us that there was a great discrepancy between the attractiveness of the man and the ferocity of his message. He had suggested to us that, road accident statistics being what they are, some of us in that stadium were unlikely to get home safe that night: so this might be our very last chance . . . He had been told that during the past week yet another unfortunate had jumped from the Suspension Bridge, which should remind us that without Christ in our lives we were all heading for destruction. The woman's fifteen-year-old son, fortunately, didn't get to the City Ground that day, as he had meant to.

The pub seemed by contrast friendly and life-affirming. But we weren't there just to enjoy the beer and the bonhomie. Those of us who had scruples about Billy Graham were quite rightly challenged to say what we had to offer instead. Evangelism there must surely be. No good just shrinking away in refined distaste from what we had just experienced. The style wasn't everything: if we really felt obliged to dissent from the content, from the fundamentalism and the threats, we ought to have the courage to say so. We needed to go back to base camp, so to say, and ask some questions about the preaching of the gospel.

The argument began to revolve, as it always does, around particular texts. What did Jesus say about it? Wasn't that the real question? And what Jesus said about evangelism is surely plain enough. The crucial text for Christian mission and evangelism must be the Great Commission, the closing verses of the Gospel according to St Matthew:

> Then the eleven disciples went away into Galilee, into a mountain where Jesus had appointed them. And when they saw him, they worshipped him: but some doubted. And Jesus came and spake unto them, saying, All power is given unto me in heaven and earth. Go ye therefore, and teach all nations, baptizing them in the name of the Father, and of the Son, and of the Holy Ghost: teaching them to observe all things whatsoever I have commanded you: and, lo, I am with you alway, even unto the end of the world. Amen.

But is that, in fact, what Jesus said?

Now let me say at once that none of us *wanted* to take issue with those verses. They are too deeply ingrained in the religious experience of every believer. There must be a special reverence due to the Last Words of the Lord. He promises his continuing presence with his followers: surely that, if anything, is the bedrock not only of Christian evangelism but of the Christian faith itself. Put a question mark against that, and what's left?

That's the point at which the student of the New Testament is under the strongest pressure to sit down and shut up. He doesn't want to threaten anyone's cherished beliefs. He doesn't want to lose his own, for that matter. He knows that biblical criticism is often regarded as sacrilegious and that academic theology is widely believed to be subversive of faith. What people want from him, he's told, is a plain exposition of scripture. He must be helpful. He must be positive.

But if you are committed to the serious study of the Bible there's a question which simply won't go away, and has to be asked of all the sayings of Jesus: Is that, in fact, what Jesus said? We need to take a deep breath and see if it can be answered.

At one level, as we've seen, it can't. Jesus of Nazareth almost certainly spoke Aramaic. His actual words are lost. What we have are a number of Greek writings, four gospels and a few words elsewhere, which between them contain many sayings attributed to Jesus. Some people think there's no way of getting behind those writings to the authentic words of Jesus, which are totally irretrievable. Other people believe that through God's inspiration the Bible has preserved those authentic words intact for us.

Most scholars take a position between those two extremes. They say, typically, that we have to take into account the editorial activity of the gospel writers, and acknowledge that in the course of transmission from oral Aramaic to written Greek the teaching of Jesus must inevitably have undergone modification; but that we don't have to despair of hearing the true voice of the Lord sounding through.

If we go along with that, we're going to have to acknowledge that some of the words attributed to Jesus are more likely to be authentic than others. And that's where the difficulties become acute. What are the criteria for discriminating between one saying and another? Indeed, how dare we attempt to judge such things? Can there be any sound basis for such judgments, or are we dependent on the subjective hunch of the individual interpreter?

With those questions in mind we have to turn our attention to this particular text from St Matthew, and see what happens when you look closely at it, before returning to the wider question of Christian evangelism, its origins in the life of the early church and the teaching of Jesus.

If we date the death and resurrection of Jesus around AD 30 and St Matthew's Gospel after AD 70 it's to the life of the church in those intervening forty or fifty years that we have to look if we're to see how the gospels came into being. We know a good deal about the church of those years from the epistles of St Paul and from St Luke's Acts of the Apostles. Three things in particular throw light on our present enquiry.

First, we discover that the first Christian leaders were decidedly reluctant to evangelize the Gentiles. Secondly, we find that their creeds or formulations of faith were very brief: a formula such as 'Jesus is Lord' may have been replaced by the end of the century with fuller statements which went as far as this, from I Timothy, 'He was manifested in the flesh, vindicated in the Spirit, seen by angels, preached among the nations, taken up in glory', but not much further. Thirdly, we gather that the worship of the earliest Christians was informal; they studied the Jewish scriptures, they handed down stories and traditions about Jesus, they gave and received careful moral instruction and exercised a ministry of healing and teaching and preaching, they celebrated the Eucharist and baptized their converts; but it's pretty clear that in the 30s, 40s and 50s of the Christian era they hadn't adopted set forms of worship, and were only gradually working their way towards an agreed policy of evangelism.

That skeletal picture can be slightly fleshed out, but not with any great certainty. What we do need to keep in mind is that the writers of the gospels belonged to communities of that sort, and wrote for them. It's only to be expected, therefore, that in their handling of the teaching of Jesus they should have kept the specific needs of their readers firmly in mind. We've seen in an earlier chapter how the Parable of the Sower was, most probably, interpreted by St Mark in terms that made sense to a struggling young church. Other parables like the Prodigal Son, while doubtless originating on the lips of Jesus, seem to have been handed down in a form that made special sense to groups afflicted with problems of apostasy and reconciliation. In other words, we find, not surprisingly, that the evangelists project back into the times and the words of Jesus concerns which didn't in fact surface until after his death and resurrection.

You can therefore, with some hope of objectivity, expect to find instances in the gospels where words of Jesus have been shaped by the evangelists to fit the needs of a later time; or, to put it the other way round, where the circumstances of the early church have been projected back into the times and the teachings of Jesus. And that may very well be what has happened in the last verses of St Matthew.

You can hardly doubt that there were indeed parting words as Jesus took leave of the eleven disciples, but the evangelists are in complete disagreement about them. What St Matthew records is

a proclamation of total authority
a requirement to evangelize the Gentiles
a command to baptize in the three-fold name
an injunction to keep commandments
an assurance of continuing presence to the end of time.

This does look very much as though it reflects the life and developed concerns of the church of St Matthew's own day. Certainly there's no evidence from earlier times of baptism in the three-fold name; and, as we've seen, the evangelization of the Gentiles took a long time to get under way. Surely, if these two requirements had been part of the Lord's parting words, as his eucharistic words in one form or another seem to have been, we would expect to find the early church acting pretty smartly upon them. But it didn't.

So, does this mean that we have to reject these final words of St Matthew as inauthentic? Surely not. But we do, I think, need to admit that they have gone through a process of adjustment in the process of becoming Holy Scripture. In other words, if someone asks you the bald question, Did Jesus actually say that? the answer has to be, Probably not. If that sounds very advanced and modern and radical and sceptical and all the rest of it, I may add that it's what many scholars have been saying about many of the Words of Jesus at least since 1800. But they don't always come out in the open about it. Here's Gerhard Barth writing about these verses in 1960, but not exactly calling a spade a spade:

> Difficulties arise for analysis because there is no direct parallel to this section by means of which additions or alterations by Matthew might be recognized. A marked editorial encroachment by the evangelists must be reckoned with by virtue of its position as the conclusion of the Gospel. Besides, the section shows a series of Matthaean thoughts and linguistic peculiarities.

And here's a very respectable old scholar, A. H. McNeile, writing in 1915; he too wraps up his words pretty carefully, but there's no doubt what he's saying:

> As to their genuineness, the divine claims made by Christ cause no difficulty, but they are closely connected with verse 19 [the command to evangelize and to baptize] which presents considerable difficulty; and the section must probably be regarded as the expression by the evangelist of truths which the Church learnt as a result of the Resurrection, and on which it still rests its faith . . . It is impossible to maintain that everything which goes to constitute even the essence of Christianity must necessarily be traceable to explicit words of Jesus.

Do, please, read that last sentence again, and reflect that the words come from an impeccably orthodox source more than seventy years ago, in what was for generations the standard commentary on St Matthew, very widely used by students and clergy. If expressed today in plain words by a church leader they would be branded as damaging and irresponsible.

So, if we're to think afresh about evangelism, we need (of course) to take the Great Commission into account. But we don't leave it at that, as though no further discussion were possible. We need to put other evidence alongside it. And we may find that some of that evidence goes back earlier than St Matthew's Gospel.

I suggested just now that we can trace in the New Testament certain fields of activity which engaged the energies of the first Christians. It would be a mistake to try and classify these too rigorously, but they would certainly include

Preaching
The study of scripture
Worship
Story-telling
Moral instruction (*paraenesis*)

Worship would have included the breaking of bread, prophecy, singing, healing. Scripture meant basically the Old Testament, but would have included letters circulating from other churches and material which would later be used in the writing of the gospels. You get a vivid picture of church life, perhaps even an exaggerated one, from what St Paul wrote to the Corinthians in answer to questions which they had addressed to him. But what I want to put before you now is something rather different from that.

In the book of the Acts of the Apostles, St Luke gives us a number of speeches, usually described nowadays as Sermons, which he attributes to the leaders of the church, to Peter and John, Stephen, Philip, Paul. Now certainly these utterances must have been well and truly worked over before they reached their present form. But scholars do think that, embedded in them, is some very early material. And this material gives us valuable evidence about the first Christian preaching, the *kerygma* or proclamation through which the message of the gospel first began to be made known. You can find this material in chapters 2, 3, 5, 7, 8 and 10 of Acts.

There's too much of this material for detailed examination here; but we need to have one specimen before us, and a sizeable one. Here it is, from chapter 2: Peter's speech in explanation of the behaviour of the disciples at Pentecost:

A

Peter, standing up with the eleven, lifted up his voice, and said unto them, 'Ye men of Judaea, and all ye that dwell at Jerusalem, be this known unto you, and hearken to my words: for these are not drunken, as ye suppose, seeing it is but the third hour of the day. But this is that which was spoken by the prophet Joel;

B

And it shall come to pass in the last days, saith God, I will pour out of my Spirit upon all flesh: and your sons and your daughters shall prophesy, and your young men shall see visions, and your old men shall dream dreams: and on my servants and on my handmaidens I will pour out in those days of my Spirit; and they shall prophesy: and I will show wonders in heaven above, and signs in the earth beneath; blood and fire, and vapour of smoke: the sun shall be turned into darkness, and the moon into blood, before that great and notable day of the Lord come: and it shall come to pass, that whosoever shall call on the name of the Lord shall be saved.

C

Ye men of Israel, hear these words; Jesus of Nazareth, a man approved of God among you by miracles and wonders and signs, which God did by him in the midst of you, as ye yourselves also know: him, being delivered by the determinate counsel and foreknowledge of God, ye have taken, and by wicked hands have crucified and slain: whom God hath raised up, having loosed the pains of death: because it was not possible that he should be holden of it. For David speaketh concerning him,

D

I foresaw the Lord always before my face, for he is on my right hand, that I should not be moved: therefore did my heart rejoice, and my tongue was glad; moreover also my flesh shall rest in hope: because thou wilt not leave my soul in hell, neither wilt thou suffer thine Holy One to see corruption. Thou hast made known to me the ways of life; thou shalt make me full of joy with thy countenance.

E

Men and brethren, let me freely speak unto you of the patriarch David, that he is both dead and buried, and his sepulchre is with us unto this day. Therefore being a prophet, and knowing that God had sworn with an oath to him, that of the fruit of his loins, according to the flesh, he would raise up Christ to sit on his throne; he seeing this before spake of the resurrection of Christ, that his soul was not left in hell, neither his flesh did see corruption. This Jesus hath God raised up, whereof we all are witnesses. Therefore being by the right hand of God exalted, and having received of the Father the promise of the Holy Ghost, he hath shed forth this, which ye now see and hear. For David is not ascended into the heavens: but he saith himself,

The Lord said unto my Lord, Sit thou on my right hand, until I make thy foes thy footstool.

Therefore let all the house of Israel know assuredly, that God hath made that same Jesus, whom ye have crucified, both Lord and Christ.

F

Now when they heard this, they were pricked in their heart, and said unto Peter and to the rest of the apostles, 'Men and brethren, what shall we do?' Then Peter said unto them, 'Repent, and be baptized every one of you in the name of Jesus Christ for the remission of sins, and ye shall receive the Holy Ghost. For the promise is to you, and to your children, and to all that are afar off, even as many as the Lord our God shall call.' And with many other words did he testify and exhort, saying, 'Save yourselves from this untoward generation.' Then they that gladly received his word were baptized: and the same day there were added unto them about three thousand souls.

G

And they continued stedfast in the apostles' doctrine and fellow-ship, and in breaking of bread, and in prayers. And fear came upon every soul: and many wonders and signs were done by the apostles. And all that believed were together, and had all things common; and sold their possessions and goods, and parted them to all men, as every man had need. And they, continuing daily with one accord in the temple, and breaking bread from house to house, did eat their meat with gladness and singleness of heart, praising God, and having favour with all the people. And the Lord added to the church daily such as should be saved.

If you anatomize that, you find that it contains many of the ingredients we've been talking about in our account of the early church. You remember what they were: preaching, the study of scripture, worship, story-telling, moral instruction. After he has set the scene for us (A), St Luke portrays the apostle as engaging in the presentation of a proof text (B) in a way characteristic of the way Jewish teachers have always done their Bible study. This is followed by a highly condensed piece of story-telling (C) in which the life and death and resurrection of Jesus is propounded in a single sentence, and supported (D) by a further exposition of scripture. The heart of the sermon is contained in the next section (E) where the claim is made that the exalted Christ has now acted, by sending the promised Holy Spirit; this, too, is supported by a proof text from scripture. The next verses (F) recount the response of the audience, which is met by the apostle's call to repent and be baptized for the remission of sin; surely another condensation, as the process of instruction and moral exhortation would doubtless have taken many weeks and months. Finally (G) there's a glowing picture of the community of the faithful, at worship, at prayer, at home, united in a joyful pattern of sharing and praise.

In passing, notice the terms in which we read of the relation between Jesus and the Father. Nothing here about 'God sending his Son'; no hint of the pre-existent Word made flesh. He is a man approved of God, who raises him up, and makes him Lord and Christ. This must surely be a very early example of the way Christ was preached. As you read it, you find yourself in the company of Christians perhaps a generation older than those for whom the closing verses of St Matthew were written. It's not a question here of finding authorization for proclaiming Christ to the Gentiles: and if, as we've claimed, the abiding presence of Christ among his disciples is the bedrock on which all faith rests, that, says St Luke, is made manifest not by the words of Jesus but by the outpouring of his spirit, 'which ye now see and hear'.

No doubt St Luke used as much freedom in his account of the first Christian Pentecost as St Matthew did in his account of

Christ's leavetaking. But it seems certain that embedded in this second chapter of Acts are sure indications of the way the earliest Christians lived and worshipped and proclaimed their gospel.

This enquiry took us away from the pub to the classroom. After Billy Graham it was what we needed. We found things we didn't want to find. The pricking of the heart, the warning to 'save yourselves from this untoward generation' were uncomfortably close to the minatory style of modern evangelism. Signs and wonders, the instant conversion of thousands, didn't fit easily with our own experience, with the long and painful path by which many of us had ourselves come to Christ. We couldn't avoid the conclusion that the outpouring of the Spirit is not something that can be controlled and channelled through the familiar patterns of conventional church life. The call to evangelize requires us to sit lightly to those patterns. The Great Commission in one way or another has to stand high on our agenda.

On the other hand, it was important for us to realize something which has been a main theme of this book: that the route by which the word of God has come down to our day is never quite as direct as it may seem. As we enter more deeply, more critically in the proper sense of that word, into the world of the New Testament writers, we find ourselves more and more able to appreciate what those writers did for us. They weren't content to be mere recorders. Perhaps, though this may seem an odd way of putting it, we shouldn't expect to learn from them What Jesus Actually Said. That may not be, for St Paul it certainly wasn't, what they were primarily interested in. What comes to us most vividly is their testimony to the new life that God had opened up for his people through the ministry and death and exaltation of Jesus of Nazareth, and through the outpouring of his Spirit. By that testimony you are delivered, if you please, from the deadening effect of 'Jesus said . . . therefore . . . end of argument', which so often takes the place of that serious study of scripture which is for us, as it was for those first communities, one of the free gifts of the Spirit.

17

Behind the Gospels

Romans 1. 1–7; Acts 13. 26–41; Psalm 2. 7

This is not a book about books, but I must acknowledge that in this chapter I'm greatly indebted to James D. G. Dunn's book *Christology in the Making* (SCM Press, 1980), particularly the section entitled 'Jesus' divine sonship in the earliest Christian writings'.

You may remember that we've already spent some time considering dates. If the crucifixion took place about AD 30, and if the first of the four Gospels wasn't written until some time around AD 70, the intervening forty years are critical for our understanding of the people who first witnessed to Jesus as Lord and formulated their ideas about him. In the various gospel passages we've studied, we've tried to penetrate the obscurity of those years and see what we can learn about those people. There's not a great deal to go on, but we're not completely in the dark. Dunn has this to say about identifying what the first Christians thought about Jesus as son of God:

> It is not always possible to penetrate back to the earliest post-Easter stage of particular traditions or motifs – our earliest documents in the NT (the letters of Paul) did not begin to appear till nearly twenty years after Jesus' death and resurrection. But in the present instance we are in the fortunate position of having some passages which by widespread consent do take us back to a pre-Pauline and probably very early stage of Christian speech and reflection about Jesus as God's Son. I refer particularly to the (probably) pre-Pauline formula used by Paul in Rom. 1.3f. and to what appears to have been the earliest apologetic use of Ps. 2.7 by the first Christians. (*Christology in the Making*, p.33)

So we are going to look at two texts. In the first we see St Paul handling already-existing Christian material. In the second we have an example of how the early church used the Old Testament. We'll be using the Revised Standard Version in this chapter, with marginal notes incorporated in the text within square brackets.

As we have it, St Paul's Epistle to the Romans begins like this:

> Paul, a servant [*or slave*] of Jesus Christ, called to be an apostle, set apart for the gospel of God which he promised beforehand through his prophets in the holy scriptures, the gospel concerning his Son, who was descended from David according to the flesh and designated Son of God in power according to the Spirit of holiness by his resurrection from the dead, Jesus Christ our Lord, through whom we have received grace and apostleship to bring about obedience to the faith for the sake of his name among all the nations, including yourselves who are called to belong to Jesus Christ; To all God's beloved in Rome, who are called to be saints: Grace to you and peace from God our Father and the Lord Jesus Christ.

This is plainly more than a mere greeting, as what's to follow is more than a mere letter. St Paul is doing three things: he presents his credentials as bringer of good news; he outlines the content of his message; he intimates to his readers what it means to receive it. It's very tightly-packed, and if we're to understand the importance of what he's saying we shall need to try and tease it out a bit.

St Paul writes as Christ's servant or slave. He starts from that, and had no need to say more, except that slavery in the ancient world was a matter of accident rather than choice, and he knew it was choice and not accident that had brought him into his service of Jesus Christ. Christ had chosen him, called him. The calling was not simply to service, but to apostleship; and that meant that he was in a particular relationship to his Lord, as an ambassador is in a special way the representative of the crown or the state. There's much more that could be said about apostles, but notice for the time being that the words 'servant', 'called', 'apostle', are central to St Paul's understanding of himself. He goes on to use another very significant word. Translated into English as 'set apart', it carries the same basic meaning in Greek as the word 'designated' which St Paul will shortly use of the Lord himself. I think there's no doubt that behind this word there's a reminiscence of the calling, the setting apart of the prophets of the Old Covenant. Jeremiah, for example, knew himself to be set apart before he was formed in the womb, and sanctified, and appointed a prophet to the nations. Paul uses just this language to describe not only his own apartness but also the unique quality of the good news entrusted to him. This gospel God has 'promised beforehand through the prophets in the holy scriptures'. This is more than a reminiscence. The Christian evangelist is making a claim, and it's easy to forget how exceedingly bold a claim it was at the time, that his message is to be set alongside the promises God gave by the prophets in holy scripture. We're used to finding Old Testament and New Testament bound together in one volume, as Holy Scripture, with the New taking precedence over the Old. In AD 50 such a thing was inconceivable. It was equally outrageous to suggest that this promised message was to be proclaimed to the heathen . . . but that comes later; first we're to be told what the message was, and who it was about.

It's about God's Son.

Here we must pause to reflect once again on capital letters. Ancient Greek was mostly written in what we would call block capitals. They didn't use a mixture of upper case and lower case, as we do. We've already reflected, in the chapter on Ezekiel, how you have to be careful not to identify Old Testament speech about the spirit/breath of God with later Christian ideas of the Holy Spirit. In the New Testament the problem of capital letters is harder still. Take as an example the passage in chapter 15 of St Mark's Gospel where the centurion says as Jesus dies 'Truly this man was the Son of God' (Authorized Version), or 'a son of God' (New English Bible), or very possibly 'a son of a god' (though translators hesitate about going quite that far). Capital letters apart, the Greek could bear any of those meanings. So what about 'God's Son' here in Romans? A Roman soldier may well have envisaged his god in small letters, as it were, but for St Paul, as for any Jew, God would be writ large, so to speak. And I think, if he'd been given the choice, he would have written of Jesus as his Son, with a large S. But to say that is to beg the whole question. For the moment, there's a further point to be stressed. We don't much distinguish, in normal Christian talk, between The Son of God and God the Son; battles about those phrases having been fought to the death in the fourth and fifth centuries. But we really must not imagine that to speak of God the Son, or God the Holy Ghost, was even remotely possible for the men of the New Testament. It's not just a matter of capital letters: theology had simply not got that far. Perhaps it never should have done; but that's another matter.

Back to St Paul. His commission as servant and apostle of Jesus Christ is to proclaim the good news about God's Son. The whole epistle develops into an exposition of that gospel, but to illuminate his greeting to the Romans he puts up four preliminary flares. Two are about the person of Jesus:

he was born of the seed of David according to the flesh;

he was designated Son of God in power according to the spirit of holiness from the resurrection of the dead.

Two are about those who receive and pass on the gospel:

through him we (I) have received grace and apostleship for the response of faith among all nations for his name's sake

among them you, called by Jesus Christ . . . to all the beloved of God in Rome . . . called saints . . . grace to you and peace from God our Father and the Lord Jesus Christ.

There are all kinds of problems in getting that from Greek into English, and at this point I've been bold enough to make my own translation. But it's not even clear what the original text was; since both ends of a roll of parchment or papyrus were easily damaged, you often get what's called 'textual corruption' at the beginning and end of a document. St Mark's Gospel is a famous example. Some scholars believe, too, that the epistle as a whole has gone through at least one drastic revision. J. C. O'Neill, in an attempt to rediscover St Paul's original thought, pruned so much that his pupils used to talk about O'Neill's Postcard to the Romans. However, it's not just a matter of trying to establish a correct text, but of trying to understand what lies behind it; and the really exciting thing here is that St Paul apparently makes use of a formula, a statement about Jesus, which was already circulating when he came to write his letter. And any formula that's earlier than St Paul is earlier than any book of the New Testament. In which case, half-buried in these verses, there may be something from those hidden years we've been thinking about. And that surely demands careful attention.

The kernel of this primitive statement is, first, that God's Son is to be identified with a man born into a Jewish family. Born 'after' or 'according to' the flesh, like any other human being. There's nothing here to suggest extraordinary circumstances surrounding the birth of Jesus. There's nothing about that pre-existent sonship which comes to be expressed in later creeds as 'begotten of his Father before all worlds'. On the other hand, there's this connection with the royal house of David, and that's something which otherwise St Paul seems never to have taken into his own theology. So we're confronted with some interesting things said and left unsaid about where Jesus the Christ comes from.

Secondly, according to this early formula Jesus is 'designated' Son of God, in power, 'after' or 'according to' the spirit of holiness. That's very difficult, because it's so unlike the creeds that we're used to. But you may find the idea of the designation of Jesus, and the reference to the spirit of holiness, beginning to come into focus as you consider that the gospels, all four of them, point to the baptism of Jesus as a moment when the spirit descends upon him and he is acknowledged as God's son, with or without capital letters. Here in Romans, however, St Paul is handing down to us a belief that the validation or designation of Jesus as God's son comes not from his baptism but 'from the resurrection of the dead'. Does that mean that he is, so to say, promoted to Sonship with effect from the date of his resurrection? or on the grounds of his resurrection? The Greek preposition *ex* could carry either meaning, and perhaps it has to be left an open question which St Paul meant. It's equally difficult to know whether he would himself have rested content with that formula. His great account of the power of the resurrection at the end of I Corinthians isn't incompatible with the idea that the resurrection of the dead is the point from which faith has to start. What is certain is that it is through the risen Christ that Paul receives grace for his apostleship, and demands the response of obedience and faith from all nations. It is Christ Risen who calls the Roman church, as God's beloved, to be saints and to receive grace and peace from God who is Our Father as surely as he is the Father of the Lord Jesus Christ.

As you'd expect, St Paul's use of this primitive formula goes beyond what the formula may have said, just as the gospels, in their use of the earliest traditions about Jesus, make claims for him which go beyond what those traditions had to say. We've just referred to the fact that all four evangelists attach great importance to the baptism of Jesus in proclaiming that he is God's son. The three synoptic gospels at this point all reflect, and St Luke directly quotes, words from Psalm 2 which had by their time become central to the preaching of the good news:

Thou art my son, this day have I begotten thee.

By the end of the century that text was being very generally used in support of claims that Jesus was Son of God. We find it quoted in the Second Epistle of Peter and in those opening words of the Epistle to the Hebrews which have for centuries been read at Mass on Christmas Day.

But most significant is St Luke's use of Psalm 2 in chapter 13 of Acts. Here we have another of those sermons in which, it seems, there has been preserved for us fragments or hints of the way the gospel was proclaimed in the generation before that of the evangelists. Those hidden years, again. If St Paul in Romans 1 has encapsulated for us something of the way in which the first believers formulated their faith, so St Luke in Acts 13 has preserved important clues as to how they interpreted their scriptures.

Acts 13 shows us the apostle Paul at worship on the sabbath day in the Jewish synagogue at Antioch in Pisidia, an inland town of what's now Southern Turkey, then a staging post on the old Royal Road from Sardis to Mesopotamia. He has reminded his Jewish audience about the establishment of the royal house of David. He emphasizes the point, as does Romans 1, that it's from this royal house that 'God has brought to Israel a Saviour, Jesus, as he promised'. He then makes direct reference to the baptism of Jesus, and to the testimony of John the Baptist, whose witness had already become influential in those parts, and continues:

Brethren, sons of the family of Abraham, and those among you that fear God, to us has been sent the message of this salvation. For those who live in Jerusalem and their rulers, because they did not recognize him nor understand the utterances of the prophets which are read every sabbath, fulfilled these by condemning him. Though they could charge him with nothing deserving death, yet they asked Pilate to have him killed. And when they had fulfilled all that was written of him, they took him down from the tree, and laid him in a tomb. But God raised him from the dead; and for many days he appeared to those who came up with him from Galilee to Jerusalem, who are now his witnesses to the people. And we bring you the good news that what God promised to the fathers, this he has fulfilled to us their children by raising Jesus; as also it is written in the second psalm, 'Thou art my Son, today I have begotten thee.' And as for the fact that he raised him from the dead, no more to return to corruption, he spoke in this way, 'I will give you the holy and sure blessings of David.' Therefore he says also in another psalm, 'Thou wilt not let thy holy one see corruption.'

For David, after he had served the counsel of God in his own generation, fell asleep, and was laid with his fathers, and saw corruption; but he whom God raised up saw no corruption. Let it be known to you therefore, brethren, that through this man forgiveness of sins is proclaimed to you, and by him everyone that believes is freed from everything from which you could not be freed by the law of Moses. Beware, therefore, lest there come upon you what is said in the prophets: 'Behold, you scoffers, and wonder, and perish; for I do a deed in your days, a deed you will never believe, if one declares it to you.'

In the so-called Nicene Creed, which many churches use in their eucharist, there's a clause referring to the Holy Spirit which says that 'he spake by the prophets', words which seem almost out of place among the large-scale pronouncements of fifth-century theologians which surround it. But there it is, part of what the church proclaims. And here it is, implicit in those early proclamations of the gospel which underlie the writings of both Paul and Luke. The good news, according to Romans, is 'promised beforehand by the prophets'. In the Antioch sermon of Acts 13 there are quotations not only from two of the Psalms but also from the prophets Isaiah and Habakkuk. The preacher not only quotes from and expounds scripture to his audience; he relates his exposition to what they are used to hearing as they worship, week by week, in their synagogue.

We've seen in an earlier chapter how the teaching of the first Christians was related to their worship. Scriptural texts weren't merely references to be dug out of old volumes. They were part of what was said and sung at moments when they were most consciously celebrating their fellowship in the spirit. And so here, in this Anatolian synagogue, a Jewish audience is challenged not by the strangeness of the good news but by the familiarity of words which were 'read every sabbath' and are now to be seen in a new light. Strict exegesis is bound to point out that Psalm 2 isn't actually about Jesus as son of God, any more than Isaiah's prophecy that 'a virgin shall conceive' is actually about the virgin birth. What mattered to the apostles and evangelists was to give their message in terms familiar to those who knew the scriptures and could recognize from their experience as worshippers how that message was 'promised beforehand through the prophets'.

The testimony of scripture is crucial to the first preaching of the gospel. That's what strikes you most forcibly as you read these sermons in the book of Acts. But there are more surprises to come. We've already noticed that the formula in Romans is remarkable as much for what it doesn't say as for what it does say about Jesus as son of God. Here in Acts we have a powerful argument linking Jesus with a figure from the scriptures who is designated as 'begotten of God' and who is not allowed 'to see corruption'. And that's just the same basis for the designation of Jesus Christ as Son of God as we found in Romans: a saviour of the house of David, as promised, raised from death by God. And yet, most surprisingly, nowhere in this sermon is Jesus specifically called God's son. Saviour, yes. Untouched by death, and raised up by God so that 'through this man' there might be forgiveness and freedom. But the testimony stops short of actually saying that Jesus is son of God. And that's remarkable. It's a reminder, to say the least, that the earliest preaching of the gospel, so far as we can judge from the occasional glimpses we catch of it, says rather less about the relationship between Jesus and the Father than we might have expected.

It seems then that in the early stages of its development the apostolic preaching portrays Jesus in terms of what has come to be called a low christology. According to this portrayal Jesus is the man raised up by God and through the resurrection exalted to be God's son, as the scriptures bear witness. Within a couple of generations a high christology has begun to take over, and this earlier way of talking of Jesus is replaced, or at least augmented, by something like this, from the Epistle to the Colossians:

> He is the image of the invisible God, the first-born of all creation; for in him all things were created, in heaven and on earth, visible and invisible . . . He is before all things, and in him all things hold

together . . . For in him all the fulness of God was pleased to dwell, and through him to reconcile to himself all things, whether on earth or in heaven, making peace by the blood of his cross.

Or these words, attributed to Jesus himself by the author of the Gospel according to St John:

The works that I do in my Father's name, they bear witness to me . . . My sheep hear my voice, and I know them, and they follow me; and I give them eternal life, and they shall never perish, and no one shall snatch them out of my hand. My Father, who has given them to me, is greater than all, and no one is able to snatch them out of the Father's hand. I and the Father are one.

Fortunately we don't have to opt for either a low christology or a high, nor do we have to make value-judgments about the various ways in which the New Testament writers speak of their Lord. But we do have to recognize that there is great variety there. In particular I think we need to keep constantly in mind that the first believers, so far as we can tell, gave their witness in a much less developed form than we find it in the epistles of St Paul or the four gospels. That's not to say that later writers have distorted or adulterated that witness; but it does mean that you need to keep a level head when people tell you about something that they call the Full Gospel. They mean, apparently, that for your faith in Jesus Christ to be complete you must take on board absolutely everything contained in the New Testament. Well, now, Christians don't of course lightly disregard anything they find in their sacred writings; but we have to tip our hats to those who in those early days found and communicated their faith on a much slenderer basis than that of the full-blown theology we find in St Paul or St John or the Epistle to the Hebrews. Their faith was not incomplete just because it was expressed in rudimentary form. People in the first Christian communities didn't come to faith in Christ because of what the formulas and the scriptures told them to believe about him: they worked out the formulas and wrote the scriptures in the light of what they had come to know of him, through their understanding of their own scriptures, through their love and knowledge of their Lord, and through their experience of his Holy Spirit. You and I are privileged to catch an occasional glimmer of that light. We are beneficiaries of their experience.

18

The Epistle to the
Ephesians

The final chapter of this book is intended as a read-through of one of the most attractive writings in the New Testament. It's quite a short document, about six pages of normal print, but the thought is highly condensed, complex and full of allusions. I've not attempted a verse-by-verse commentary: you'll find recommendations for detailed study in the Appendix. What I am offering is some notes to help you to see the Epistle as a whole, in its setting, rather than as a collection of well-known texts.

It's tempting to part company with the Authorized Version at this point, since the obscurities of the epistle can in places be unscrambled in a modern translation. On the other hand, if you know Ephesians at all, you're likely to know it for its magnificent phraseology:

> Walk worthy of the vocation wherewith ye are called . . . being rooted and grounded in love . . . till we all come in the unity of the faith, and of the knowledge of the Son of God, unto a perfect man, unto the measure of the stature of the fulness of Christ.

The epistle is full of such marvellous high speech, and the King James Version captures it to perfection. As we'll see, beauty of language has its drawbacks as well as its delights.

> Paul, an apostle of Jesus Christ by the will of God, to the saints which are . . . to the faithful in Christ Jesus: grace be to you, and peace, from God our Father, and from the Lord Jesus Christ (1.1–2).

'In the steps of St Paul,' says the travel brochure, 'we visit

Ephesus. His best-loved epistle was written to the Ephesians.'
But many scholars will tell you, and I think they're right, that this
epistle is not in fact a letter from St Paul to the church at Ephesus;
that it was probably written some twenty years after St Paul's
death; that it's an Encyclical or circular letter, a sort of Round
Robin, perhaps intended as a compendium or digest of the great
apostle's teaching.

There are good reasons for believing that. As a small instance,
in Greek the first verse doesn't make sense as it stands. There's a
hole waiting to be filled in, as I've shown by inserting some dots
where the Authorized Version has put 'at Ephesus', words
missing in the best manuscripts. That's a slight point, and there
will be more important evidence for us to consider as we go
along. But first, at risk of being tedious, I want to emphasize what
has already been said about those books in the Bible which
weren't written by the people whose names appear at the top of
the page. They are none the worse for that. They are not
forgeries. If the author of Ephesians puts out his epistle under the
name of Paul, or someone else does so for him, it's because he
wants to claim for this work a place within the great tradition of
the apostolic church. Remaining anonymous, he points away
from himself to the important message he has to give: and that
message, as we shall see, is profoundly 'Pauline'. Pseudonymity
in no way diminishes the value of Ephesians. On the contrary,
you may find yourself marvelling that among Christians of the
later first century, apart from those whose names we know, there
are unknown writers and thinkers of high quality whose work is
able to stand alongside that of Luke or John or Paul. Ephesians
was written by such a man or woman, and it ranks as one of the
great achievements of the second generation of Christian believers.

(In case you're curious to know, the epistles which are
nowadays generally agreed to have been written by St Paul
himself, probably in this order, are: I Thessalonians, Galatians, I
and II Corinthians, Romans, Colossians, Philemon, Philippians.
Almost certainly written by somebody else are: II Thessalonians,
Hebrews, Ephesians, and the Pastoral Epistles to Timothy and
Titus. Perhaps it should be added that there are two main sources
of information about St Paul himself: his own letters, and the
second volume of St Luke, known as The Acts of the Apostles.
They don't always agree. A third source, obviously, is the work of

'Pauline' writers like the author of Ephesians. If you want to
know more about the fascinating task of piecing together and
assessing these fragments of evidence, you'll find suggestions in
the Appendix. For our present purpose we have to leave the case
mostly unargued.)

> Blessed be the God and Father of our Lord Jesus Christ, who hath
> blessed us with all spiritual blessings in heavenly places in Christ:
> according as he hath chosen us in him before the foundation of the
> world, that we should be holy and without blame before him in
> love: having predestinated us unto the adoption of children by
> Christ Jesus to himself, according to the good pleasure of his will,
> to the praise of the glory of his grace, wherein he hath made us
> accepted in the beloved, in whom we have redemption through
> his blood, the forgiveness of sins, according to the riches of his
> grace; wherein he hath abounded toward us in all wisdom and
> prudence; having made known unto us the mystery of his will,
> according to his good pleasure which he hath purposed in himself:
> that in the dispensation of the fulness of times he might gather
> together in one all things in Christ, both which are in heaven, and
> which are on earth; even in him; in whom also we have obtained
> an inheritance, being predestinated according to the purpose of
> him who worketh all things after the counsel of his own will: that
> we should be to the praise of his glory, who first trusted in Christ:
> in whom ye also trusted, after that ye heard the word of truth, the
> gospel of your salvation: in whom also, after that ye believed, ye
> were sealed with that holy Spirit of promise, which is the earnest
> of our inheritance until the redemption of the purchased posses-
> sion, unto the praise of his glory (1.3–14).

Yes, that's just how it is in the Greek. One thumping great
sentence, rather like the slow movement of a Bruckner sym-
phony, with ideas following one another without a great deal of
apparent connection. It's typical of the style of this writer. He
gives you memorable phrases to stick in your mind, even when
you're not sure what they mean exactly. He uses a lot of
repetition and rhetorical devices of all sorts. In particular he
achieves great effect by accumulations of what I've earlier
described as A of B statements: 'the good pleasure of his will', 'the
praise of the glory of his grace' and so forth. This can make for
heavy reading, and translators have tried to make it easier by

breaking up his units into manageable lengths. But the style is part of the message, and we need to reckon with it.

He starts with Thanksgiving and Blessing: not God blessing us, but us blessing God, in the Jewish manner, for what he is and does. Commentators have pointed out three things about this:

1. All the verbs of *doing* have God as their subject. He's the one who blesses, chooses, adopts, abounds, makes known.

2. You and I are on the *receiving* end. We hear, obtain, trust, believe.

3. Christ is present as the centre of activity, as the one *through* whom everything happens, rather than as the initiator.

That last point gives support to the idea that the whole epistle may have been intended for use in public worship, 'through Jesus Christ our Lord' having been from the start an essential ingredient of Christian praise. Certainly the speech is solemn and churchy, serene, not anguished as St Paul's often is. We'll see that the language of baptism figures largely in the epistle, that of eucharist less so.

What matters primarily is that 'we' are incorporated into Christ. Look back through that Blessing, and the words jump out at you: chosen, predestinated, adopted, accepted, redeemed, forgiven, gathered together, sealed; we are offered grace, wisdom, an inheritance, a gospel, a promise.

And who are 'we'? Well, that varies a bit. Sometimes the writer identifies himself with 'us'; sometimes he talks to 'you' as newly-arrived from the dark. But in the end it will appear that we are those who are recipients of all this great divine activity, both Jews and Gentiles, old stagers and newcomers, men and women. That's one of the most important things Ephesians has to say to us, that we all share the experience of being accepted in the beloved; which is why this community of the redeemed, the church, means so much to him. So he continues:

> Wherefore I also, after I heard of your faith in the Lord Jesus, and love unto all the saints, cease not to give thanks for you, making mention of you in my prayers; that the God of our Lord Jesus Christ, the Father of glory, may give unto you the spirit of wisdom and revelation in the knowledge of him: the eyes of your understanding being enlightened; that ye may know what is the hope of his calling, and what the riches of the glory of his

inheritance in the saints, and what is the exceeding greatness of his power to usward who believe, according to the working of his mighty power, which he wrought in Christ, when he raised him from the dead, and set him at his own right hand in the heavenly places, far above all principality, and power, and might, and dominion, and every name that is named, not only in this world, but also in that which is to come: and hath put all things in subjection under his feet, and gave him to be the head over all things to the church, which is his body, the fulness of him that filleth all in all (1.15–23).

Another great mammoth of a sentence. Prayer once again acts as a pivot. It swings you backwards to what God has done, and forwards to your future hope. In Ephesians there's plenty of future, in this life and beyond the grave. Where St Paul speaks of a world which was shortly to come to an end, this writer is settling down in anticipation of Christian generations to come. Therefore love matters more than judgment, as the programme of God's salvation gradually unfolds. Repeatedly he uses the word 'mystery' for this process. It has been described as 'a new evolving unity' between God and man, and between men. He sees this unfolding in the context of eternity, the fulness of time. He will have much to say about the breaking down of barriers: here already one frontier is on the way to being removed, that between earth and heaven. The scene of Ephesians, like *A Midsummer Night's Dream*, moves easily between this world and 'the heavenly places' because the church is required to be at home in both, as the body of Christ who is the fulfilment of that mystery as of everything else.

And you . . . who were dead in trespasses and sins; wherein in time past ye walked according to the course of this world, according to the prince of the power of the air, the spirit that now worketh in the children of disobedience: among whom also we all had our conversation in times past in the lusts of our flesh, fulfilling the desires of the flesh and of the mind; and were by nature the children of wrath, even as others – God, who is rich in mercy, for his great love whereby he loved us, even when we were dead in sins, hath quickened us together with Christ, (by grace ye are saved;) and hath raised us up together, and made us sit together in heavenly places in Christ Jesus: that in the ages to come he might shew the exceeding riches of his grace in his kindness towards us through Christ Jesus. For by grace ye are saved through faith; and that not of yourselves: it is the gift of God: not of works, lest any man should boast. For we are his workmanship, created in Christ Jesus unto good works, which God hath before ordained that we should walk in them (2.1–10).

I've taken liberties with the punctuation to show that in the Greek text there's a great build-up through the first five verses before we're told what God has actually done. 'He hath quickened us.' Made us alive. That's the clincher; and the writer makes it very strong, first piling on the indictment against our depraved condition before wiping the slate clean with one mighty word: *Synezoöpoiēsen.* We can't do it in English in less than eight words: 'he has brought us to live together with . . .' Together with Christ. Sometimes the rhetoric of Ephesians grows turgid, and confuses the thinking: here it illuminates brilliantly.

The A of B phrases aren't always easy to decipher. 'Children of disobedience' are presumably disobedient children; but are 'children of wrath' angry children, or children you're angry with? You see the difficulty? Grammarians call it the difference between a subjective genitive and an objective genitive. In plainer terms, I remember John Burnaby, who was a great authority on St Augustine and wrote a fine book about him which he called *Amor Dei*, 'The Love of God', saying at the end of his life that he often couldn't decide, when Augustine spoke of the love of God, whether he meant God's love for us or our love for God. The difference can sometimes be crucial.

We'll come across this problem again. The point here is that through the piling up of word upon word we are being told that the drama of God's activity is played out not only against 'the prince of the power of the air', on that cosmic stage where good and evil are locked in eternal conflict, but in the lesser arena of our own personal lives: and that there the victory is won simply through God's grace given to us through faith in Christ, in unity with whom we are brought to life and exalted to glory. 'Simply' indeed! The rest of the chapter is given to explaining something of what that unity means. It's a cardinal point for the whole argument: 'from this point the epistle moves away from the privileges of the Christian as an individual to the privileges of the community. Awareness of the corporate nature of the Christian faith now becomes prominent.'

Wherefore remember, that ye being in time past Gentiles in the flesh, who are called Uncircumcision by that which is called the Circumcision in the flesh made by hands; that at that time ye were without Christ, being aliens from the commonwealth of Israel, and strangers from the covenants of promise, having no hope, and without God in the world: but now in Christ Jesus ye who sometimes were afar off are made nigh by the blood of Christ. For he is our peace, who hath made both one, and hath broken down the middle wall of partition between us; having abolished in his flesh the enmity, even the law of commandments contained in ordinances; for to make in himself of twain one new man, so making peace; and that he might reconcile both unto God in one body by the cross, having slain the enmity thereby: and came and preached peace to you which were afar off, and to them that were nigh. For through him we both have access by one Spirit unto the Father. Now therefore ye are no more strangers and foreigners, but fellowcitizens with the saints, and of the household of God; and are built upon the foundation of the apostles and prophets, Jesus Christ himself being the chief corner stone; in whom all the building fitly framed together groweth unto a holy temple in the Lord: in whom ye also are builded together for an habitation of God through the Spirit (2.11–22).

The word 'flesh' can be something of a puzzle, as it's used in a variety of ways in the New Testament. It doesn't necessarily imply anything we'd call carnal or sensual. For instance, quarrelsomeness and backbiting are said by St Paul to be sins of the flesh. And in this passage from Ephesians we're asked to consider as fleshly the barrier between Jew and Gentile which has now been broken down by the cross of Christ. Sadly we have to admit that what seemed to this writer an accomplished fact seems to us a long way from fulfilment. We have to confess ourselves bedevilled by a further range of fleshly divisions; black and white, male and female, protestant and catholic, we're a long way from being fitly framed together as a living temple to the Lord. These verses, for all their exalted language, ring hollow in our world, unless we can accept them as a glimpse of a spiritual truth as yet only half-realized; as Dante did, evoking out of the turmoil and violence of mediaeval Italy an echo of these words: *E la sua voluntate e nostra pace*. Christ is our peace.

For this cause I Paul, the prisoner of Jesus Christ for you Gentiles, if ye have heard of the dispensation of the grace of God which is given me to you-ward; how that by revelation he made known to me the mystery; (as I wrote afore in few words, whereby, when ye read, ye may understand my knowledge in the mystery of Christ) which in other ages was not made known unto the sons of men, as it is now revealed unto his holy apostles and prophets by the Spirit; that the Gentiles should be fellow-heirs, and of the same body, and partakers of his promise in Christ by the gospel: whereof I was made a minister, according to the gift of the grace of God given unto me by the effectual working of his power. Unto me, who am less than the least of all saints, is this grace given, that I should preach among the Gentiles the unsearchable riches of Christ; and to make all men see what is the fellowship of the mystery, which from the beginning of the world hath been hid in God, who created all things by Jesus Christ: to the intent that now unto the principalities and powers in heavenly places might be known by the church the manifold wisdom of God, according to the eternal purpose which he purposed in Christ Jesus our Lord: in whom we have boldness and access with confidence by the faith of him. Wherefore I desire that ye faint not at my tribulation for you, which is your glory (3.1–13).

The writer steps out boldly in his Pauline shoes. He speaks in role, as an apostolic witness. But the more you look at it, the more unlikely it seems that St Paul himself would have written to the Ephesians in these terms. He knew them intimately. He had lived with them for long periods, yet there's no hint here of any personal knowledge or of the dramatic experiences which they had shared. 'If ye have heard', indeed! St Paul writing to Ephesus could never have had recourse to written testimony in support of his gospel; he was too sure of his message, if not always of himself. But the argument at this point of Ephesians is so vital that the writer has no hesitation in calling on the highest apostolic authority to validate what he is saying. The fellowship of the church, as Ephesians presents it, has to be based on the bedrock of the apostles precisely because it has grown beyond anything that the apostles themselves knew of. The message for the church is now no longer just for Philippi or Corinth or Ephesus. It is for all mankind. More than that, it is for the principalities and powers in the heavenly places. It's a cosmic proclamation, entrusted no longer to the little company gathered in So-and-so's house, but to the Universal Church, to be described in due course as no less than the Bride of Christ. To make such a claim requires the highest possible warranty: and that is Paul.

We should pause for a moment to consider 'principalities and powers'. Once again, part of the problem is that in the New Testament these ideas carry different meanings at different times. Everyone believed in a world where you were likely to encounter all sorts of spiritual beings, good and bad. Sometimes, particularly in a late writing like the Book of Revelation, it's the Roman Empire that's seen as the embodiment of supernatural evil. At other times this malignancy is an internal matter. St Paul is apt to speak of Satan as a kind of Super-Power. The synoptic gospels are full of demons who behave like rustic imps. Ephesians is different again: the enemy is located somewhere between earth and heaven, literally in the Upper Air, but still within range of the saving activity of God and never out of earshot of his church.

> For this cause I bow my knees unto the Father of our Lord Jesus Christ, of whom the whole family in heaven and earth is named, that he would grant you, according to the riches of his glory, to be strengthened with might by his Spirit in the inner man; that Christ may dwell in your hearts by faith; that ye, being rooted and grounded in love, may be able to comprehend with all saints what is the breadth, and length, and depth and height; and to know the love of Christ, which passeth knowledge, that ye might be filled with all the fulness of God. Now unto him that is able to do all that we ask or think, according to the power that worketh in us, unto him be glory in the church by Christ Jesus throughout all ages, world without end, Amen (3.14–21).

That sounds remarkably final: a blessing, followed by a doxology or ascription of praise. In fact it marks the end of the first half of the epistle, and does so in those solemn tones which suggest public worship. The words do in fact sound uncommonly fine booming round some cathedral at the end of a festival service. But the writer hasn't finished by any means. What follows is known technically as *paraenesis*, or exhortation; guidelines for putting doctrine into practice. St Paul's letters almost always end like this, and the effect can be something of an anticlimax after the magnificence of the thought that has gone before.

However, St Paul usually peppers his practicalities with remarks
of deep import; the writer of Ephesians likewise keeps up the
exalted tone to the very end. Evidently the final chapters are
meant not only for a group of converts in an Aegean port but for
that 'whole family in earth and heaven' which, in this epistle, is
the context of the Good News of Jesus Christ. And for this
purpose he once again invokes the authority of the great apostle
whose teaching he so faithfully interprets.

> I therefore, the prisoner of the Lord, beseech you that ye walk
> worthy of the vocation wherewith ye are called, with all lowliness
> and meekness, with longsuffering, forbearing one another in love;
> endeavouring to keep the unity of the Spirit in the bond of peace.
> There is one body, and one Spirit, even as ye are called in one hope
> of your calling; one Lord, one faith, one baptism, one God and
> Father of all, who is above all, and through all, and in you all (4.1–
> 6).

I don't know of any more eloquent words anywhere in scripture.
As an appeal to unity you'd think it irresistible, if you didn't
know how Christian history has turned out. What follows is in its
way equally powerful, but rather harder to understand. A proof-
text from Psalm 68 is taken and altered and used as a way of
investing the church's ministry with massive spiritual authority.

> Unto every one of us is given grace according to the measure of the
> gift of Christ. Wherefore he saith, 'When he ascended up on high,
> he led captivity captive and gave gifts unto men.' (Now, that he
> ascended, what is it but that he also descended first into the lower
> parts of the earth? He that descended is the same also that
> ascended up far above all heavens, that he might fill all things.)
> And he gave some, apostles; and some, prophets; and some,
> evangelists; and some pastors and teachers; for the perfecting of
> the saints, for the work of the ministry, for the edifying of the body
> of Christ: till we all come in the unity of the faith, and of the
> knowledge of the Son of God, unto a perfect man, unto the
> measure of the stature of the fulness of Christ: that we henceforth
> be no more children, tossed to and fro, and carried about with
> every wind of doctrine, by the sleight of men, and cunning
> craftiness, whereby they lie in wait to deceive; but speaking the
> truth in love, may grow up into him in all things, which is the
> head, even Christ: from whom the whole body fitly joined

together and compacted by that which every joint supplieth, according to the effectual working in the measure of every part, maketh increase of the body unto the edifying of itself in love (4.7–16).

If that had been part of a sermon by one of my pupils, I'd have advised some radical cuts. Too much is being said, and the main point obscured. That main point, surely, is to do with growing up. Maturity in Christ. Try reading through the paragraph again, and see if that's not what everything else leads to: the quotation from the psalm, the list of ministries, the warnings against deception, the analogy of the parts of the body, it all builds up to the Full Grown Man. And that certainly needs a word of explanation.

The word used here for '*man*' isn't the usual *anthrōpos*, meaning a human being of whichever gender. It's *anēr*. And that word usually has a specifically male meaning. It's true that it is the common word for 'husband'. But it's also true that in ancient religious language you find a phrase *teleios anēr*, 'perfect man', which is not specifically male. 'Perfect Man-hood' is not a matter of gender. It doesn't signify physical ultra-virility, or moral supermanhood. It's humanity fulfilled. Male and female. Obviously, for a male person that fulfilment may well include being a husband, *anēr* in that sense; it's in the context of what we now call 'committed human relationships', marriage or whatever, that human beings of either sex characteristically find their fulfilment. But what distinguishes Perfect Man, the measure of the stature of the fulness of Christ, is maturity not gender. Do observe that here in Ephesians the opposite of 'man' is not 'woman' but 'children tossed to and fro'. It may be that this writer hadn't got very far towards finding a really satisfactory doctrine of human nature which would include the full range of our sexuality. Nor had his contemporaries; nor ours, for that matter. The church has a long way to go, in its understanding of human nature, before it can properly represent the fulness of Christ.

This I say therefore, and testify in the Lord, that ye henceforth walk not as other Gentiles walk, in the vanity of their mind, having the understanding darkened, being alienated from the life of God through the ignorance that is in them, because of the blindness of their heart: who being past feeling have given themselves over unto lasciviousness, to work all uncleanness with greediness. But ye have not so learned Christ; if so be that ye have heard him, and have been taught by him, as the truth is in Jesus: that ye put off concerning the former conversation the old man, which is corrupt according to the deceitful lusts; and be renewed in the spirit of your mind; and that ye put on the new man, which after God is created in righteousness and true holiness. Wherefore putting away lying, speak every man truth with his neighbour: for we are members one of another. Be ye angry, and sin not: let not the sun go down upon your wrath: neither give place to the devil. Let him that stole steal no more: but rather let him labour, working with his hands the thing which is good, that he may have to give to him that needeth. Let no corrupt communication proceed out of your mouth, but that which is good to the use of edifying, that it may minister grace to the hearers. And grieve not the holy Spirit of God, whereby ye are sealed unto the day of redemption. Let all bitterness, and wrath, and anger, and clamour, and evil speaking, be put away from you, with all malice: and be ye kind one to another, tenderhearted, forgiving one another even as God for Christ's sake hath forgiven you. Be ye therefore followers of God, as dear children; and walk in love, as Christ also hath loved us, and hath given himself for us an offering and a sacrifice to God for a sweetsmelling savour (4.17–5.2).

You may feel that he lays it on a bit thick. Like St Paul before him, he is content to use the moralistic language which was in common use in Greek, Roman and Jewish circles at that time. But there are some special insights. I find it rings absolutely true when he identifies those four causes of human degeneracy: a sense of futility, alienation from God, hardness of heart, greed. And when he urges us to have done with lust and anger and theft and slander 'so that we may have to give to him that is in need', that strikes me as a good motive for moral improvement.

And there's another thing. More than once in this epistle you come across the notion of sealing and redemption. It has been suggested that in Ephesians this takes the place of St Paul's characteristic teaching of justification, which doesn't figure here at all. The basic idea of sealing is that you mark a piece of property with its owner's mark. You can then claim or redeem it only if you have the owner's authorization. It's a lively metaphor for Christian baptism. If the goods are damaged or misappropriated, the owner suffers loss; so we should be careful not to grieve the

Spirit. More than that, we have to see that our attempts to lead a better life are motivated primarily by love, because Christ has loved us, and in so doing has incorporated us into his offering of himself to God.

The moralizing, then, is less conventional than it appears to be. What follows looks like more of the same. And so it is, except that he plays the tune on different stops.

Fornication, and all uncleanness, or covetousness, let it not be once named among you, as becometh saints; neither filthiness, nor foolish talking, nor jesting, which are not convenient: but rather giving of thanks. For this ye know, that no whoremonger, nor unclean person, nor covetous man, who is an idolater, hath any inheritance in the kingdom of Christ and of God. Let no man deceive you with vain words: for because of these things cometh the wrath of God upon the children of disobedience. Be not ye therefore partakers with them. For ye were sometimes darkness, but now are ye light in the Lord: walk as children of light: (for the fruit of the Spirit is in all goodness and righteousness and truth;) proving what is acceptable unto the Lord. And have no fellowship with the unfruitful works of darkness, but rather reprove them. For it is a shame even to speak of those things which are done of them in secret. But all things that are reproved are made manifest by the light: for whatever doth make manifest is light. Wherefore he saith, 'Awake thou that sleepest, and arise from the dead, and Christ shall give thee light.' See then that ye walk circumspectly, not as fools, but as wise, redeeming the time, because the days are evil (5.3–16).

Two things are very familiar from other New Testament writings: the contrast between darkness and light, so characteristic of St John; and the sense of urgency in the face of evil times, which is a mark of St Paul. Ephesians doesn't usually contain much sense of crisis, nor does the contrast of darkness and light figure very much. But at this point the *paraenesis* reflects very accurately the kind of pressure under which Christians did have to live at the end of the first century AD. This pressure came from two directions.

On the one hand, it's evident that the prevailing patterns of social behaviour in the Roman Empire, however much they have been exaggerated, did make it difficult for Christians to maintain standards of purity. We're not so differently placed today. But it's hard for us to take on board the requirement, which you'll find many times in the epistles, that believers should dissociate themselves from unbelievers, and have no fellowship with them. Hard, particularly, because the gospels seem to offer us a picture of Jesus which goes clean contrary to that sort of disengagement. We've seen in an earlier chapter how the early church was preoccupied with the problem of relations with outsiders. Here in Ephesians we find a community still struggling to come to terms with the problem.

On the other hand, and from an apparently opposite direction, there was pressure on 'the enlightened' to go overboard in an excess of religious freedom and shake off the old restraints, whooping it up as though the rules no longer mattered and there was no tomorrow. At first this seems to have affected mainly those who believed that the world was coming to a speedy end. Later it apparently went hand-in-hand with certain enthusiastic and possibly alcohol-induced forms of spiritual excitement within the church. Perhaps that's why this part of the epistle, having quoted what looks like part of a baptismal hymn, 'Awake Thou that Sleepest', ends with a reminder of what it ought to mean to be filled with the Spirit. Being filled with the Spirit, significantly, is a phrase not much used in the New Testament, apart from the writings of St Luke.

> Wherefore be ye not unwise, but understanding what the will of the Lord is. And be not drunk with wine, wherein is excess; but be filled with the Spirit; speaking to yourselves in psalms and hymns and spiritual songs, singing and making melody in your heart to the Lord; giving thanks always for all things unto God and the Father in the name of our Lord Jesus Christ; submitting yourselves one to another in the fear of God (5.17–21).

Time and again the teaching of this epistle is grounded in the need to build up the church, to preserve its unity and the association of its members in Christ. What follows next makes this very clear indeed. The teaching here on marriage and the family is emphatically not Guidelines for the Last Days, such as you find in the Corinthian epistles. Ephesians gives a blueprint for domestic life in the on-going Christian community, what the Germans call a *Haustafel*. Some of it doesn't transfer easily to our own times. We can't really maintain today the dominance of husband over wife, or argue from the premiss that no man ever hated his own flesh. What does remain impressive is the insistence on mutual love, on life in Christ, and on the building-up of the church. A morality based on those grounds deserves to be taken seriously on its own terms, even though the details may no longer apply.

> Wives, submit yourselves unto your own husbands, as unto the Lord. For the husband is the head of the wife, even as Christ is the head of the church: and he is the saviour of the body. Therefore as the church is subject unto Christ, so let the wives be to their own husbands in everything. Husbands, love your wives, even as Christ also loved the church, and gave himself for it; that he might sanctify and cleanse it with the washing of water by the word, that he might present it to himself a glorious church, not having spot, or wrinkle, or any such thing; but that it should be holy and without blemish. So ought men to love their wives as their own bodies. He that loveth his wife loveth himself. For no man ever yet hated his own flesh; but nourisheth and cherisheth it, even as the Lord the church: for we are members of his body, of his flesh, and of his bones. For this cause shall a man leave his father and mother, and shall be joined unto his wife, and they two shall be one flesh. This is a great mystery: but I speak concerning Christ and the church. Nevertheless let every one of you in particular so love his wife even as himself; and the wife see that she reverence her husband. Children, obey your parents in the Lord: for this is right. 'Honour thy father and mother'; which is the first commandment with promise; 'that it may be well with thee, and that thou mayest live long on the earth.' And, ye fathers, provoke not your children to wrath: but bring them up in the nurture and admonition of the Lord. Servants, be obedient to them that are your masters according to the flesh, with fear and trembling, in singleness of your heart, as unto Christ; not with eyeservice, as menpleasers; but as the servants of Christ, doing the will of God from the heart; with goodwill doing service as unto the Lord, and not to men: knowing that whatsoever good thing any man doeth, the same shall he receive of the Lord, whether he is bond or free. And, ye masters, do the same things unto them, forbearing threatening: knowing that your Master also is in heaven; neither is there respect of persons with him (5.22–6.9).

It's sad to think how much inhumanity, both within the family and between masters and servants, has claimed justification from

those words. But the word of God doesn't come 'in commandments contained in precepts', and the author of Ephesians is
careful to insist that he is handling a mystery, that he speaks
'concerning Christ and his church'. He can only do this within his
own situation and with his own insights, which are different from
ours. Maybe there's not much we can now learn from this
document about marriage, or being a good employer. Something,
perhaps. For my own part I'm less troubled by this than I am by the
military metaphors which follow and which are still so much
beloved by those who prepare material for Sunday School and
Confirmation Class.

> Finally, my brethren, be strong in the Lord, and in the power of his
> might. Put on the whole armour of God, that ye may be able to stand
> against the wiles of the devil. For we wrestle not against flesh and
> blood, but against principalities, against powers, against the rulers
> of the darkness of this world, against spiritual wickedness in high
> places. Wherefore take unto you the whole armour of God, that ye
> may be able to withstand in the evil day, and having done all, to
> stand. Stand, therefore, having your loins girt about with truth, and
> having on the breastplate of righteousness; and your feet shod with
> the preparation of the gospel of peace; above all, taking the shield of
> faith, wherewith ye shall be able to quench all the fiery darts of the
> wicked. And take the helmet of salvation, and the sword of the
> Spirit, which is the word of God: praying always with all prayer and
> supplication in the Spirit, and watching thereunto with all
> perseverance and supplication for all saints . . . (6.10–18).

I can't say that I find it easy to respond to that. If my
circumstances were different, if I lived under an evil and
oppressive regime, I should certainly feel otherwise. And even
now, I don't mind singing those words when they come in the
shape of a good bouncy hymn. But I remain uneasy when
Christian faith adopts an ideology which dresses itself up as
warfare against an invisible foe. That seems to me to question the
victory of Christ's cross. When the enemy is palpable, concrete –
yes, certainly: I need to be stirred up against whatever violates love
and justice and truth. But these verses do seem to me to pass the
point at which rhetoric turns into bombast.

However, my sympathies are re-engaged by the words which
end the epistle. The anonymous author in all humility puts on once
again the clothes of his apostolic predecessor. He writes in the

name of Paul, and borrows a few personal greetings from
Colossians to make the identification complete. He speaks, as we
all do, as an ambassador in chains, paradoxically both bound and
free. And his last words are what any of us would like our last
words to be: about boldness in proclaiming the mystery of the
gospel, about comfort and peace, knowledge, sincerity, faith and
grace; and, above all, about the love of the Lord Jesus Christ.

. . . praying for me, that utterance may be given unto me, that I
may open my mouth boldly, to make known the mystery of the
gospel, for which I am an ambassador in bonds; that I may speak
boldly, as I ought to speak. But that ye also may know my affairs,
and how I do, Tychicus, a beloved brother and faithful minister in
the Lord, shall make known to you all things: whom I have sent
unto you for the same purpose, that ye might know our affairs,
and that he might comfort your hearts. Peace be to the brethren,
and love with faith, from God the Father and the Lord Jesus
Christ. Grace be with all them that love our Lord Jesus Christ in
sincerity. Amen.

Suggestions for Further Reading

Details of books mentioned here are given in the Acknowledgments

You should have a good Study Bible, with Concordance, such as *The Oxford Annotated Bible* or *The Jerusalem Bible, Standard Edition with Notes*.

An *Atlas of the Bible* can be an eye-opener. Grollenberg's is the easiest to handle. Other more elaborate ones are available.

Stacey's *Groundwork of Biblical Studies* and Hooker's *Studying the New Testament* were both written to help Methodist Local Preachers. They are excellent aids to study.

Anderson's conclusions in *The Living World of the Old Testament* are rather conservative, but the book is delectably produced and illustrated and a joy to use. Schmidt's *Introduction to the Old Testament* is less attractive, but excellent. For the New Testament, try Perrin and Duling's *Introduction*: it's an intriguing book, though not to everybody's taste.

For individual commentaries, the *Cambridge Bible Commentaries* are usually well done, if not always very lively. Nineham on St Mark always is, and should not be missed. Ziesler's *Pauline Christianity* is a good introduction, so is Verney's *Water into Wine*. For Ephesians, J. L. Houlden (*SCM Pelican Commentaries*) and C. L. Mitton (*New Century Bible Commentary*) are reliable guides.

James Dunn's *The Living Word* is a challenging recent book; Bornkamm's *Jesus of Nazareth* is an enduring classic. The two great volumes by Edward Schillebeeckx, *Jesus* and *Christ* are very hard work, and should be taken in small doses, but are immensely rewarding: the first of them is, sad to say, out of print, but you'll find it in libraries.

Acknowledgments

This is not a full bibliography of the sort which you will find, for instance, in Schmidt's *Introduction to the Old Testament* and Perrin and Duling's *New Testament*. What follows is a list of books which I have used and found valuable.

W. F. Arndt and F. W. Gingrich, *A Greek–English Lexicon of the New Testament*, Chicago University Press 1957

F. Blass and A. Debrunner, *A Greek Grammar of the New Testament*, Chicago University Press 1961

G. Kittel and G. Friedrich, *Theological Dictionary of the New Testament*; 1-volume abridgment by G. W. Bromiley, Eerdmans 1985

J. H. Hayes and C. R. Holladay, *Biblical Exegesis*, SCM Press 1982

B. Gerhardsson, *The Ethos of the Bible*, Darton, Longman & Todd 1981

L. Grollenberg, *The Penguin Shorter Atlas of the Bible*, Penguin 1959

D. E. Nineham, *The Use and Abuse of the Bible*, SPCK 1976

W. D. Stacey, *Groundwork of Biblical Studies*, Epworth 1979

B. W. Anderson, *The Living World of the Old Testament*, Longman, third ed. 1978

J. Blenkinsopp, *A History of Prophecy in Israel*, SPCK 1984

B. S. Childs, *Introduction to the Old Testament as Scripture*, SCM Press 1979

R. E. Clements, *Prophecy and Tradition*, Blackwell 1978

W. Dyrness, *Themes in Old Testament Theology*, Paternoster 1979

M. Noth, *The History of Israel*, Black, second ed. 1959, SCM Press 1983

W. O. E. Oesterley and T. H. Robinson, *An Introduction to the Books of the Old Testament*, SPCK 1934

R. H. Pfeiffer, *Introduction to the Old Testament*, Black, revised ed. 1948

G. von Rad, *Old Testament Theology*, Oliver & Boyd, 2 vols. 1962/65, SCM Press 1975

T. H. Robinson, *Prophecy and the Prophets in Ancient Israel*, Duckworth 1923

H. H. Rowley, *The Old Testament and Modern Study*, Oxford University Press 1951

H. H. Rowley, *The Faith of Israel*, SCM Press 1956

W. H. Schmidt, *Introduction to the Old Testament*, SCM Press 1984

D. Winton Thomas (ed.), *Documents from Old Testament Times*, Harper 1958

G. Vermes, *The Dead Sea Scrolls in English*, Penguin, second ed. 1975

C. K. Barrett, *The Signs of an Apostle*, Epworth 1970

G. Bornkamm, *Jesus of Nazareth*, Hodder & Stoughton 1960

R. E. Brown and J. P. Meier, *Antioch and Rome*, Chapman 1983

F. F. Bruce, *New Testament History*, Oliphants, second ed. 1977

R. Bultmann, *Theology of the New Testament*, SCM Press, 2 vols 1952/55

R. Bultmann, *Primitive Christianity in its Contemporary Setting*, Thames & Hudson 1956

H. Conzelmann, *An Outline of the Theology of the New Testament*, SCM Press, second ed. 1968

B. S. Childs, *The New Testament as Canon*, SCM Press 1984

W. D. Davies, *Paul and Rabbinic Judaism*, SPCK, second ed. 1955

C. H. Dodd, *The Parables of the Kingdom*, Collins 1935

C. H. Dodd, *The Apostolic Preaching and Its Development*, Hodder & Stoughton, second ed. 1944

J. Drury, *The Parables in the Gospels*, SPCK 1985

J. K. Elliott, *Questioning Christian Origins*, SCM Press 1982

J. D. G. Dunn, *Christology in the Making*, SCM Press 1980

J. D. G. Dunn, *The Living Word*, SCM Press 1987

B. Gerhardsson, *The Origins of the Gospel Traditions*, SCM Press 1977

H. Hendrickx, *The Parables of Jesus*, Chapman, second ed. 1986

M. Hooker, *Studying the New Testament*, Epworth 1979

M. Hengel, *The Son of God*, SCM Press 1975

E. Hoskyns and F. N. Davey, *The Riddle of the New Testament*, Faber & Faber, second ed. 1936

J. Jeremias, *The Parables of Jesus*, SCM Press 1962

J. Jeremias, *The Prayers of Jesus*, SCM Press 1967

J. Jeremias, *New Testament Theology*, SCM Press, vol. 1 1971

E. Käsemann, *New Testament Questions of Today*, SCM Press, second ed. 1965

W. G. Kümmel, *Introduction to the New Testament*, SCM Press 1965

W. G. Kümmel, *The New Testament: The History of the Investigation of its Problems*, SCM Press 1970

T. W. Manson, *The Teaching of Jesus*, Cambridge University Press, second ed. 1935

B. M. Metzger, *The Text of the New Testament*, Oxford University Press, second ed. 1968

B. M. Metzger, *A Textual Commentary on the Greek New Testament*, United Bible Societies 1971

C. F. D. Moule, *An Idiom Book of New Testament Greek*, Cambridge University Press, second ed. 1959

C. F. D. Moule, *Worship in the New Testament*, Lutterworth 1961

C. F. D. Moule, *The Birth of the New Testament*, Black 1962

C. F. D. Moule, *The Origin of Christology*, Cambridge University Press 1977

C. F. D. Moule, *New Testament Interpretation*, Cambridge University Press 1982

R. C. Musaph-Andriesse, *From Torah to Kabbalah*, SCM Press 1973

D. E. Nineham (ed.) *Studies in the Gospels*, Blackwell 1955

N. Perrin, *What is Redaction Criticism?*, Fortress 1970

N. Perrin and D. C. Duling, *The New Testament: An Introduction*, Harcourt Brace, second ed. 1982

A. Richardson, *An Introduction to the Theology of the New Testament*, SCM Press 1958

C. Rowland, *The Open Heaven*, SPCK 1982

E. P. Sanders, *Paul, the Law and the Jewish People*, SCM Press 1983

E. P. Sanders, *Jesus and Judaism*, SCM Press 1985

E. Schillebeeckx, *Jesus*, Fount 1974

E. Schillebeeckx, *Christ*, SCM Press 1977

R. Schnackenburg, *The Church in the New Testament*, Burns & Oates 1965

J. Stewart, *A Man in Christ*, Hodder & Stoughton 1935

V. Taylor, *The Text of the New Testament*, Macmillan, second ed. 1963

C. Tuckett, *Reading the New Testament*, SPCK 1987

D. E. H. Whiteley, *The Theology of St Paul*, Blackwell, second ed. 1974

J. Ziesler, *Pauline Christianity*, Oxford University Press 1983

Commentaries on individual books of the Bible

G. von Rad, *Genesis*, SCM Press 1956

O. Kaiser, *Isaiah 1–12*, SCM Press 1973

O. Kaiser, *Isaiah 13–39*, SCM Press 1963

C. Westermann, *Isaiah 40–66*, SCM Press 1966

P. Ackroyd, *Doors of Perception* (Psalms), Faith Press 1978, SCM Press 1983

A. F. Kirkpatrick, *The Psalms*, Cambridge University Press 1902

P. D. Miller, *Interpreting the Psalms*, Fortress 1986

R. E. Prothero, *The Psalms in Human Life*, Murray 1906

A. Weiser, *The Psalms*, SCM Press 1962

W. Eichrodt, *Ezekiel*, SCM Press 1970

G. von Rad, *Wisdom in Israel*, SCM Press 1970

J. L. Crenshaw, *Old Testament Wisdom*, SCM Press 1981

A. H. McNeile, *The Gospel According to St Matthew*, Macmillan 1915

J. C. Fenton, *St Matthew*, Penguin 1963

G. Bornkamm, G. Barth, H. J. Held, *Tradition and Interpretation in Matthew*, SCM Press 1960

C. F. Evans, *The Beginning of the Gospel* (St Mark), SPCK 1968

R. H. Lightfoot, *The Gospel Message of St Mark*, Oxford University Press 1950

D. E. Nineham, *St Mark*, Penguin 1963

V. Taylor, *The Gospel According to St Mark*, Macmillan, 1952

A. R. Vidler, *Read, MARK, Learn*, Fount 1980

G. B. Caird, *St Luke*, Penguin 1963

J. M. Creed, *The Gospel According to St Luke*, Macmillan 1930

H. Conzelmann, *The Theology of St Luke*, Faber & Faber, second ed. 1957

I. H. Marshall, *The Gospel of Luke*, Paternoster 1978

S. Verney, *Water into Wine* (St John), Fount 1985

E. Haenchen, *The Acts of the Apostles*, Blackwell 1970

C. S. C. Williams, *A Commentary on the Acts of the Apostles*, Black 1957

C. H. Dodd, *The Epistle of Paul to the Romans*, Fontana 1932

K. Barth, *The Epistle to the Romans*, Oxford University Press 1933

C. F. D. Moule, *Colossians and Philemon*, Cambridge University Press 1957

J. L. Houlden, *Paul's Letters from Prison*, SCM Press 1970

C. L. Mitton, *Ephesians*, Eerdmans 1973

C. Masson, *L'Épitre de St Paul aux Éphésiens*, Delachaux & Niestlé 1953